Advanced Ana
with
Excel 2019

Perform Data Analysis Using
Excel's Most Popular Features

by

Manisha Nigam

FIRST EDITION 2020

Copyright © BPB Publications, India

ISBN: 978-93-89845-80-8

All Rights Reserved. No part of this publication may be reproduced or distributed in any form or by any means or stored in a database or retrieval system, without the prior written permission of the publisher with the exception to the program listings which may be entered, stored and executed in a computer system, but they can not be reproduced by the means of publication.

LIMITS OF LIABILITY AND DISCLAIMER OF WARRANTY

The information contained in this book is true to correct and the best of author's & publisher's knowledge. The author has made every effort to ensure the accuracy of these publications, but cannot be held responsible for any loss or damage arising from any information in this book.

All trademarks referred to in the book are acknowledged as properties of their respective owners.

Distributors:

BPB PUBLICATIONS
20, Ansari Road, Darya Ganj
New Delhi-110002
Ph: 23254990/23254991

DECCAN AGENCIES
4-3-329, Bank Street,
Hyderabad-500195
Ph: 24756967/24756400

MICRO MEDIA
Shop No. 5, Mahendra Chambers,
150 DN Rd. Next to Capital Cinema,
V.T. (C.S.T.) Station, MUMBAI-400 001
Ph: 22078296/22078297

BPB BOOK CENTRE
376 Old Lajpat Rai Market,
Delhi-110006
Ph: 23861747

Published by Manish Jain for BPB Publications, 20 Ansari Road, Darya Ganj, New Delhi-110002 and Printed by him at Repro India Ltd, Mumbai

About the Author

Manisha Nigam is a seasoned management professional with twenty plus years of information technology experience, working with multinationals across the globe. Her expertise in Excel comes from the vast experience she has in using and understanding the software over the years, that helped her in working efficiently and managing complex programs. A certified PMP (PMI – Project Management Professional), CSM (Scrum Alliance – Scrum Master), TOGAF 9.1 (The Open Group – Enterprise Architecture) and holds a post graduate degree in computer science and business management from prestigious universities in India.

Her LinkedIn Profile: linkedin.com/in/mnigam10

Preface

*"Spreadsheets are corporate poetry; when constructed elegantly enough,
they can be used to communicate sophisticated ideas to audiences who wouldn't
otherwise be receptive to details."*
— *Eric Seufert, "Freemium Economics"*

*"The best tool available today for exploring real-life questions of quantity and change is
the spreadsheet."*
— *Bret Victor, "Kill Math"*

*"Excel is the best tool non-programmers have in order to write code,
that's why it wins."*
— *antirez on HackerNews*

These lines truly define the characteristics of Microsoft Excel, which is one of the most popular and vastly used spreadsheets. Microsoft Excel's first version Excel v1.0 was released on Macintosh in 1985 and a Windows version 2.0 in 1987. It has come a long way since then and the latest version, that is, Excel 2019 contains a wide assortment of new and improved features and capabilities.

Who should read this book?

Anyone from a student, teacher, manager, entrepreneur, job seeker, retailer, distributor, freelancer to a housewife, who is searching for shortcuts & advanced methods to resolve their daily problems. Using Excel, you can easily and quickly do mundane tasks, complex calculations, analyze huge data from internal or external sources, take decisions based on predictions, do forecasting, create plans, charts, reports, dashboards for progress and status and so on.

The intend of this book is to explain and simplify the usage of Excel features and functionalities, with the help of examples. Few examples are extracts of the actual problems that people had faced in real life and found a solution via Excel. We assume that the users reading this book have basic knowledge of working with Excel like opening Excel, navigating around, enter data etc. Microsoft's official support website has been used as a reference for this book. For understanding a subject in depth, like the statistical or financial terms used in this book, we advise users to refer to subject related documentation or an expert.

How is the book organized?

Chapters 'Getting Started with Excel' and 'Performing functions with shortcut keys' will help you in getting started with Excel. You will learn about the basic components of Excel, the available menu options and tools, some customizations, working with multiple workbooks and worksheets, most frequently used and useful keyboard shortcuts.

Chapter 'Formulas and Functions' gives an initial understanding of what are operators, formulas, functions, their components and in the later sections it goes on to explain important functions under different categories. Error handling and formula auditing have also been covered to help you review and avoid errors. Multiple examples have been used to explain the usage in real world scenario.

Chapters 'Data Visualization with new Charts types', 'Gantt and Milestone chart', 'SmartArt and Organization Chart' give details on the different chart types available in Excel and how best you can use them for creating different views of data, good graphics or visualizations for dashboards etc. Using Gantt and Milestone chart, you can plan and track your projects efficiently.

Chapter 'Get creative with Icons, 3D models, Digital Inking' details multiple new and improved features that got introduced to enhance the visual presentation.

Chapters 'Putting Data in Perspective with Pivots', 'Complex data analysis using ToolPak' and 'Forecasting in Excel' help in learning the different ways and methods to consolidate data, do complex analysis and predict or forecast based on trends. These chapters are very helpful for people who require to do lot of data analysis and based on results or predictions make important decisions.

Chapters 'Mail Merge using Excel', 'Create Custom Excel Template' and 'Macros in Excel' explain the Excel features that help in automating tasks. You will learn how to generate multiple documents automatically with customization, create and use your own templates and use of macros to do repeated task automatically.

Chapter 'Get help for your problem' lists few problem statements and their probable solutions with references to the Excel feature or functionality that can be used to resolve the problem. Hoping that these examples might trigger new ideas or thoughts for finding solution to your problems.

Version of Excel referred in this book

This book has been written for desktop version of Microsoft Excel 2019 for Windows (not Mac).Information is relevant to Excel 2019,which is available as part of perpetual Office 2019 and to subscription-based Office 365 (with latest version of Excel). Excel 2013 & 2016 users may also find information in this book relevant and useful.

Note that this book does not cover the touch screen gestures. In case you are working on a device that has touch screen enabled, then you will need to follow the touch screen commands instead of the keyboard and mouse actions given in this book. For example, 'Click' may be equivalent to 'Tap' in your touch screen.

References

Microsoft's official support website has been used as a reference for this book.

The more a user gets deeper in learning the benefits of Excel, the more they tend to develop smarter ways to implement excel in daily life.

Thanks for selecting this book! Excel with EXCEL!!

Manisha Nigam (Author)

https://in.linkedin.com/in/mnigam10

Table of Contents

CHAPTER 1

Getting Started with Excel

1.1 Workbook and Worksheets

When we talk about working in Excel, we basically work in a workbook, that is, the file that is created by Excel with the default extension '.xlsx'. Each workbook contains one or more worksheets and by default, they are named as **Sheet1**, **Sheet2**, **Sheet3**, and so on, in the sequence in which they get created. The users can rename the worksheets by right-clicking on the sheet name and selecting '**Rename**' from the options, with a condition that each sheet name in a workbook is unique.

Sheets are structured as two-dimensional matrix with the columns named alphabetically (A-Z, AA-AZ, BA ..., ZZ, AAA, AAB, and so on) and the rows numerically (1 through 1048576). Each sheet contains individual cells which can contain number, text, or formula. The intersection of a row and a column is a single cell which is referenced using the column letter and row number. For example, the first cell in the worksheet is referenced as A1, that is, column A row 1. A worksheet also has an invisible drawing layer which holds charts, images, and diagrams. Objects on the drawing layer sit over the top of the cells, however, they are not inside the cells like a number or a formula.

An open Excel workbook screen looks like the following screenshot. It also shows the important and useful elements that are often used:

Figure 1-1: Workbook Screen

1.2 Navigation with Keyboard

Users are quite familiar with and find it easy to navigate through the cells using their mouse. But you can also use the standard navigation keys on the keyboard to move around the worksheet. For example, the down arrow moves the active cell down by one row, the right arrow moves it one column to the right, and so on, the PgUp and PgDn keys move the active cell up or down by one full window. There are a lot of useful keyboard shortcuts available which are listed in Chapter 2 Perform Functions with Shortcut Keys .

1.3 Tabs and Ribbons

The user interface of Excel, like all other Microsoft products such as Word, PowerPoint, and so on, has Tabs and Ribbons. Each tab (Home, Insert, Page Layout, and so on) has an associated Ribbon with several group of buttons for working. For example, if you click the Formulas tab, you get a Ribbon with buttons that are useful for working with formulas. Also, when you hover the mouse pointer over a Ribbon button, it will show the description that contains the command's name along with a brief description.

Figure 1-2: Tabs and Ribbons

1.3.1 Contextual Tabs

In addition to the standard tabs, Excel includes contextual tabs. Whenever an object (such as a chart, a table, or a SmartArt diagram) is selected, specific tools for working with that object are made available in the Ribbon of the Contextual tab. For example, when you select a chart, two tabs 'Chart Design' and 'Format' become visible. As shown in screenshot below, the Ribbon for the contextual tab 'Chart Design' is shown with options to modify the design of the selected chart.

Figure 1-3: Contextual Tabs and Ribbons

1.3.2 Tab and Ribbon Visibility

If you need more space, you can right-click on any Ribbon and select 'Collapse the Ribbon' button, you can then restore it in the same way. Also, note that depending on the width of the Excel window, some Ribbons might not show fully, however, everything is still available. To toggle the Ribbon's visibility, use the keyboard shortcut Ctrl + F1 (or double-click the Tab at the top). You can also change the Tab and Ribbon visibility option using a control named 'Ribbon Display Options' (next to the Minimize button) on the title bar. The control has three options: 'Auto-Hide Ribbon', 'Show Tabs' and 'Show Tabs and Commands'.

There is also an option for customizing the Ribbons; you can right-click on any Ribbon and select 'Customize the Ribbon...' or go to 'File->Options' to launch the Excel Options dialog box.

Figure 1-4: Customizing Ribbons

1.4 File Menu

The File menu takes you to the backstage view where you can perform file operations. You can also open the 'Excel Options' dialog box from there. To go back and leave backstage view, simply click on the back arrow at the top left.

Figure 1-5: File Menu

1.5 Quick Access Toolbar (QAT)

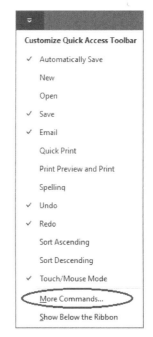

There is a Quick Access Toolbar (QAT) at the top-left corner of the Excel window. You can put your favorite buttons on this toolbar so that they are always visible and available. The QAT comes with a few favorite buttons, however, you can add more. The QAT can be customized by clicking on the drop-down arrow to the right of your QAT. You will see a list to the right, of the most used buttons, which you can then check to add them to your QAT.

You can also click on the 'More Commands' item in this list, as shown in preceding screenshot, to launch the dialog box which contains several other buttons that you can add to your QAT.

Figure 1-6: More Commands option in QAT

Figure 1-7: Quick Access Toolbar

Adding Superscript and Subscript commands

Excel allows you to add shortcuts to the Superscript and Subscript commands to your Quick Access Toolbar. Note that this feature is not available in previous versions of Excel, that is, Excel 2016 and older.

Go to 'Excel Options -> Quick Access Toolbar' and select Subscript or Superscript from the commands list and click 'Add>>'.

Figure 1-8: *Inserting Subscript and Superscript in QAT*

Although Excel doesn't have quick keyboard shortcuts to these commands, you can navigate the menus and dialogs with just the keyboard. Use Alt+HFNE for Superscript, and Alt+HFNB for Subscript.

1.6 Excel Options

Excel has many options for changing the software's behavior. Click on the 'File' button in the upper-left corner of the screen and then on 'Options' to see all the options. Options are grouped in categories: General, Formulas, and others. Though the option names are self-explanatory, for more details on what each option means, you can either click on the information icon or the help button on the upper-right corner of the screen.

For example, under the Advanced group, you will see many Editing options which you can change based on your style of working, such as using the Enter key to move the selection down, allowing Automatic flash fill, and so on.

Figure 1-9: Advance Editing options

Most of the options are for Excel as a whole, not for any workbook or worksheet you might have opened. However, there are a few that are workbook-specific or worksheet-specific. For example, in the Advanced group, there are two sets of options, 'Display options for this workbook' and 'Display options for this worksheet' that can be varied from one workbook/worksheet to another.

Figure 1-10: *Advance Options at Worksheet & Workbook level*

You can also change the look and feel of all your Office programs by changing the Office Theme or Background. Go to 'File > Options > General > Office Theme'

Figure 1-11: *Change Office Theme / Background*

The Black theme provides the highest-contrast visual for your Office theme. Note that the Black theme is not available in previous versions of Excel, that is, Excel 2016 and older.

1.7 Create a New Workbook, Print and Save

1.7.1 Create New File

You can create a new Excel file in your Window's explorer by going to the New option on the Home Tab or by right-clicking on any empty space in the explorer and choose 'New-> Microsoft Excel Worksheet'. Or launch Microsoft Excel application, select a Blank Workbook or use an existing Template, Take a Tour, and so on, as shown in the following screenshot. You can also use the shortcut key CTRL+N, to create a new workbook:

Figure 1-12: Create New Excel file

You can create as many worksheets required in a workbook and rename them as discussed earlier. There are many useful keyboard shortcuts for working in a worksheet, as detailed in Chapter 2 Perform Functions with Shortcut Keys. Working with data within the worksheet will be discussed in the later chapters of this book.

1.7.2 Print File

You can print the entire workbook, active sheets, or the selected area. The Print option is available on the File menu or you also can use the keyboard shortcut CTRL+P to launch the Print dialog box with all the print settings that can be configured, as in other Microsoft products.

Figure 1-13: Print Settings

1.7.2.1 Print Active Sheets

Select the worksheets that you want to print. Click on the tab of the sheet for selecting a single worksheet or press the SHIFT key and click the tabs of the adjacent sheets for multiple sheets selection or in case you want to select multiple non-adjacent sheets then press the CTRL key and click on the sheet tabs.

Go to 'File->Print' menu or use the keyboard shortcut CTRL+P to launch the Print dialog box, select 'Print Active Sheets' in 'Settings' (Figure 1-13) and then click on 'Print'.

1.7.2.2 Print Entire Workbook

Open the workbook and go to 'File->Print', select 'Print Entire Workbook' (as shown in Figure 1-13) and click on 'Print'. In case you want to print multiple workbooks, in the File Explorer, select the file, right-click and select 'Print' option. You can also Print the workbook as a file, using the 'Print to File' option in the Print dialog box under the 'Printer' setting as shown in below screenshot.

Figure 1-14: Printer setting

1.7.2.3 Print Selection

Open the worksheet and select the range of data that you want to print. Go to 'File->Print' menu, in the Print dialog box, select 'Print Selection' (as shown in Figure 1-13) and click on 'Print'.

Print Selection with defined Print Area

Another way to print selection is by defining print area. A worksheet can have multiple print areas defined and each print area will print as a separate page. When the print areas are defined, only those are printed when you print the worksheet. You can add cells to expand the print area as needed, and you can clear the print area to print the entire worksheet.

Open the worksheet and select a single data range or multiple data ranges by pressing the CTRL key. Go to the 'Page Layout' tab, in the 'Page Setup' group, select 'Print Area' and click on 'Set Print Area' to define the print area as shown in screenshot below. Now, go to 'File->Print' to open the Print dialog box and select 'Print Active Sheets' which will print only the defined data ranges as the print area.

Figure 1-15: Set / Clear Print Area

Even if the file is closed and opened again, the defined print areas are saved, and you do not need to do the selection again and define. Note that in order to remove the print area, you need to click on 'Clear Print Area' as shown in preceding screen shot (Figure 1-15).

Print Tables and Objects

When you select an Excel table in the worksheet and go to 'File->Print' menu, under 'Settings' you will see a new option 'Print Selected Table' as shown in screenshot below.

Figure 1-16: *Print Selected Table option*

Sometimes you may find that certain objects like text boxes, buttons, and arrows do not get printed. To correct that, right-click on any such object, select 'Size and Properties', and click on the Properties tab. This contains a 'Print object' option that you can check or uncheck.

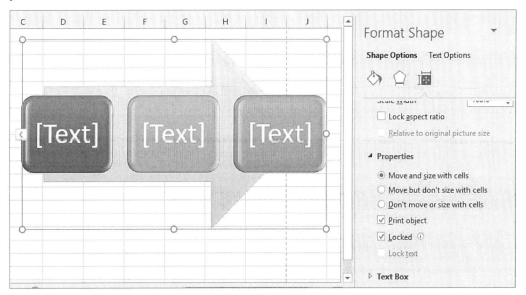

Figure 1-17: *Print Object option*

1.7.3 Save and Save As File

Saving the Excel file is as simple as printing and similar to what you see in other Microsoft products, with only difference that it shows the relevant file types. The first time you save an Excel workbook, Excel takes you to the Backstage screen that lets you choose the location for the file; online location or local computer and launches a Save dialog box. In the dialog box you can enter the Filename and the file type or extension you want to save the file in, click on 'Save' button to save the file.

By default, Excel also saves a backup copy of your work automatically in every 10 minutes. AutoRecover setting can be changed, go to 'File -> Options' and click on the Save tab of the Excel Options dialog box.

The default file extension is '.xlsx', however, it also gives other files type options as well, as shown in below screenshot. If you want to save in a version compatible with older Excel version, then you can choose Excel 97-2003 Workbook (*.xls) or if you require a macro-enabled version, then choose Excel Macro-Enabled Workbook (*.xlsm) or a comma delimited files as CSV UTF-8 (*.csv), and so on.

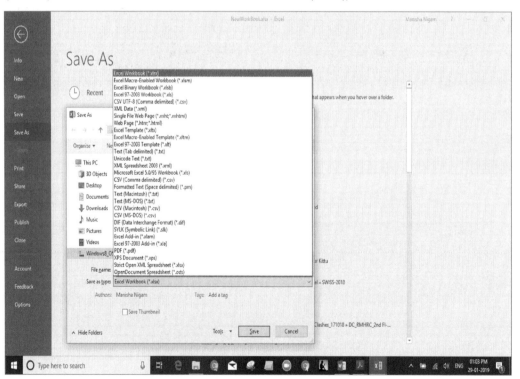

Figure 1-18: Save As options

On saving a file as CSV, Excel used to show a warning, that is, "This file may contain features that are not compatible with CSV...". Excel has now removed this warning in the latest version of Excel that is Excel 2019.

1.8 Understanding Worksheet Basics

Worksheets are the playground for entering, editing, formatting, analyzing, and visualizing information or data. You can perform a lot of operations in the worksheet like renaming the sheet, adding/deleting a sheet, controlling the worksheet view, inserting/deleting rows and columns, grouping/ungrouping data, formatting data, and so on. In this chapter, we will learn the worksheet basics with the help of examples.

1.8.1 Commands for entering/editing data

You can use the mouse as well as keyboard to enter, modify, or delete data in the worksheet. There are many keyboard commands (see Chapter 2 Perform Functions with Shortcut Keys), but here, we will list only a few that are frequently used, will help in your daily work with Excel and in the following chapters.

Operation	Keyboard Commands
Edit a cell	Select the cell, double-click with the mouse or press F2 on the keyboard
Insert a new line within a cell	Press ALT+ENTER within the cell to insert a new line
Go to next cell	Single click with mouse to select or use arrow keys or press the ENTER key
Cut/Copy/Paste/ Paste Special in cell	Select the source/destination cell, right-click with mouse for the desired options or press CTRL+X / CTRL+C / CTRL+V / CTRL+ATL+V on the keyboard
Add a new Table	Press CTRL+T to add a new table
Insert/Delete in Table	Press CTRL+'+' and CTRL+'-' to insert or delete a table respectively
Copy same text in cells below	Select the cell, press CTRL+C and then select the cells below where you want to paste the value and press CTRL+D
Undo/Redo change	Press CTRL+Z to undo a change and CTRL+Y to redo a change
Flash fill cells	Select the cell with mouse, click on the '+' sign at the lower-right corner and drag the mouse selecting the cells you want to fill with data

You can also change few settings like pressing the ENTER key will move the selection in the right side instead of down, using 'File->Options->Advanced->Edit Options'. In this book, we assume the preceding commands hold true, unless specified.

1.8.2 Insert/Delete Cells

Excel gives options in the 'Home' tab to insert new sheets, rows, columns, and even specific cells relative to the selection. Similarly, you can delete sheets, rows, columns, and cells.

Figure 1-19: Insert / Delete Rows & Columns menu options

These options are also available on right-click of the mouse.

Figure 1-20: Insert / Delete Rows & Columns options on right click

1.8.2.1 Insert/Delete/Rename Sheet

Open the workbook in which you want to insert/delete worksheets. By default, it has one worksheet named 'Sheet1'.

To Insert, go to the 'Home' tab, in the 'Cells' group and click on 'Insert Sheet'. The new sheet gets added on the left of the existing sheet with name 'Sheet2'. The sheet number (in the sheet name) depends on the number of sheets that were already created in the workbook. Assuming your worksheet has 'Sheet1', 'Sheet2', and 'Sheet3', then the new sheet will be 'Sheet4'. Now delete all the sheets except Sheet1 and again insert a new sheet. The new sheet in this case will be 'Sheet5', as Sheet4 was the last one that was created, even though you deleted it.

To Delete a single sheet, select the sheet tab and click on 'Delete Sheet'. In case you want to delete multiple sheets, press CTRL and select the sheet tabs (non-adjacent) or press SHIFT and select the sheet tabs (adjacent) and click on the 'Delete Sheet' option. On delete, the sheets and its content are removed from the workbook.

You can Rename the sheet, either by double-clicking on the sheet tab and typing the new name or right-clicking on the mouse and selecting the 'Rename' option.

Figure 1-21: Rename Sheet

1.8.2.2 Insert/Delete Rows and Columns

The 'Insert Sheet Rows' option inserts an empty row above the selected row. In case you selected multiple adjacent rows (by pressing SHIFT key), say three in number, then it will insert the same number of empty rows, that is, three empty rows above the row on top of the selection. In case you selected multiple non-adjacent rows (by pressing CTRL key), then it inserts a single empty row above each selected row.

The 'Insert Sheet Columns' works in the same way; new columns are inserted on the left of the selected column.

To Delete, select the rows/columns to delete (single or multiple) and click on 'Delete Sheet Rows' / 'Delete Sheet Columns'. Note that Insert and Delete options are also

1.8.2.4 Deselect a selection

Sometimes when you're selecting multiple cells or ranges in Excel, you accidentally select one or more that you didn't intend. You can deselect any cell within the selected range with the Deselect Tool. Pressing the Ctrl key, you can click, or click-and-drag to deselect any cells or ranges within a selection. If you need to reselect any of those cells, continue holding the Ctrl key and reselect those cells.

1.8.3 Formatting Cells

Formatting in worksheet can be very helpful in understanding the purpose of the worksheet and help in preventing data entry errors. The options are available on the 'Home' tab in the 'Font', 'Alignment', 'Number', 'Cell Styles', and 'Format Cells' groups.

These options can also be seen in the mini toolbar above the shortcut menu, when you right-click on the cells.

Most of the formatting can be done directly using these menu items, however, sometimes you need the 'Format Cells' dialog box. The Format Cells dialog box contains six tabs, Number, Alignment, Font, Border, Fill, and Protection.

Figure 1-22: Format Cells Dialog box

The Format Cell dialog box can be launched from multiple places. Select the cell range to format and use any one of the following ways to launch the dialog box:

- Using the keyboard shortcut - Press CTRL+1.
- Click on the dialog box launcher in 'Home->Font', 'Home->Alignment', or 'Home->Number'. The dialog box launcher is the small downward-pointing arrow icon displayed to the right of the group name in the Ribbon.
- Right-click on the selected cell or range and choose 'Format Cells' from the shortcut menu
- Click on the 'More command' in some of the drop-down controls in the Ribbon. For example, in the Number group, clicking on the drop-down menu gives the 'More Number Formats...' option.

1.8.3.1 Using fonts to format

You can use different fonts, font sizes, or text attributes in your worksheets to make various parts stand out, such as the headers for a table.

Figure 1-23: *Format Cells - Font*

You can select the font from the given list, make it bold or italics, select the size, color of the font, and effects such as strikethrough, superscript, and so on. You can see the preview of how your text will look in the preview section. You can also use the shortcut keys for changing the text, that is, Ctrl+B: Bold, Ctrl+I: Italic, Ctrl+U: Underline, and Ctrl+5: Strikethrough.

If a cell contains text, you can also apply formatting to individual characters in the cell by selecting the character and using the formatting options as described earlier.

1.8.3.2 Change text Alignment

The contents of a cell can be aligned horizontally and vertically. By default, Excel aligns numbers to the right and text to the left. All the cells use bottom alignment by default. You can overwrite the defaults by using the Alignment tool.

Figure 1-24: *Format Cells - Alignment*

The following are a few examples of how your text will look like with different alignments. You can try different styles and use whichever is more appropriate for your use.

	A	B	C	D	E
1	Text is aligned Top	Text is aligned Middle	Text is aligned Bottom	I am text in merged cells, cols D & E	
2	Text is aligned Left	Text is aligned Center	Text is aligned Right		I am wrap text
3	Text is Counterclockwise	Text is Clockwise	T h i s	I am example of how the distributed text looks like. I am distributed.	
4					

Note that for merging the cells, you need to select all the adjacent cells which you want to merge and then use the merge option. Merge will ask for confirmation before merging, sometimes it only keeps the text of the first cell selected and discards the text in other selected cells for merge. So, you need to be careful while merging text in cells. You can merge the cells before entering text. Similar rule applies to unmerge, select all the merged cells and then click on the unmerge option.

1.8.3.3 Using Number formatting

Numbers can be in different categories and there is a default setting in Excel for each category. For example, if you format the number in a cell say 42381 as Date, it will get converted to '12 January 2016' and if it is formatted as a Number, it will be converted as 42381.00. You can also make your own format by using the Custom option. There is some custom formatting already available, however, you can also create by typing a new one in the Type field. Type 'mm-dd-yyyy' and click on OK. Instead of 12 January 2016, it will be converted to 01-12-2016.

Figure 1-25: *Format Cells - Number*

Each category has different settings and you can use any based on your requirements. Category names are self-explanatory and hence easy to identify which category to use when:

Format	Description
General	This is the default number format that Excel applies when you type a number. For most part, numbers that are formatted with the General format are displayed just the way you type them. However, if the cell is not wide enough to show the entire number, the General format rounds the numbers with decimals. The General number format also uses scientific (exponential) notation for large numbers (12 or more digits).

Contd…

Number	This is used for the general display of numbers. You can specify the number of decimal places that you want to use, whether you want to use a thousands separator, and how you want to display negative numbers.
Currency	This is used for general monetary values and displays the default currency symbol with numbers. You can specify the number of decimal places that you want to use, whether you want to use a thousands separator, and how you want to display negative numbers.
Accounting	This is also used for monetary values; however, it aligns the currency symbols and decimal points of numbers in a column.
Date	This displays date and time serial numbers as date values, according to the type and locale (location) that you specify.
Time	This displays date and time serial numbers as time values, according to the type and locale (location) that you specify.
Percentage	This multiplies the cell value by 100 and displays the result with a percent (%) symbol.
Fraction	This displays a number as a fraction, according to the type of fraction that you specify.
Scientific	This displays a number in an exponential notation, replacing a part of the number with E+n, where E (which stands for Exponent) multiplies the preceding number by 10 to the nth power.
Text	This treats the content of a cell as text and displays the content exactly as you type it, even when you type numbers.
Special	This displays a number as a postal code, ZIP Code, phone number, or Social Security number.
Custom	This allows you to modify a copy of an existing number format code. Use this format to create a custom number format that is added to the list of number format codes.

1.8.3.4 Changing Cell Styles

Excel has several built-in cell styles that you can apply or modify. You can also modify or duplicate a cell style to create a custom cell style. A cell style is a defined set of formatting characteristics, such as fonts and font sizes, number formats, cell borders, and cell shading. To prevent anyone from making changes to specific cells, you can also use a cell style that locks cells.

Figure 1-26: Format Cells – Cell Styles

In the following example, we have used Heading 1 and Ascent 6 cell styles to format the cells:

In the 'New Cell Style' dialog box, the settings are the default Excel settings for font, alignment, and so on. You can enter a name for your own style and by using the 'Format' option, you can change the formatting for a Number, Alignment, Font, Borders, shading, and so on as given in the screenshot below:

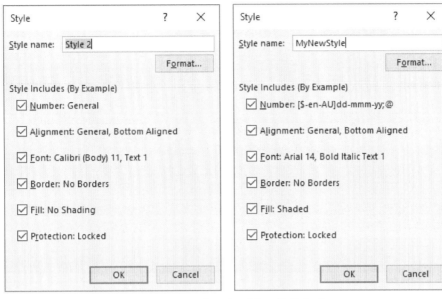

Figure 1-27: Creating New Cell Style

1.8.3.5 Changing Borders and lines

Excel has another tool called Borders that you can add around the cells. There are 13 preset styles of borders in Excel, which are available under the 'Home' tab, in the 'Font' group's 'Borders' drop-down list.

Figure 1-28: Format Cells: Borders and Lines

You can either select the existing styles or draw them yourself using the 'Draw Borders' option as shown in preceding screenshots.

1.8.3.6 Translate Text into different Languages

You can translate words or phrases in your worksheet into different languages using 'Review->Translate' option.

Figure 1-29: Translate text

Highlight the cell or text you want to translate, go to 'Review->Translate' and in the Translator option pane choose the language from the 'To' list in which you want to translate. Excel automatically detects the language of the highlighted text, which is shown in the 'From' field. You can select any language from the available list in the 'To' field. You can reverse the 'From' and 'To' by clicking on the double arrows.

Copy the translated text from the 'To' text box and paste it in any cell of the worksheet.

1.8.4 Data Tools

1.8.4.1 Data Cleansing (Sort, Filter, Remove Duplicates)

Excel allows you to sort the data in ascending or descending order. You can also define a custom sort specific to your needs. It also lets you filter data so that only those items are visible that meet your filter criteria and all other items are hidden. The 'Sort' and 'Filter' options are available under the 'Home' tab, in the 'Editing' group and under the 'Data' tab, in the 'Sort & Filter' group.

Figure 1-30: *Sort and Filter options in the 'Home' and 'Data' tabs*

Using these options, we will sort and filter our data, as shown in the screenshot below:

	A	B	C
1	Vendor 1	Apples	12
2	Vendor 2	Mangos	10
3	Vendor 3	Strawberries	6
4	Vendor 4	Banana	7
5	Vendor 5	Orange	3
6	Vendor 5	Apples	34
7	Vendor 1	Mangos	26
8	Vendor 2	Strawberries	75
9	Vendor 3	Banana	23
10	Vendor 4	Orange	11
11	Vendor 4	Apples	21
12	Vendor 5	Mangos	42
13	Vendor 1	Strawberries	8
14	Vendor 2	Banana	2
15	Vendor 3	Orange	9

Figure 1-31: *Sort and Filter – Example data*

We have data in three columns A (Vendors list), B (Fruits list), and C (number of items).

Sorting

Select the data range from A1 to C15 and click on 'Sort A to Z'. Excel will sort the data in ascending order, with reference to the first column in the selected range, that is, column A, where it will first put all 'Vendor 1' rows, followed by 'Vendor 2' and so on. In case the 'Sort Z to A' option was selected, it will put all the 'Vendor 5' rows first, followed by 'Vendor 4' and so on in descending order.

Now if we want to sort based on two columns that is, all Vendors in ascending order and for each Vendor, fruits sorted based on the number of items in descending order. Excel allows you to do that with the help of 'Custom Sort'. Select the data range and go to custom sort. In the Sort dialog box, add the required levels for sorting by using 'Add Level'. The resulting Sort criteria and results are as shown in the following screenshot:

Figure 1-32: Custom Sort

	A	B	C
1	Vendor 1	Mangos	26
2	Vendor 1	Apples	12
3	Vendor 1	Strawberries	8
4	Vendor 2	Strawberries	73
5	Vendor 2	Mangos	10
6	Vendor 2	Banana	2
7	Vendor 3	Banana	23
8	Vendor 3	Orange	9
9	Vendor 3	Strawberries	6
10	Vendor 4	Apples	21
11	Vendor 4	Orange	11
12	Vendor 4	Banana	7
13	Vendor 5	Mangos	42
14	Vendor 5	Apples	34
15	Vendor 5	Orange	3

Since we wanted to sort Vendors first, the 'Sort by' field shows Column A in ascending order that is, A-Z in the Order field. Next, we wanted to sort the data for each Vendor based on the number of items, hence in second level, we specified Column C and 'Largest to Smallest' in the fields.

Filtering

Adding a filter to change the view of data is very simple in Excel. Select the data and go to the 'Filter' option (see Figure 1-30). It adds a little arrow in the first row of your data range. By clicking on the arrow, you get options to add different filters based on the type of data in the column. In columns with text, it shows 'Text Filters' and in columns with numbers it shows 'Number Filters':

As in the preceding example, the filter lists all unique values for that column and allows you to select or deselect items by clicking on the checkbox. Based on your selection, the items are displayed in that column. Another way is to use one of the Text/Number filter options and add criterias like, make visible if the text contains 'berries' or number is greater than '10'.

In the custom filter, you can add another critera and combine the two using the AND operator (for both criterias to be true) or the OR operator (any one of the criteria is true) connectors.

Clear & Reapply Filter

You can remove the filter by clicking on 'Clear' (as shown in Figure 1-30). In case your data is changed in the filtered data, you can update the view by clicking on 'Reapply'.

Using Advanced Fitering

If you want to filter the data based on complex criteria, then you can use the 'Advanced' filter option (as shown in Figure 1-30). When you use the Advanced Filter option, you need to set up the criteria range. A criteria range is a designated range on a worksheet that conforms to certain requirements. Criteria range should have the same column headers as the dataset and you need to make sure there is at least one blank row between the criteria range and dataset. The fields in each row of the criteria range (except for the header row) are joined with an AND operator. If you enter more than one row in the criteria range, the rows of the criteria are joined with an OR operator.

In the following example, we have entered two criterias: first creates a filter to view only Vendor 5 where the number of Apples is greater than 20 and second creates a filter to view only Vendor 1 where it can be any fruit having number greater than 10. Click on 'Advanced' and in the 'Advanced Filter' dialog box enter the values as shown in the screenshot below:

Figure 1-33: Advanced Filtering

Specify the 'List Range' and 'Criteria Range' and select the option labeled 'Filter the List, In-Place'. Click on OK, and the list is filtered by the criteria that you specified.

	A	B	C
1	Name	Item	Qty
2	Vendor 5	Apples	>20
3	Vendor 1		>10
4			
5			
6	Name	Item	Qty
7	Vendor 1	Mangos	26
8	Vendor 1	Apples	12
20	Vendor 5	Apples	34

You can also copy your filtered dataset to another location by selecting the option 'Copy to another location' and specifying the destination range in 'Copy To' field. In case your data contains duplicates and you want to see unique records only, select the 'Unique records only' checkbox in the 'Advanced Filter' dialog box.

Remove Duplicates

Remove Duplicates helps you to clean your data, the duplicate data will be permanently deleted. Hence, it is preferable to backup or copy the original data in another worksheet before removing duplicates so you don't accidentally lose any information.

Select the range of cells that has duplicate values you want to remove. Go to the 'Data' tab, in the 'Data Tools' group select 'Remove Duplicates'. In the Remove Duplicates dialog box, under Columns, check or uncheck the columns where you want to remove the duplicates and click on OK.

Figure 1-34: Remove Duplicates

Excel will display a message with the number of duplicates removed and unique values remaining and remove the duplicates from the data range.

◢	A	B	C	D	E	F	G	H	I
10									
11		Product	Jan Sales						
12		Part #1	12	Microsoft Excel					✕
13		Part #2	5						
14		Part #3	45	ⓘ 2 duplicate values found and removed; 5 unique values remain.					
15		Part #4	23						
16		Part #5	42	OK					
17									
18									

1.8.4.2 Data Grouping

You can group and summarize your list of data using the Outline or grouping feature of Excel. You can create an outline of up to eight levels, one for each group. Each inner level, represented by a higher number in the outline symbols, displays detailed data for the preceding outer level, represented by a lower number in the outline symbols. You can also Ungroup once the grouping has been created. Group & Ungroup options are available under the 'Data' tab in the 'Outline' group.

Figure 1-35: Outline - Grouping

Grouping/Ungrouping Rows and Columns

Select the rows you want to group, click on 'Group' and select 'Rows' in the Group dialog box. An outline is created and represented by a level number. Similarly, select the columns you want to group, click on 'Group' and select 'Columns' in the Group dialog box. Grouping can be removed by selecting the 'Ungroup' option and selecting 'Rows' or 'Columns' in the Ungroup dialog box:

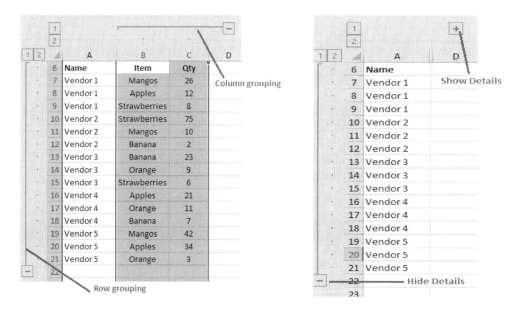

Show/Hide Details

To hide a group, click on the minus sign or select the 'Hide Detail' option. To show a hidden group, click on the plus sign or select the 'Show Detail' option in the 'Data->Outline' group.

Subtotal

Subtotal has been explained in a later chapter, see Chapter 3.10.7, Example #2 (Figure 3-33).

1.8.4.3 Conditional Formatting

Conditional formatting helps you to apply cell formatting selectively and automatically to cells, rows, columns, or tables based on the cell value or based on another cell's value. Conditional formatting is more flexible than the usual cell formats in a sense that it allows you to format only the data that meets certain criteria or conditions. The 'Conditional Formatting' option is available under the 'Home' tab in the 'Styles' group.

Select the cells and use one of the commands from the Conditional formatting drop-down menu to set, manage, or create new rules that will get applied based on selected cell content.

Figure 1-36: *Conditional Formatting*

The table below gives description of the different conditional formatting choices and some examples for reference.

Choices	Description/Examples
Highlight Cells Rules	Highlighting cells that are greater than, less than, are between two values, equal to, contain a specific text string, contain a date occurring, or duplicated values
Top/Bottom Rules	Highlighting the top/bottom 10 items, top/bottom 10% items, and the items that are above/below average.
Data Bars	Show graphic bars directly in the cells, proportional to the cell's value.
Color Scales	Changes background color, proportional to the cell's value.
Icon Sets	Displays icons directly in the cells, depending on the cell's value.
New Rule	To add new conditional formatting rules, including rules based on a logical formula.
Clear Rules	Deletes all conditional formatting rules from the selected cells.
Manage Rules	Displays the Conditional Formatting Rules Manager dialog box in which you can create, edit, or delete conditional formatting rules

We will explain how to use conditional formatting using some examples. Not all rules can be covered, however, the method to do or apply others is the same as the following examples.

Example #1:

In this example, we will use different conditional formatting that is, Data bars, Icons Sets, and Color Scales to indicate the trend in data. Select the 'Total Sales' that is, cells H12 to H16 and then select 'Conditional Formatting->Data Bars->Gradient Fill->Green Data Bar'. The longest data bar is for the highest number and all other bars are relative to that. Similarly, select the other cells and apply the conditional formatting styles that is, E12:E16 – Icon Sets: Shapes, B12:B16 – Color Scales and B17:G17, which is the Total for each month, is shown using Icons Set – Directional.

	A	B	C	D	E	F	G	H
10								
11	Product	Jan	Feb	Mar	Apr	May	Jun	Total Sales
12	Part #1	12	21	15	13	3	10	74
13	Part #2	5	43	74	41	12	11	186
14	Part #3	2	23	34	12	43	23	137
15	Part #4	23	16	23	45	34	66	207
16	Part #5	42	29	54	32	44	43	244
17	Total	84	132	200	143	136	153	
18								

Data Bars Gradient Fill

Icons Set Directional

Colour Scales

Icon Sets - Shapes

Example #2:

We will highlight the Total Sales that are greater than 150. Select the cells H12:H16, go to 'Conditional Formatting->Highlight Cell rules->Greater Than…' and specify the condition of 150 and highlight the text using green color.

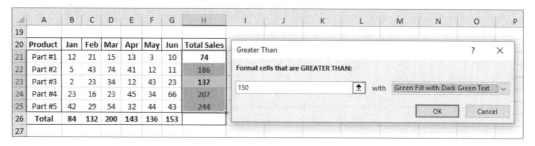

Example #3:

We will highlight all the sale values between 25 and 100. In this case, we will select the complete data range from B21:G25 and go to the 'Conditional formatting->New Rule' option. In the 'New Formatting Rule' dialog box, we will select one of the rule types, 'Format only cells that contain', and create the new rule where the cell contains values between 25-100 and fill those cells with light green color. Using the 'Format' option, select Fill color.

Example #4:

We will highlight the low performing product, that is, the one with the lowest Total Sales. Using the Icons Set – Directional arrows we will show the least performing product. Select the Total Sales cell range H21:H25 and apply conditional formatting using the Icons Set -Directional indicators, that is, go to 'Conditional Formatting->Icons Sets >Directional'. The arrows are shown for all cells, but we need to display only the least sales, that is, the down arrow.

	A	B	C	D	E	F	G	H	I
19									
20	Product	Jan	Feb	Mar	Apr	May	Jun	Total Sales	
21	Part #1	12	21	15	13	3	10	⬇ 74	
22	Part #2	5	43	74	41	12	11	⇨ 186	
23	Part #3	45	23	34	12	43	23	⇨ 180	
24	Part #4	23	16	23	45	34	66	⬆ 207	
25	Part #5	42	29	54	32	44	43	⬆ 244	
26	Total	127	132	200	143	136	153		
27									

Add a New Rule, if the cell value is greater than the average of all the selected cells, then don't add any formatting to the cells. That is, in the New Formatting Rule, select 'Format only cells that contain' and add a condition that cell value is greater than "=AVERAGE(H21:H25)". Do not add any formatting so that it displays 'No Format set' and click on OK.

Now, go to 'Conditional Formatting->Manage Rules...' and tick into the 'Stop if True' checkbox which is next to the rule you have just created. Click on OK.

Now, only the down arrow is displayed in the cell that has the lowest sale, as shown in screenshot below. Since we ticked the checkbox 'Stop if True', as soon as the condition is found to be True, Excel stops processing the other rules and hence the Icon Set rule is not applied to cells that have values greater than average.

◢	A	B	C	D	E	F	G	H
19								
20	Product	Jan	Feb	Mar	Apr	May	Jun	Total Sales
21	Part #1	12	21	15	13	3	10	⬇ 74
22	Part #2	5	43	74	41	12	11	186
23	Part #3	45	23	34	12	43	23	180
24	Part #4	23	16	23	45	34	66	207
25	Part #5	42	29	54	32	44	43	244
26	Total	127	132	200	143	136	153	
27								

1.8.4.4 Data Validation

Data validation is helpful to restrict the type of data or the values that users enters in a cell. 'Data Validation' option is available on the 'Data' tab, in the 'Data Tools' group. In the Data Validation dialog box, there are three tabs: Settings, Input Message, and Error Alert. In the Settings tab, there are two fields: 'Validation criteria' and 'Data' where you can set the specific conditions. In the 'Input Message', enter the message you want users to see on cell selection and in the 'Error Alert' enter the message you want the users to see in case a wrong value is entered.

In the Settings tab, under Allow, the options available are:

- Whole Number: To restrict the cell to accept only whole numbers
- Decimal: To restrict the cell to accept only decimal numbers
- List: To pick data from the drop-down list
- Date: To restrict the cell to accept only date
- Time: To restrict the cell to accept only time
- Text Length: To restrict the length of the text.
- Custom: For custom formula

The conditions that can be set under Data are:

- between, not between, equal to, not equal to
- greater than, less than, greater than or equal to, less than or equal to

We will explain the use of data validation with the help of the following examples:

Example #1:

We want to enter the sales data for multiple products and want to restrict users from entering zero or negative values. Select the cells you want to add data validation to. Open the Data Validation dialog box. In the 'Settings' tab, under Allow, select the 'Whole Numbers' option and in Data select 'greater than' with Minimum value as 0.

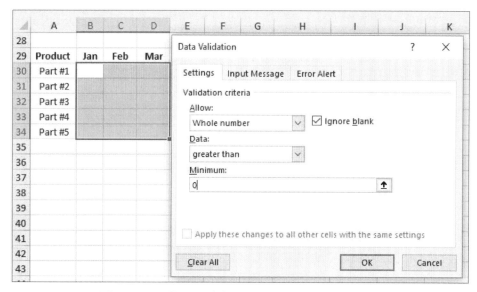

Figure 1-37: Data Validation – Allow Whole Number

Click on Ok to apply data validation to the cells. Now try entering 0 or any negative number in any of the selected cells B30:D34, Excel shows a generic error message.

This does not help the user to know the exact restrictions on the cell. You can customize the Input message and the Error alert to make it more helpful, as given in the screenshot below:

Figure 1-38: Data Validation: Input Message and Error alert tabs

Now select any cell in the data validation range of cells. You will see the message you added in the 'Input Message' and on entering 0 in any of the cells you will see the error message you entered in the 'Error Alert'.

Similarly, you can restrict using the other conditions of allowing only Decimals, Date, and so on.

Example #2:

Set the data validation as in Example #1, Figure 1-37, however, in the Input Message and Error Alert tabs, Figure 1-38, remove the tick from the checkboxes that allow to 'Show Input Message when a cell is selected' and 'Show error alert after invalid data is entered'. Now enter 0 and -1 in cells within the data validation cell range that is, B30:D34. Select the data range, then go to 'Data->Data Tools->Circle Invalid Data'. All the cells with 0 and -1 values will be circled as below.

Example #3:

In this example, we want to restrict the user to select only from the drop-down list provided in the cell. For each student, the teacher needs to select their class (Class 1, Class 2, or Class 3) and specify their attendance (Present or Absent) for the day. In order to provide drop-down for class and attendance, we will first make two lists: List 1 & List 2, separately in either the same worksheet of a different worksheet.

◢	A	B	C	D	E	F	G	H
37								
38	**Name**	**Class**	**Attendance**			**List 1**		**List 2**
39	Mike					Class 1		Present
40	Tom					Class 2		Absent
41	Gary					Class 3		
42	Neha							
43	Puja							

Select the cells B39:B43, go to 'Data Validation' and in the 'Settings' tab under Allow, select List. In 'Source', select the cell range F39:F41 and click on OK. Similarly select the cells C39:C43 and in 'Source' select the cell range H39:H40 and click on OK. Select any one of the cells in the data validation range, they now have a drop-down list.

◢	A	B	C
37			
38	**Name**	**Class**	**Attendance**
39	Mike		
40	Tom		▼
41	Gary	Class 1	
42	Neha	Class 2	
43	Puja	Class 3	
44			

◢	A	B	C	
37				
38	**Name**	**Class**	**Attendance**	
39	Mike			▼
40	Tom		Present	
41	Gary		Absent	
42	Neha			
43	Puja			

Creating the data validation list (like List 1 and List 2) in the same worksheet is not preferable as any deletion or addition of rows in the sheet may change the list and hence disrupt the data validation. A good practice is to keep all the lists to be used in the workbook in a separate sheet. Also using defined names or named ranges (see Chapter 3.3) is very helpful in this case.

In a new sheet, name it as List, copy List 1, and List 2. Using the Name Manager, define the lists names as "Class_List" (for cells B3 to B5) and "Attendance_List" (for cells D3 to D4). See Chapter 3.3 on how to create defined names.

Now go back to the worksheet where you want to add data validation. Select the cells B39:B43, go to 'Data Validation' and in the 'Settings' tab under Allow, select List. In 'Source', enter the corresponding list name that is, type "=Class_List" and click on OK. Similarly, select cells C39:C43 and in 'Source', enter the corresponding list name that is, type "=Attendance_List" and click on OK. Select any one of the cells in the data validation range, they now have a drop-down list.

Figure 1-39: Data Validation with Source as defined names

An advantage of this method is that with any addition or deletion of rows or columns in the data sheet, the lists are not touched. Also, in case you want to add items to the list, you can do so without disrupting your validation. See Chapter 3.3.1 on defined names for details. One of the most common use of data validation is to create a drop-down list.

Example #4:

Now we want to remove all data validations or validation circles added in the sheet. Select the cell ranges where data validation has been added. Go to the 'Data' tab, in the 'Data Tools' group select 'Data Validation'. In the Data Validation dialog box click on 'Clear All' button. All validations will be removed.

To remove the validation circles, select the data range from where you want to erase. Go to the 'Data' tab, in the 'Data Tools' group, select 'Clear Validation Circles'. All the circles that were displayed on invalid cells will be removed.

1.8.5 Working with Excel tables

Excel table is a powerful feature that helps grouping of data into rows and columns. When the data is designated as a table, Excel gives it special properties that enable quick and easy options to analyze the data and help prevent errors.

Figure 1-40: Excel Table components

Table can consist of a set of rows and columns in a sheet that are specifically designated as Excel tables using the create options. There can be multiple tables in a sheet. Table components are the following,

'Header Row' – It is the first row within the table that has names identifying the columns. Generally, the header row color would be different than other rows, also depends on the table style chosen. Excel automatically adds filter buttons and subtotals to the table that adapt as you filter your data.

'Banded Rows or Data' – One or more rows of data. By default, the rows are banded that is, formatted with alternating colors. When we add new data to the table, the existing formatting, formulas, conditional formatting, data validation, and so on, all get applied to the new data. This is a very big advantage of having tables.

'Resizing Handle' – It is at the bottom right of the last cell of the table. You can drag this handle to extend the table that is, can add empty rows as well as columns and

the new cells inherit the same formatting, color and so on from the existing. You can also decrease the size of the table that is, less rows columns will be considered as part of the table. Decreasing the size does not delete the data in the removed cells but they are no longer considered as part of the table and will not get included in calculation, formulas, and so on.

1.8.5.1 Create a table

To convert data to a table, the first step is to identify the data range that you want to convert. For Excel to work correctly, the data range should not have any row or column that is completely blank. Select any cell in the data range, go to the 'Home' tab, in the 'Styles' group select 'Format as Table' and choose from the different styles for the table. Upon selection of the style, Excel automatically selects the adjoining cells and launches the 'Format as Table' dialog box. Confirm the table settings, data range and tick the checkbox if your data has a header row and click on OK. Data range is converted into a table, with banded rows and sort & filter control.

Figure 1-41: *Format as Table*

Another method to convert a range to table is by selecting any cell in the data range and pressing CTRL+T on the keyboard. A 'Create Table' dialog box is launched where you can give the data range and specify if selection has a header row or not.

Figure 1-42: *Create Table*

Click on OK to create the table. You can change the table style from the 'Table Design' tab, using the 'Table Styles' group options. For users working with older versions of Excel i.e., 2016 and before, you will see 'Table Styles' under 'Table Tools->Design' tab.

Excel also allows you to create a table first, with empty rows and columns using the 'Format as Table' and 'Create Table' options, and then entering the data. By default, the column names are added as Column1, Column2, and so on. You can change the names of columns as required.

1.8.5.2 Use table styles

By clicking anywhere in the table, you can see a contextual 'Table Design' tab. Click on the 'Table Styles' drop-down and select any one of the style thumbnails to apply the selected color scheme to your data. For users working with older versions of Excel i.e., 2016 and before, you will see 'Table Styles' under 'Table Tools->Design' tab.

Figure 1-43: Table Styles

These quick styles make it easier and faster to change the look of your table and to make a good data representation.

1.8.5.3 Convert to Range

Excel allows you to convert a table to a data range. Upon conversion, all the special properties associated with the table are lost, the data remains as is. The 'Convert to Range' option is available on the 'Table Design' tab, in the 'Tools' group and on mouse right click. For users working with older versions of Excel i.e., 2016 and before, you will see 'Tools' under 'Table Tools->Design' tab. Excel converts table to range only after getting confirmation from user

Figure 1-44: Convert table to range

After the table is converted to a range, all the table properties get removed but the row colors or bands may remain based on the style that was selected for the original table.

1.8.5.4 Add name to table

By default, the table names given by Excel are Table1, Table2, and so on. You can change the table name, which is preferable as it makes it easier to identify and reference the table data in formulas. To change the table name, go to the 'Table Design' tab, in the 'Properties' group on left-hand side of the Ribbon and type the name in the 'Table Name' field. Table name should be a single word that is, no spaces are allowed. For users working with older versions of Excel i.e., 2016 and before, you will see 'Properties' under 'Table Tools->Design' tab.

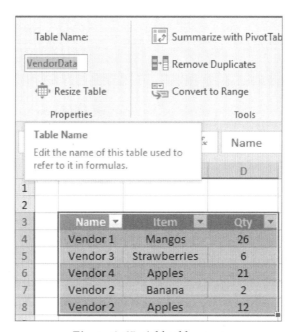

Figure 1-45: Add table name

Table name can be used in formulas as reference and when the table changes with new rows or columns, these references get updated as well.

1.8.5.5 Add or Delete data from table

You start typing text in the cell adjacent to the last row or column of the table and as you click ENTER, Excel automatically expands the Table and applies all the formatting, formulas, data validations to the new added row or column.

Using the resizing handle also you can expand or reduce the Table. Click on the resizing handle using the mouse and drag to add or delete rows or columns. Adding applies all formatting, formulas, and so on while deleting removes the cells from all special properties of the table.

You can also add or delete rows and columns in the Table using the insert or delete menu options (see Chapter 1.8.2.2). You can also use the keyboard shortcuts CTRL+'+' and CTRL+'-' ; click on any cell within the table and press the keyboard shortcuts.

There is also an option to 'Resize Table' under the 'Table Design->Properties' group. For users working with older versions of Excel i.e., 2016 and before, you will see 'Resize Table' option under 'Table Tools->Design->Properties' group.

Select the new data range for the Table and click OK. The new added columns will be given the default name as Column1, Column2 etc.

1.8.5.6 Sorting & Filtering data

Sorting and Filtering of data in tables are like the normal range sort and filter. See Chapter 1.8.4.1. Filtering makes it easy to copy a subset of a larger Table and paste it to another location. Note that when you copy data from a filtered Table, only the visible data is copied and the pasted data is a normal range, not a Table.

1.8.5.7 Filtering using Slicers

Another way of filtering is, using slicers. Slicers can be inserted by selecting any cell within the Table and then selecting 'Insert Slicer' option in the 'Table Design->Tools' group. For users working with older versions of Excel i.e., 2016 and before, will see 'Insert Slicer' under 'Table Tools->Design->Tools' group. Excel responds with a dialog box that displays each header in the Table. Tick the checkbox for which you want to create the slicer and click on OK.

You can create a slicer for each column. To use a slicer, just click one of the buttons and the Table displays only the rows that have a value that corresponds to the button. In case of more than one slicer, data is filtered by the selected buttons in each slicer. You can remove filtering for a slicer by clicking on the Clear Filter icon in the upper-right corner of the slicer.

1.8.5.8 Quick Analysis

Quick Analysis tools are very helpful, wherein you don't have to add formulas for calculating sum or averages however, you can add them quickly using the options. These work on the complete data designated as a Table. Select any cell in the Table and select the 'Quick Analysis' option on mouse right-click menu options.

Figure 1-46: *Quick analysis on Table*

This allows you to add conditional Formatting, create Charts, add Totals, create PivotTables and create Sparklines. Here we will discuss adding Totals in Tables, all other options are discussed under different chapters of PivotTable, Pivot Charts, and so on.

In 'Quick analysis', click on 'Totals', move your cursor across the buttons to see the calculation results for your data, and then click on the button to apply the totals. For example, the row and column sums are shown by selecting the two sum options:

Figure 1-47: *Sum the columns*

Figure 1-48: Sum the rows

This is easier and faster than adding totals manually using formulas. The totals automatically apply to the complete data in the Table. In case you add data in new rows or columns or delete from existing, the totals are updated automatically.

1.8.6 Controlling View of Worksheet

Excel includes few options under the 'View' tab that enables you to view multiple sheets at a time. The Zoom in and Zoom out options are available under the 'Zoom' group. The Split, Arrange all, Freeze Panes, and more such options are available under the 'Windows' group.

Figure 1-49: Zoom and Windows options

1.8.6.1 Zoom Options

By default, the view is displayed at 100%. You can change the zoom percentage and make it big with 'Zoom In' or make it small with 'Zoom Out'. These options do not change the font or picture size, the original content remains the same. Zoom factor of the active sheet can be changed either using the zoom slider on the status bar or by pressing CTRL and using the mouse wheel button, or using the options under the 'Zoom' group in the 'View' tab.

The 'Zoom to Selection' option zooms in the selected cell range to a factor that fits in the Excel window. As the name suggests, the '100%' option displays the content in 100% mode. The 'Zoom' option launches a dialog box where you can either select from the existing percentage or specify your own under the 'Custom' option.

You can have different Zoom percentages for different worksheets and different windows (displaying the same worksheet).

1.8.6.2 Windows Options

New Window

A worksheet may have lots of information that is not easily visible and fits the screen for your analysis or you may want to see multiple sheets of the workbook simultaneously. Excel gives an option to launch a new window or multiple windows to the workbook using the 'New Window' option (see Figure 1-49). In each of the new window, you can have a different view of the same worksheet or have different sheets opened. Changes made in any of the new windows and on saving the file gets reflected in all windows. As soon as a new window is launched, Excel changes the name of the original file by appending the number, '1', to the name. All the new workbooks will have the same name as the original file but with a number appended, based on the creation sequence. For example, if the workbook name is 'Myfile.xlsx' and two new windows are launched then the original file will be renamed to 'Myfile. xlsx:1' and the new ones as 'MyFile.xlsx:2' and 'MyFile.xlsx:3'.

Hide/Unhide

Open a new workbook named 'MyFile.xlsx' and launch two new windows as explained in the preceding section. Go to each of the new workbooks—MyFile.xlsx:2 and MyFile.xlsx:3—and click on the 'Hide' option in the 'Windows' group under 'View' tab (see Figure 1-49), the workbooks are no longer visible. In order to make those workbooks visible, go to 'Unhide' option in the workbook that is open. In the Unhide dialog box, the hidden workbooks are listed under 'Unhide workbook', select the workbook to unhide and click on OK.

The workbook selected to unhide is now visible.

Arrange All

You can arrange all open windows in different ways, Tiled, Horizontal, Vertical, or Cascade. In any one of the open windows, go to the 'View' tab, in the 'Windows' group and select 'Arrange All', a dialog box is launched where you can select the arrangement style and click on OK.

Split window

Split window is a very helpful feature, wherein you can split the active window into two or four panes and have different views of the same worksheet. Select the worksheet you want to split and then go to the 'View' tab, in the 'Windows' group and select 'Split'. The worksheet will be divided into four panes, the split is done at the position of the active cell. You can drag the split lines and change the view size of the panes.

◢	A	B	C	D	E	N	O
1	Product ▼	Unit Pric ▼	Quantit ▼	Sales ▼	Pane 1	Pane 2	
2	Apple	120	2	240			
3	Banana	65	4	260			
4	Grapes	97	1	97			
5	Mango	154	5	770			
6	Orange	42	2	84			
7							
11					Pane 3	Pane 4	
12			Split Lines				
13							

Freeze Panes

Freeze Panes option helps in keeping the column headers and row labels visible even when the user scrolls the worksheet up or down. For example, we have a sales data with column headers in the first row and the data goes beyond the rows that are currently visible in the window. In order to see the rows below, we will scroll down and in this process the column header also scroll ups. To avoid this, go to the 'View' tab, in the 'Windows' group, select 'Freeze Panes->Freeze Top Row'.

Now the top row is fixed and on scrolling down, the rows below move up, but the first header row is always visible. Similarly, if you select 'Freeze First column', then the first column is always visible even when the user scrolls to extreme right. In case of 'Freeze Panes', based on the cell that is selected, the rows and columns are fixed while rest of the worksheet scrolls.

View Side by Side and synchronous Scrolling

When you have multiple windows or workbooks open, you can tile them side-by-side for comparison using the 'View Side by Side' option in the 'View->Window' group. The 'Synchronous Scrolling' option gets enabled after you click on 'View Side by Side'. Synchronous scrolling means that the scrolling happens at the same pace in both the open windows simultaneously.

1.8.7 Accessibility Features

1.8.7.1 Using Accessibility Checker

You can improve accessibility of your spreadsheet with the Accessibility Checker. Before sharing your document or spreadsheet, run the Accessibility Checker to make sure your Microsoft Office content is easy for people of all abilities to read and edit. Go to 'Review->Check Accessibility'.

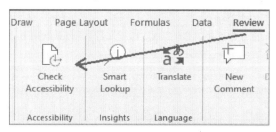

In the Accessibility window you can review your results. You will see a list of Errors, Warnings, and Tips with how-to-fix recommendations for each under the 'Additional Information' section. For example, in the screenshot below, the Accessibility Checker is giving a warning that 'Table 2' in Sheet4 has some text that is hard to read.

To see the recommendations, click on the arrow next to the selected warning as shown in screenshot below.

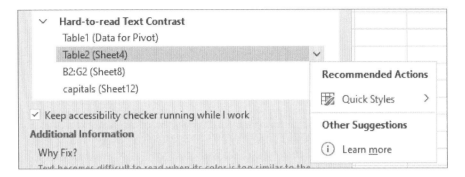

To be notified of accessibility issues in your document as you continue working on it, tick the 'Keep accessibility checker running while I work' check box. This adds the Accessibility button to your status bar and keeps track of accessibility issues in real time. You can open the Accessibility Checker whenever you want by selecting the status bar button.

1.8.7.2 Turn on Audio Cues

You can enhance your productivity in Microsoft Office by providing audio cues. To turn on the audio cues, go to 'File->Options'. In the Excel Options dialog box go to 'Ease of Access' and under 'Feedback options' select the 'Provide feedback with sound' checkbox.

For example, a sound cue might notify you when options on the screen change. Or, a sound can confirm that an action (such as send a mail, delete something, or paste content) completed.

1.9 Protecting Excel Workbook and Worksheet

You can protect your workbook to control the changes that can be made to the workbook, go to 'File->Info' menu and the first option on right-hand side pane is

Protect Workbook. It has a drop-down menu, which gives options like opening the file in Read-only mode, Encrypt with password, Protect Current Sheet, and Workbook Structure (which we will discuss in details later in this chapter), Restrict Access (using Azure Rights Management System), Add digital signatures (digitally signing the document using a Microsoft Partner) and the last option is Mark as Final. The 'Mark as Final' option is used to designate the workbook as 'final'. The document is saved as a read-only file to prevent changes and useful to let others know that you're sharing a completed version of a workbook.

Figure 1-50: Protect Workbook Options

Excel gives multiple options for unprotecting and protecting your work, under the Protect section in the Review tab; Protect Sheet, Protect Workbook, Allow Edit Ranges, and Unshare Workbook.

1.9.1 Protect Workbook

Protect Workbook launches the 'Protect Structure and Windows' dialogue box. You can add your password and click on OK to save it. It will ask you to re-enter the password for confirmation and finally setting the same. Next time you try to open the workbook, Excel will ask for the password and if correctly entered it will open the workbook else it will disallow. So, it is important to remember your password.

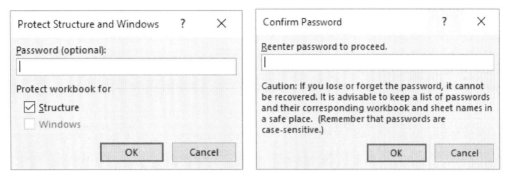

Figure 1-51: *Protect Workbook with Password*

1.9.2 Protect Sheet & Allow Edit Ranges

Select the sheet to be protected, right-click and select 'Protect Sheet' option. It launches a dialog box with different options. You can protect a sheet and its contents with password and set permissions for user operations like selecting locked cells, changing format of cells, or allow inserting/deleting rows/columns and so on. For example, if the "Select locked cells" were unchecked, users wouldn't even be allowed to select locked cells, so any formulas in these cells would be hidden.

The 'Allow Users to Edit Ranges' menu option allows you to add or modify the range of cells and set permissions for users to allow/disallow operations.

Figure 1-52: *Protect Sheet with Password / Edit Ranges*

By default, all the cells are locked in Excel. But in order to restrict the user from making any changes, you need to also protect the locked cells. This also means that if a cell is not locked and you protect it, the user would be able to make changes.

1.10 Importing data into Excel

Data you want to analyze may not always be in Excel format, it could be in a text file, website, in a database, or other sources. Excel allows you to import data using the 'Get Data' option under Data. More detailed information on importing data will be discussed later in the data analysis chapter (Chapter 8) of this book.

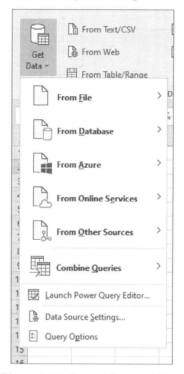

Figure 1-53: Import External Data

1.10.1 Importing from Text

Refer to Chapter 8.15.1 Import data from Text/CSV

1.10.2 Importing from Web

Refer to Chapter 8.15.2 Import data from Web

1.10.3 Import from Database

Refer to Chapter 8.15.4 Import data from Other sources

1.11 Exporting Data from Excel

1.11.1 Export to file

You can Export data from Excel in PDF format (Adobe Acrobat document) or different file types as given in the following screenshot. Go to 'File' menu and select the 'Export' option:

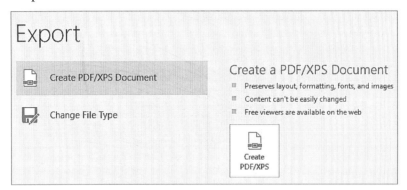

Click on 'Create PDF/XPS document' for exporting the workbook in PDF format. A file Save dialog is launched.

Using the 'Options' setting in the Save dialog you can specify what to publish in the PDF from Excel like page numbers, entire workbook, the active sheet, or selection as shown in screenshot below.

Click Ok and on the Save dialog click on 'Publish' to print the Excel in PDF format.

If you want to save the workbook in a different file type (excluding PDF), select the file type and click on 'Save As' (see details in Chapter 1.7.3).

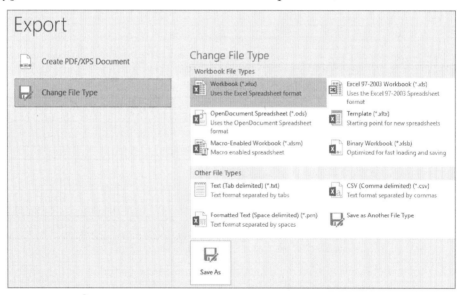

Figure 1-54: Export from Excel

1.11.2 Export table to SharePoint List

There is an option to export an Excel Table to a SharePoint List. When you export the list, Excel will create a new SharePoint list on the site for you to work. For doing this, you need a SharePoint site and the correct permissions.

Select the Table in the sheet and from the 'Table Design' tab, select 'Export-> Export Table to SharePoint List…'.

Figure 1-55: Export to SharePoint List

Specify the URL of the SharePoint site in 'Address', type the 'Name' and 'Description' and click on 'Next' or 'Finish'. When you click on 'Next', it might ask for Office credentials. Review the information given in Columns and Data Types and then click on Finish. Click on OK to complete. A message indicating that your Table is published, along with the Uniform Resource Locator (URL) appears.

1.12 Sharing in Excel

You can share and collaborate in Excel using a feature called 'Co-authoring' that is, multiple people can open and work on the same shared Excel workbook and see each other's changes quickly. In older versions of Excel, the feature was named "Shared Workbooks" that had many limitations and hence was replaced by co-authoring in newer versions, starting Excel 2016. This feature has been further enhanced in the latest version, that is, Excel 2019. We will discuss Co-authoring and see how to enable the old legacy features. Microsoft recommends using Co-authoring now.

1.12.1 Co-authoring

Co-authoring is only available with Office 365 subscription and in a later version on Excel, including Excel 2016. If you're using a version of Excel that supports co-authoring, you can see the 'Share' option in the upper-right corner.

Figure 1-56: Share option

Before sharing, we will need to save the Excel file in OneDrive (can also be done in SharePoint Online library). Note that you will need to have OneDrive software installed on your system and correct permissions to copy.

To save the Excel file in OneDrive, first open the Excel file you want to save. Go to 'File->Save a Copy' option and select OneDrive. In order to increase efficiency and help users to quickly save the file, Excel displays the list of recently accessed folders that you can save to. Select the Location or Folder, specify the   File Name, File Type and click 'Save'.

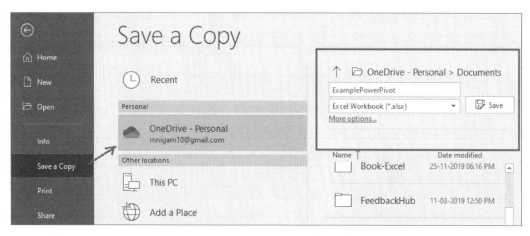

Close the workbook and verify on OneDrive that the file has got saved in the specified location.

Now in order to share this workbook with other users so that all can work on it simultaneously, open the workbook from OneDrive location and click 'Share' option on the upper-right corner of the window. A window is launched that allows you to share the file with other users.

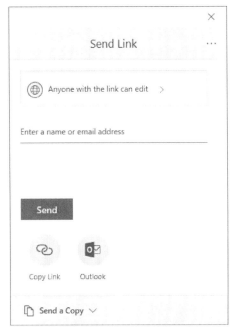

Figure 1-57: *Send Link dialog box*

Excel gives multiple options for sharing the file. It allows you to 'Send Link' of the file to multiple users, 'Copy Link' for sharing, use Outlook for directly sending the link to file and 'Send a Copy' of the file in either PDF or Excel Workbook format via email. You can also set edit permissions to file for users, to enable or disable file modifications.

1.12.1.1 Send Link

In order to send link of the file to multiple users, specify the users email addresses in the text box, as shown in snapshot below and click the 'Send' button.

In the preceding example, users 'abc@gmail. com' and 'xyz@yahoo.com' will receive the link to the file via email. As it was sent with option 'Anyone with the link can edit', these users will be able to make changes in the shared file.

Figure 1-58: *Send Link with Edit permissions*

You can modify the edit permissions for the users, before sending the file link, by clicking 'Anyone with the link can edit' option that is located above the user email addresses. A Link settings dialog box is launched. Uncheck 'Allow editing' box and click 'Apply' button to disable users from editing the shared file.

Figure 1-59: Link setting dialog box   *Figure 1-60:* Send Link with View Permissions

In the preceding screenshot, users 'abc@gmail.com' and 'xyz@yahoo.com' will receive a view only link to the file.

Excel also allows you to specify the expiration date of the link, that is, the link will not be accessible to users after the specified date. In order to add additional security, you can also set a password. Users with whom you have shared the password will only be able to access the shared file.

Figure 1-61: Link settings dialog with Expiration date and password set

In the preceding screenshots, both expiration date (i.e., Monday Jan 13, 2020) and password (encrypted) have been set. Status of checkbox 'Allow editing' will determine if the link is view only or allows editing of the file. Click 'Apply' button in the Link settings dialog box to return to Send Link dialog box.

You will notice that two icons are displayed indicating that along with edit permissions, the expiration date and password have also been set for file sharing. Click on the 'Send' button in the Send Link dialog box, the file is shared with the specified permissions.

1.12.1.2 Copy Link

You can copy the link to the file and share it with individuals or set of users separately. Click on 'Share' and in the Send Link dialog box click on 'Copy Link' button. Excel creates a shareable link to the file and you can set the permissions as edit or view only in the Link settings dialog box as shown in Figure 1-61. Click on 'Copy' to copy the link and you can paste it in an email, message or any document as required.

 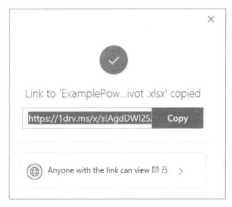

1.12.1.3 Use Outlook to share

You can share the link to the file using Outlook messaging application by clicking 'Outlook' button in the Send Link dialog box. You can specify the user email addresses either in the Send Link dialog box or directly specify them in the 'To / CC/ BCC' sender fields in Outlook.

Figure 1-62: Share link to file using Outlook

As explained in preceding examples, you can set the file permissions as edit or view only, with or without expiration date and password by modifying the settings in the Link settings dialog box as shown in Figure 1-61.

1.12.1.4 Send a Copy as PDF or Excel

You can share the file as a Copy in either PDF or Excel format. In the 'Send Link' dialog box, click on 'Send a Copy'. Excel shows two options 'Excel Worksheet' and 'PDF'. Click on the format in which you want to share the file to users. Outlook will be launched with the file attached in the selected format.

Figure 1-63: *Send a Copy option*

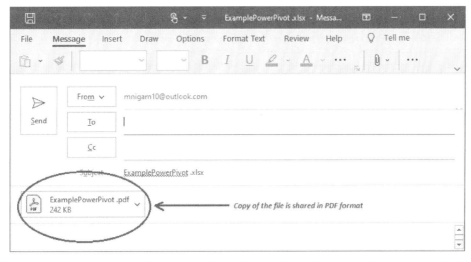

In the preceding example, the copy of the file is shared in PDF format. Similarly, on selecting 'Excel Workbook' the copy of the file will be shared in Excel format. As explained in preceding examples, you can set the file permissions as edit or view only, with or without expiration date and password by modifying the settings in the Link settings dialog box as shown in Figure 1-61.

1.12.1.5 Manage Access

You can edit the user permissions using the Manage Access option. In the 'Send Link' dialog box, click on the three dots near 'Send Link' and click on 'Manage Access'.

All existing user permissions set for the file are shown in the 'Manage Access' dialog box.

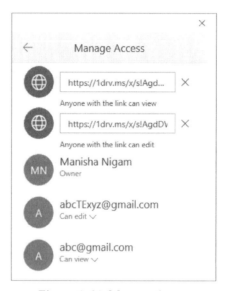

Figure 1-64: Manage Access

You can delete the permissions by clicking on the cross next to it or change the file sharing from edit to view only and visa-versa or stop sharing of the file.

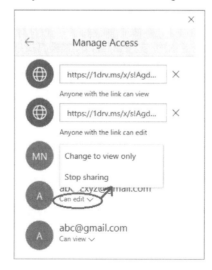

1.12.2 View and restore changes in workbooks that are shared

Excel maintains the version history of cloud-based files, that is, files that are stored in OneDrive or SharePoint Online. Click 'File > Info > Version history' and select a version to open it in a separate window.

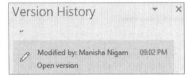

If you want to restore a previous version you've opened, select Restore.

1.12.3 Shared Workbooks (legacy)

In latest versions of Excel like Excel 2019, the buttons related to the "Shared Workbook" feature are no longer available on the Review tab by default as this has been replaced by Co-authoring feature. Excel still gives an option to enable those.

1.12.3.1 Adding legacy features on QAT

We will enable the legacy features and add them to the Quick Access Toolbar. Go to 'File->Options' and select 'Quick Access toolbar'.

Figure 1-65: Adding Shared Workbook legacy commands in QAT

In 'Choose commands from' select 'Commands Not in the Ribbon'. This will display all commands in the list that are not currently seen in the Ribbons tab. Now select the Shared Workbook-related commands one-by-one that is, Share Workbook (Legacy), Track Changes (Legacy), Protect Sharing (Legacy), Compare and Merge Workbooks, and add them to the right-hand side using the 'Add>>' button. After you have added all the commands, click on OK to see the command buttons in the QAT.

Figure 1-66: QAT with Shared workbook buttons

- Share Workbook button:
- Protect and Share button:
- Compare and Merge Workbooks button:
- Track Changes button:

1.12.3.2 Share Workbook

Create a new workbook or open an existing workbook and upload it on a network location, like what we did in co-authoring example. From the Quick Access Toolbar (QAT), click on the 'Share Workbook' button. There are two tabs in the 'Share Workbook' dialog box: Editing and Advanced.

In the Editing tab, click on the checkbox to enable use of old features. In the Advanced tab, modify the settings as per your requirements and click on OK to save.

You can see that next to the file name, 'Shared' is mentioned in brackets to indicate that now the file is in sharing mode.

As per the official Microsoft website, the following are the unsupported features and hence, it is advised to use the new feature Co-authoring.

Unsupported items	Unsupported actions
Creating or inserting tables	Inserting or deleting blocks of cells
Adding or changing conditional formats	Deleting worksheets
Adding or changing data validation	Merging cells or splitting merged cells
Creating or changing charts or PivotChart reports	Sorting or filtering by format
Inserting or changing pictures or other objects	Using drawing tools
Inserting or changing hyperlinks	Assigning, changing, or removing passwords
Creating, changing, or viewing scenarios	Protecting or unprotecting worksheets or the workbook
Inserting automatic subtotals	Grouping or outlining data
Creating data tables	Writing, recording, changing, viewing, or assigning macros
Creating or changing PivotTable reports	Changing or deleting array formulas
Creating or applying slicers	Adding, renaming, or deleting XML maps
Creating or modifying sparklines	Mapping cells to XML elements
Adding or changing Microsoft Excel 4 dialog sheets	Using the XML Source task pane, XML toolbar, or XML commands on the Data menu
	Using a data form to add new data
Adding threaded comments	Editing, or deleting threaded comments

1.12.3.3 Protect Shared Workbook

You can enable the option to prevent the change history to be removed by clicking on the 'Sharing with track changes' checkbox in the 'Protect Shared Workbook' dialog box.

Figure 1-67: Protect Shared Workbook

1.12.3.4 Compare and Merge Workbooks

Open the Shared Workbook into which you want to merge changes. Click on the 'Compare and Merge Workbooks' button on QAT, browse to select the copy of the workbook (can select multiple files) that contains the changes to merge and click on OK. The changes will be merged in the original shared workbook.

1.12.3.5 Track Changes

Track changes gives two options: Highlight changes and Accept or Reject changes. You can change 'When', 'Who', and 'Where' fields to selectively track the changes made by everyone or individuals or for specific cell ranges as selected in 'Where'.

Figure 1-68: Track changes in Shared Workbooks

Again, a word of caution that the old features that is, these legacy features have some limitations and hence, it is advisable to use the new co-authoring feature to take full advantage of Excel.

CHAPTER 2
Perform Functions with Shortcut Keys

Excel provides many shortcut keys to help users perform major functions or operations on cells, columns, rows, or objects in worksheets and workbooks.

Benefits of Excel shortcut keys that are often overlooked:

- Faster operations that save time, increases productivity, and therefore saves money

- Reduced dependency on computer mouse that minimizes the hand movement and the number of steps or clicks to perform a function

- Improved work posture and prevents strain associated with repetitive strain injury

Excel has been a popular tool for many years and basic shortcuts for functions like copy, paste, and select all, are well known. In this section, we will discuss important shortcuts keys that are not very often used.

2.1 Keys for Menus

Show a shortcut menu	SHIFT+F10
Make the menu bar active	F10 or ALT

Contd…

Show the program icon menu (on the program title bar)	ALT+SPACEBAR
Select the next or previous command on the menu or submenu	DOWN/UP ARROW
Select the menu to the left or right, or, with a submenu visible, switch between the main menu and the submenu	LEFT/RIGHT ARROW
Select the first or last command on the menu or submenu	HOME or END
Close the visible menu and submenu at the same time	ALT

2.2 Move on a Worksheet or Workbook

Move to the first/last cell on the worksheet	CTRL+ {HOME / END}
Move up/down one screen	PAGE {UP / DOWN}
Move one screen to the right/left	ALT+ PAGE {DOWN / UP}
Move to the next/previous sheet in the workbook	CTRL+PAGE {DOWN / UP}
Move to the next workbook or window	CTRL+F6 or CTRL+TAB
Move to the previous workbook or window	CTRL+SHIFT+F6

2.3 Select Cells, Columns, Rows or Objects

Select the entire column/row	{CTRL/ SHIFT} + SPACEBAR
Select the entire worksheet	CTRL+A
Select the current region around the active cell (the current region is an area enclosed by blank rows and blank columns)	CTRL+SHIFT+* (ASTERISK)
Extend the selection by one cell	SHIFT+ arrow key
Extend the selection to the last nonblank cell in the same column or row as the active cell	CTRL+SHIFT+ arrow key
Extend the selection to the beginning of the row	SHIFT+HOME
Extend the selection to the first/last cell used on the worksheet (lower-right corner)	CTRL+SHIFT+ {HOME / END}

2.4 Select Cells with Special Characteristics

Select the current array, which is the array that the active cell belongs to	CTRL+/

Contd...

Select all cells with comments	CTRL+SHIFT+O (the letter O)
Select cells whose content are different from the comparison cell in each row (for each row, the comparison cell is in the same column as the active cell)	CTRL+\
Select cells whose contents are different from the comparison cell in each column (for each column, the comparison cell is in the same row as the active cell)	CTRL+SHIFT+	
Select only cells that are directly referred to by formulas in the selection	CTRL+ [
Select only cells with formulas that refer directly to the active cell	CTRL+]
Select all cells with formulas that refer directly or indirectly to the active cell	CTRL+SHIFT+}
Select only visible cells in the current selection	ALT+SEMICOLON
Show all cells that have formulas	CTRL+ ` (that is to the left of the 1 key on your keyboard)

2.5 Format Data

Display the Style command (Format menu)	ALT+' (APOSTROPHE)
Display the Cells command (Format menu)	CTRL+1
Apply bold style to all cells in the highlighted section	CTRL+2
Apply italics to all cells in the highlighted section	CTRL+3
Underline all cells in the highlighted section	CTRL+4
Apply or remove strikethrough formatting	CTRL+5
Apply the General number format	CTRL+SHIFT+~
Apply the Currency format with two decimal places (negative numbers appear in parentheses)	CTRL+SHIFT+$
Apply the Percentage format with no decimal places	CTRL+SHIFT+%
Apply the Exponential number format with two decimal places	CTRL+SHIFT+^
Apply the Date format with the day, month, and year	CTRL+SHIFT+#
Apply the Time format with the hour and minute, and indicate A.M. or P.M.	CTRL+SHIFT+@
Apply the Number format with two decimal places, 1000 separator, and – for negative values	CTRL+SHIFT+!
Hide rows	CTRL+9

Contd…

Unhide rows	CTRL+SHIFT+ (
Hide columns	CTRL+0 (ZERO)
Unhide columns	CTRL+SHIFT+)
Changes between displaying cell values or formulas in the worksheet	CTRL+`

2.6 Filling data in cells

Fill down. Fills the cell beneath with the contents of the selected cell. To fill more than one cell, select the source cell and press Ctrl+Shift+Down to select multiple cells. Then press Ctrl+D to fill them with the contents of the original cell.	CTRL+D
Fill right. Fills the cell to the right with the contents of the selected cell. To fill more than one cell, select the source cell and press Ctrl+Shift+Right to select multiple cells. Then press Ctrl+R to fill them with the contents of the original cell.	CTRL+R
Copies a formula from the cell above	CTRL+'
Copies value from cell above	CTRL+SHIFT+"

2.7 Working on Tables

Creates table of selected cells	CTRL+L / CTRL+T
Insert, (Rows, Columns, or Cells) Depends on selection	CTRL++ / CTRL+SHIFT+=
Delete, (Rows, Columns, or Cells) Depends on selection	CTRL+-
Apply the outline border	CTRL+SHIFT+&
Remove all borders	CTRL+SHIFT+_

Chapter 3
Formulas and Functions

3.1 Understanding Formulas

Formulas in Excel worksheets are very important and useful features of Excel that makes it so powerful. Formulas help to calculate results from the data stored in the worksheet. A formula consists of special code entered in a cell, performs calculations, and returns the result in the displayed cell. When data changes, the formulas calculate updated results dynamically. Formulas use a variety of operators and worksheet functions to work with values and text which can be in other cells. The formula itself appears in the Formula bar when you select the cell.

A formula always begins with an equal sign and can contain any of these elements:

- Mathematical operators, such as + (for addition) and * (for multiplication)
- Cell references (including named cells and ranges)
- Values or Text
- Worksheet functions (such as SUM and COUNT)

3.2 Operators in Formula

Operators specify the type of calculation that you want to perform on elements in a formula. They are categorized into four different types: Arithmetic, Logical /

Comparison, Text concatenation, and Reference. There is also a Double Minus (or Double Unary) operator that is a little uncommon and used more in advanced Excel formula.

3.2.1 Arithmetic Operators

Operator		Meaning
%	(percent sign)	Percentage
^	(caret)	Exponentiation
*	(asterisk)	Multiplication
/	(forward slash)	Division
+	(plus sign)	Addition
–	(minus sign)	Subtraction

3.2.2 Logical / Comparison Operators

Operator		Meaning
=	(equal sign)	Equal to
>	(greater than sign)	Greater than
<	(less than sign)	Less than
>=	(greater than or equal to sign)	Greater than or equal to
<=	(less than or equal to sign)	Less than or equal to
<>	(not equal to sign)	Not equal to

3.2.3 Text Concatenation & Reference Operators

Operator		Meaning
&	(ampersand)	Connects, or concatenates, two values to produce one continuous text value
:	(colon)	Range operator, which produces one reference to all the cells between two references, including the two references.
,	(comma)	Union operator, which combines multiple references into one reference.
	(space)	Intersection operator, which produces a reference to cells common to the two references.

Contd…

#	*(pound)*	The # symbol is used in several contexts:
		Used as part of an error name.
		Used to indicate insufficient space to render. In most cases, you can widen the column until the contents display properly.
		Spilled range operator, which is used to reference an entire range in a dynamic array formula.
@	*(at)*	Reference operator, which is used to indicate implicit intersection in a formula.

3.2.4 Operators Precedence

Operators that are used in formulas are listed in the following table with their precedence that is, when Excel calculates the value of a formula, it uses certain rules to determine the order in which the various parts of the formula are calculated.

Excel performs the operations in the order shown in the following table. If a formula contains operators with the same precedence, for example, if a formula contains both a multiplication and division operator, Excel evaluates the operators from left to right.

Operator	Name	Precedence
:	Range Operator	1
(space)	Intersection Operator	
,	Union Operator	
-	Negation (as in -1)	2
%	Percentage	3
^	Exponentiation	4
*	Multiplication	5
/	Division	
+	Addition	6
–	Subtraction	
&	Concatenation	7
=	Logical comparison (equal to)	8
>	Logical comparison (greater than)	
<	Logical comparison (less than)	
>=	Logical comparison (greater than or equal to)	
<=	Logical comparison (less than or equal to)	
<>	Logical comparison (not equal to)	

Figure 3-1: Operators & Precedence

Note that the parentheses can be used to override Excel's built-in order of precedence. Expressions within parentheses are always evaluated first. You can also nest parentheses within formulas and Excel evaluates the most deeply nested expressions first and then works its way out.

For example, in the following picture we have taken five values and are using different operators and parentheses to create multiple formulas, including nested parentheses to show how the result changes in each case. Note that the formula is displayed in the formula bar for the selected cell.

D2				f_x	=B2-B3*B4+B5/B6
	A	B	C		D
1		Values	Formula		Result
2		10	=B2-B3*B4+B5/B6		-6
3		5	=(B2-B3)*B4+B5/B6		24
4		4	=((B2-B3)*(B4+B5))/B6		30
5		8	=((B2-B3)*(B4+B5/B6))		40
6		2	=(B2-(B3*(B4+B5)/B6))		-20
7					

Figure 3-2: Operator precedence examples

So, based on the precedence Excel calculates the result for the above formulas. In the first formula, that is, "=B2-B3*B4+B5/B6", first the multiplication and division calculations will happen (result 20 and 4), then addition and subtractions (=10-20+4). In the last formula, we have nested parentheses, "=(B2-(B3*(B4+B5)/B6))". Working from inner most parentheses, Excel first calculates (B4+B5) = 12, then 12/B6 = 6, B3*6 = 30 and finally B2-30 = -20.

3.2.5 Double Minus / Unary Operator

There is another, not so common operator, that is 'Double Minus / Double Unary' operator. The double minus (--) can be used to transform TRUE and FALSE values into their corresponding 1 and 0 equivalents in more advanced formulas, especially formulas that work with arrays.

E13	▼	⋮	×	✓	*fx*	=SUMPRODUCT(--(B13:B16=C13:C16))			
◢	B	C	D	E			F	G	H
11									
12	Column 1	Column 2		Match					
13	1	2		2					
14	3	3							
15	4	4							
16	5	6							
17									

In the preceding example, there are two columns that contain four values each. Two values match (3 & 4) and two are different. The formula used to count matching values is: '=SUMPRODUCT(--(B13:B16=C13:C16))' Where, B13:B16 is compared to C13:C16 in a simple expression that creates an array of TRUE, FALSE values, that is '=SUMPRODUCT(--({FALSE;TRUE;TRUE;FALSE}))'. And the double unary changes the TRUE, FALSE values to ones and zeros, that is '=SUMPRODUCT({0;1;1;0})'. With only one array to work with, SUMPRODUCT simply returns the sum of all items, 2. Function SUMPRODUCT is detailed in Chapter 3.10.5.

3.3 Defined Names

Excel gives an option of defined names where the user can define a descriptive name for a cell range, function, constant, or table. Defined name, range name, or named range refer to the same thing. Using named range in formulas, charts are easier to understand and maintain. Another benefit in using named range is that they do not change when the formula is copied to another location, so there is no chance of messing your formulas.

Note that the name cannot have spaces, however, you can use underscore or period. Excel will not allow names that conflict with the names it uses internally; it will show an error if it conflicts. There are multiple ways of defining a name that we will discuss in this chapter.

3.3.1 Create New, Delete, Edit Named Range

3.3.1.1 Directly typing name in Name box

Select the range of cells and type in the descriptive name that you want in the Name Box that is, on left corner above the first column A in the sheet. In the following example, we selected the cell range A2 to A6 and typed in the name 'fruits' in the Name Box and hit Enter.

Figure 3-3: Define name in Name Box

Now, how do you confirm that this name you typed has been added correctly? Go to menu 'Formulas -> Name Manger' under Defined Names group. This name should be displayed in the list of named ranges.

Figure 3-4: Defined Names -Name Manager

3.3.1.2 Using Name Manager or Define Name

You can also define a named range using the Name Manager or Define Name option under menu 'Formulas -> Defined Names' group. On clicking Names Manager, a window is displayed as given above in Figure 3-4. Click on New in the Names Manager window to launch the 'New Name' dialog box. Same dialog box is launched if you select the Define Name option.

Figure 3-5: Named Range: Define New Name

In the New Name dialog box, you can specify the name like 'fruits_sales' as in our preceding example, for the range of cells specified that is, D2 to D6 in the 'Refers to' field. You can define the range by clicking on the arrow button next to the field and selecting the cells. Click on OK in the New Name dialog box to save and return to the sheet. Note that additionally you can define the scope of the named range, it can be at workbook or specific sheet level. Workbook level is preferred as you would generally want to use the named ranges across sheets. There is a comments section also for describing the purpose of the named range or any text that you would like to put for future reference.

Name Manager can also be used for deleting the existing named range by selecting the named range in the Name Manager window and clicking on the Delete button (see Figure 3-4) and confirming by clicking on OK in the delete dialog box. It also allows us to Edit the existing named range that is, you can modify the name, comments, and the cell range.

Figure 3-6: Named Range: Edit

3.3.1.3 Using Create from Selection

There is another option for creating names automatically from existing row or column labels. In the following example, we will create names from the column labels that is, Unit Price, Quantity, and Sales columns. Select the cells in range B1 to D6 and click on the 'Create from Selection' option from the Formulas ribbon. In the 'Create Names from Selection' dialog box, select the checkbox 'Top Row' as we want to use the labels in top row of the selected range for defining the named ranges and click on OK.

	A	B	C	D
1	Product	Unit Price	Quantity	Sales
2	Apple	120	2	240
3	Banana	65	4	260
4	Grapes	97	1	97
5	Mango	154	5	770
6	Orange	42	2	84
7				

Create Names from Selection

Create names from values in the:

☑ Top row
☐ Left column
☐ Bottom row
☐ Right column

Figure 3-7: Named Range: Create from Selection

Now open the Name Manager window to view the named ranges created. Note that since column B had a space in the name that is, "Unit Price", Excel has created the named range as "Unit_Price" that is, with an underscore as named ranges cannot have space.

Figure 3-8: Create from selection: New named ranges

3.3.2 Using Named Range

We have seen how to create, edit, and delete named ranges. In this section, we will see how to use the named ranges in a formula and apply them.

3.3.2.1 Use in formula

Taking the same example as discussed before for creating named ranges, now we want to find the Total Sales and we will use 'Sales' named range in the function SUM.

Click on the cell where you want to enter the formula which is D7 in our case. Type '=SUM(', go to Formulas Ribbon and select 'Use in Formula' option to select the named range 'Sales' as shown in screenshot below. Close the function bracket and press Enter. The formula in cell will look like '=SUM(Sales)'.

Figure 3-9: Named Range: Use in formula

3.3.2.2 Apply Name in formula

We can insert a named range into an existing formula. This is particularly helpful when you want to replace cell references with named ranges to make formulas easier to manage and look more user-friendly.

Figure 3-10: Named Range: Apply Names

In the preceding example, we are calculating the Tax amount on the Sales using the formula D2*F1, based on the Tax rate specified in cell F1 (i.e., 10%).

Now we will define name for the Tax rate in cell F1 as 'taxrate' and apply to the formula in cell range E2 to E6. Select the cell range E2 to E6 as shown in the screenshot below. From Formulas ribbon, click on 'Define Names-> Apply Names' option, select named range 'taxrate' and click on OK.

By clicking on OK in the 'Apply Names' dialog box, Excel modifies the formula in the cell range E2 to E6 from '=D2*$F$1' to '=D2*taxrate' respectively.

Figure 3-11: Named Range: Apply names

3.4 Calculations

By default, Excel automatically recalculates formulas only when the cells that the formula depends on have changed. However, you can control when and how Excel recalculates formulas using the 'Calculation' Ribbon option in the Formulas tab.

Figure 3-12: *Formulas: Calculations*

- 'Calculation Options ->Automatic' is the default setting. This means that all dependent formulas will be recalculated every time you make a change to a value, formula, or name that is referenced in the formula.

- 'Calculation Options ->Automatic Except for Data Tables' if set, then all dependent formulas, except the data tables, will be recalculated every time you make a change to a value, formula, or name that is referenced in the formula.

- 'Calculation Options ->Manual' if set, will turn off automatic recalculation and you will have to manually do it explicitly by pressing F9 or clicking on 'Calculate Now' (to recalculate) or 'Calculate Sheet' options.

- 'Calculate Now' recalculates all open worksheets, including data tables, and updates all open chart sheets.

- 'Calculate Sheet' recalculates only the active worksheet, charts and any chart sheets linked to this worksheet.

3.5 Functions in Formula

Formulas also use Excel functions that enable users to perform complex calculations that are difficult to perform using just the operators or not otherwise possible, like finding tangent of an angle, which can easily be done using Excel TAN function. Excel has more than 400 built-in functions and you can use additional functions from third-party vendors or create custom formulas using visual basic (VBA). On regular basis, we only use few of the functions and in the following section we will discuss those, how to find the correct function and their usage.

Excel functions are grouped into categories, including Math and Trig, Financial, Logical, Statistical, Web, and so on. In this chapter, we will look at some important functions that can be used separately or in combination, in order to do complex calculations/searches.

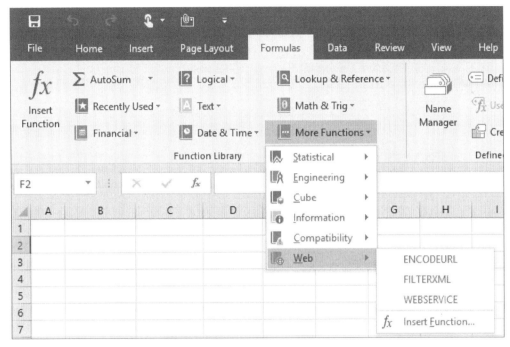

Figure 3-13: Functions Categories

Using the Insert function option from the Formula tab or the Formula bar, you can search a function, select a category to see all the relevant functions and its corresponding help using the link Help On this Function.

Figure 3-14: Insert function

Excel has an Auto Complete feature. As the user starts typing the formula/function in the cell, Excel will show the possible options.

Figure 3-15: Excel auto complete

3.6 Relative and Absolute addressing

Before we go ahead on discussing the different functions, we need to know about the Relative and Absolute addressing that is used quite often in functions. Absolute addressing is indicated in formula by dollar sign, which indicates that part of the formula to stay fixed and not change relative to the cell position. While Relative addressing lacks the dollar sign which indicates that part of the formula to change relative to the cell position.

Figure 3-16: Relative Addressing

In the preceding example, the Price is calculated with relative addressing where the Price and Qty of each product is changing and if we enter the formula C12*D12 in first cell E12 and drag to fill or copy the formula in the cells below, it will change to C13*D13 and C14*D14.

Now the Discount (10%) is same for all and we want to use it to calculate the Discounted price.

F12			✕	✓	*fx*	=E12*$D$9	
	A	B	C	D	E	F	G
7							
8							
9			Discount	10%			
10							
11		Product	Unit Price	Qty	Price	Discount	Discounted Price
12		P1	100	20	2000	200	1800
13		P2	80	10	800	80	720
14		P3	120	5	600	60	540
15							

Figure 3-17: *Absolute Addressing*

In cell F12, the formula we enter is E12*$D$9 and using the same technique if we drag to fill or copy the formula in cells below, it will change to E13*$D$9 and E14*$D$9. Note that here D9 does not change as we have dollar sign there before the row and column, making it fixed. In case the dollar sign was just before the column letter like $D9, then column is fixed but not the row. Hence, copying the formula in the cell below would have resulted in 0 as Excel would have copied it as E13*$D10. Based on what you want to be fixed, place the dollar sign before the row/column or both.

3.7 Referencing Cells Outside the Worksheet

Excel allows you to refer a cell in another worksheet in the same workbook. Format "=SheetName!CellAddress" can be used in the formulas to refer the cell. For Example, =B2*'Sales Data'!A12. If the worksheet name in the reference includes one or more spaces, enclose SheetName in single quotation marks.

3.8 Referencing Cells Outside the Workbook

In order to add a reference to a cell in another workbook, use the format "=[WorkbookName]SheetName!CellAddress". For Example, = B2*'[Financial Data] Sales Date'!A12.

3.9 Logical Functions

3.9.1 Using IF

This function tests a condition and if condition is met it is considered TRUE, else it is considered FALSE. We will understand its usage with the help of an example.

Syntax is "=IF (Criteria, True, False)"

Example #1:

The following table shows the Sales figures and Targets for sales reps. Using IF we will compare Sales with Targets and see who Achieved their targets and who did not.

	A	B	C	D	E	F	G	H	I
1									
2									
3		Name	Sales	Target	Result				
4		Joey	1000	3000	Not Achieved	=IF(C4>=D4,"Achieved","Not Achieved")			
5		Ross	6000	5000	Achieved	=IF(C5>=D5,"Achieved","Not Achieved")			
6		Rachel	3000	4000	Not Achieved	=IF(C6>=D6,"Achieved","Not Achieved")			
7									

Figure 3-18: Example using IF with values

Let us understand the formula, in row 4 column F, the formula checks if C4 [i.e., 1000] is greater than or equal to D4 [i.e., 3000], since the result is "False", the IF function will return the value given as third argument. And in row 5 column F the condition is "True", hence the IF function returns the value given as second argument.

Example #2:

Now we want to calculate the commission, it is 10% of Sales if the Sales are greater than or equal to the Target, else it is 5%.

	A	B	C	D	E	F	G	H	I
8									
9		**Name**	**Sales**	**Target**	**Commission**				
10		Joey	1000	3000	50	=IF(C10>=D10,C10*10%,C10*5%)			
11		Ross	6000	5000	600	=IF(C11>=D11,C11*10%,C11*5%)			
12		Rachel	3000	4000	150	=IF(C12>=D12,C12*10%,C12*5%)			
13									

Figure 3-19: Example using IF with reference

Note that you can have text or formula as values for the "True" and "False" parameters. In this example, the value returned for "True" condition is the multiplication of the Sales figures with 10% as the commission and 5% if "False".

3.9.2 Using nested IF

Syntax is
"=IF(condition1,expression1,IF(condition2,expression2,expression3))"

Expressions can have nested IF functions. If condition1 is true, the relevant value is expression1. Otherwise, condition2 is checked. If it is true, the relevant value is expression2. Otherwise, the relevant value is expression3.

Example #1:

For example, there might be three possibilities, depending on whether the value in cell A1 is negative, zero, or positive. A nested IF formula can then be used as follows. When the value in cell A1 is negative, value returned is 10.

B1	▼	⋮	✕	✓	*fx*	=IF(A1<0,10,IF(A1=0,20,30))

	A	B	C	D	E	F	G
1	-1	10					
2							
3							

When the value in cell A1 is zero, value returned is 20. That is the nested IF statement is executed.

B1	▼	⋮	✕	✓	*fx*	=IF(A1<0,10,IF(A1=0,20,30))

	A	B	C	D	E	F
1	0	20				
2						

When the value in cell A1 is neither negative nor zero, value returned is 30.

B1		:	✕	✓	*fx*	=IF(A1<0,10,IF(A1=0,20,30))

◢	A	B	C	D	E	F
1	3	30				
2						

Figure 3-20: Example using nested IF

3.9.3 Writing conditional expressions: IF combined with AND / OR

The IF function is many times used in combination of AND/OR, where we have multiple conditions to consider.

Example #1:

In this example, we will see how to use IF() with AND() and OR(). A vendor gives 10% discount on certain product lines.

The discount is given in either of the two conditions:

    i.   Products are on Special Offer and the Order Value is 1000 or above

    ii.   Customer is eligible for Loyalty Bonus

◢	A	B	C	D	E	F	G	H	I	J	K	L
20												
21												
22			Loyalty	Special	Order							
23		Product	Bonus	Offer	Value	Discount	Total					
24		Wood	No	Yes	3,000.00	300.00	2,700.00					
25		Glass	Yes	No	2,000.00	200.00	1,800.00					
26		Cement	No	Yes	500.00	-	500.00					
27		Turf	Yes	Yes	2,000.00	200.00	1,800.00					
28						=IF(OR(AND(D26="Yes",E26>=1000) , C26="Yes"), E26*10% , 0)						

Condition #1   Condition #2

Figure 3-21: Example of IF with AND / OR

Condition #1 is a case of AND, where both conditions given in (i) above must be satisfied. If either of Condition #1 or Condition #2 is satisfied, then 10% discount will be given.

3.9.4 Using IFS

Using nested IF functions gets complicated, especially when there are more than two levels of nested IF statements. IFS function is the better alternative of nested IF functions. With this function, conditions are tested in the order that you specify. The IFS function checks whether one or more conditions are met and returns a value that corresponds to the first TRUE condition. You can also specify an else "catch all" if none of the conditions are met.

Syntax is

"=IFS(logical test1, value if true1, [logical test2, value if true2], [logical test3, value if true3],...)"

where,

- ◦ logical test1 (required) – Condition that evaluates to TRUE or FALSE
- ◦ value if true1 (required) – Result to be returned if logical_test1 evaluates to TRUE. Can be empty.
- ◦ logical test2...logical test127 (optional, allows to test up to 127 different conditions)
- ◦ value if true2...value if true127 (optional)

| B8 | ▼ | ⋮ | ✕ | ✓ | *fx* | =IFS(A8>90,"A",A8>80,"B",A8>60,"C",A8>40,"D",TRUE,"F") |

	A	B	C
7	Student Marks	Grade	
8	95	A	"A" as A8>90
9	55	D	"D" as A9>40
10	66	C	"C" as A10>60
11	81	B	"B" as A11>80
12	34	F	"F" because it doesn't meet any of prior conditions.

Figure 3-22: Example for IFS

In the preceding example, the formula "=IFS(A8>90,"A", A8>80,"B",A8>60,"C", A8>40,"D",TRUE,"F")" is equivalent to multiple IF statements, that is IF(A8 is greater than 90, then return "A", IF(A8 is greater than 80, then return "B", and so on and for all other values less than 40, then return "F").

The last condition "TRUE" is for the default result. If none of the other conditions are met, the corresponding value will be returned. And if no TRUE conditions are found, this function returns #N/A error.

Note: IFS is a new function introduced in Excel 2019. It is available on Windows or Mac if you have Office 2019 or Office 365 subscription with latest version of Office.

3.9.5 Using SWITCH

This function evaluates an expression against a list of values in order and returns the first matching result. If no results match, the "else" is returned.

Syntax is

"=SWITCH(expression, value1, result1, [default or value2, result2],...[default or value3, result3])"

where,

- ° expression - the value (such as a number, date or some text) that will be compared against
- ° value1...value126 - valueN is a value that will be compared against expression.
- ° result1...result126 - resultN is the value to be returned when the corresponding valueN argument matches expression.
- ° default – this is optional. Default is the value to return in case no matches are found in the valueN expressions. Default must be the final argument in the function.

B26		*fx*	=SWITCH(A26,"A","Excellent","B","Good","F","Fail","Fair")	
	A	B	C	D
25	Grade	Result		
26	A	Excellent	corresponds to switch value = A	
27	D	Fair	corresponds to defult value	
28	C	Fair	corresponds to defult value	
29	B	Good	corresponds to switch value = B	
30	F	Fail	corresponds to switch value = F	

Figure 3-23: Example of SWITCH

In the preceding example, the formula "=SWITCH(A26,"A","Excellent","B", "Good","F","Fail","Fair")" returns "Excellent" if the expression or the value in cell to be compared is "A", "Good" if the value is "B" and "Fail" if the value is "F". For "C" and D" there is no match, hence the function returns the default value that is, "Fair". If the expression or value to be compared is not specified in the list of switch values, then the function returns the default value. If there are no matching values, and no default argument is supplied, the SWITCH function returns the #N/A! error.

Both SWITCH and IFS functions allow us to test more than one condition without nesting, unlike nested IF. These functions are much simpler to use and easy to understand. SWITCH should be used in cases of exact matching, as it is not possible to use operators like "<" less than or ">" greater than in the logic.

Note: SWITCH is a new function introduced in Excel 2019. It is available on Windows or Mac if you have Office 2019 or Office 365 subscription with latest version of Office.

3.10 Summarizing Functions

3.10.1 COUNT, COUNTA, COUNTBLANK

Commonly used functions for counting number of cells are COUNT (for counting cells that contain numbers), COUNTA (for counting non-blank cells), and COUNTBLANK (for counting empty cells).

Syntax is

"=COUNT (value1, [value2], ...)"
"=COUNTA (value1, [value2], ...)"
"=COUNTBLANK (value1, [value2], ...)"

Example #1:

The following example shows how these functions work in case data is text and numbers. Note that you can count individual values, cell references or ranges or a mix of all three.

Since COUNT only counts cells with numbers, for Student column it returns 0, while for Scores column it returns the value 6, even though total cells considered are 7 from rows 18 to 24. Note that in column Scores, 0 is considered as non-blank cell and hence COUNTA returns 6.

	A	B	C	D
16				
17		Student	Scores	
18		Ankit	8	
19		Puja	10	
20		Ishan	9	
21		Arav	9	
22			0	
23				
24		Mani	6	
25		Total		
26		0	6	=COUNT(C18:C24)
27		5	6	=COUNTA(C18:C24)
28		2	1	=COUNTBLANK(C18:C24)
29				

Figure 3-24: Example of COUNT, COUNTA, COUNTBLANK functions

3.10.2 COUNTIF, COUNTIFS

These functions are used for counting number of cells that satisfy the given criteria(s) or conditions.

Syntax is

"=COUNTIF (Data Range, Criteria to be matched)"
"=COUNTIFS (Data Range1, Criteria1, [Data Range2, Criteria2] …)"

Example #1:

Use of COUNTIF and COUNTIFS are explained with the help of the following data. In the COUNTIFS () function, we can write multiple Range and Criteria pairs.

	A	B	C	D	E	F	G	H	I	J	K
30											
31		Item	Date	Cost							
32		Brakes	Jan	80							
33		Tyres	May	50							
34		Brakes	Feb	80							
35		Mirror	Mar	150							
36		Mirror	Jan	300							
37		Window	Jun	50							
38		Tyres	Apr	200							
39		Tyres	Mar	100							
40		Clutch	May	250							
41											
42		How many Brakes Have been bought.				2	=COUNTIF(B32:B40,"Brakes")				
43		How many Tyres have been bought.				3	=COUNTIF(B32:B40,"Tyres")				
44		How many items cost 100 or above.				5	=COUNTIF(D32:D40,">=100")				
45											
46		Type the name of the item to count		mirror		2	=COUNTIF(B32:B40,E46)				
47											
48		How many Tyres have been bought that cost				2	=COUNTIFS(B32:B40,"Tyres",D32:D40,">=100")				
49											

Figure 3-25: Example of COUNTIF & COUNTIFS functions

In the preceding example, the rows #42, 43, 44, and 46, the COUNTIF(S) function uses a single criterion, specified directly and as a parameter for counting the number of cells. Note that the criteria can be a simple text or a formula as in row #44 or a reference to a cell like in row #46. In row #48, there are two criterions to be satisfied, one for Item and the other for Cost. The range of cells to look for are specified before each criterion.

3.10.3 SUM, AVERAGE, PRODUCT

The SUM function as the name suggests, sums all values in one or more ranges. The AVERAGE function calculates the average of all the numeric cells in a range and the PRODUCT function is like the SUM function, however, instead of adding it multiplies all the values in the range.

Syntax is

"=SUM (Data Range)"
"=AVERAGE (Data Range)"
"=PRODUCT (Data Range)"

Note that you can add individual values, cell references, or ranges, or a mix of all three as you can see in the following examples. In case of PRODUCT, since it only multiplies the values in the range, mentioning Absent in cell E35 will neither give an error nor will the result change if Absent text is removed.

	A	B	C	D	E	F
31						
32		Student	Maths	Science	English	
33		Puja	8	7	10	
34		Ishan	10	9	8	
35		Ankit	0	6	Absent	
36						
37		Total Puja Score		25	=SUM(C33,D33,E33)	
38		Total Ishan Score		27	=SUM(C34:E34)	
39		Average Science Score		7.3	=AVERAGE(D33:D35)	
40		Product of English Score		80	=PRODUCT(E33,E34:E35)	
41		Product of Maths Score		0	=PRODUCT(C33:C35)	
42						

Figure 3-26: Example of SUM, AVERAGE, PRODUCT functions

3.10.4 SUMIF, SUMIFS

The SUM function is the most commonly and widely used function for adding all values in the given range. Although SUMIF and SUMIFS are not that popular, these functions are very helpful in complex situations where we only want to add values in a range based on given criteria(s).

Syntax is

"=SUMIF (Range, Criteria to Match, Sum Range)"
"=SUMIFS (Sum Range, Criteria Range1, Criteria1, Criteria Range2, Criteria2 ...)"

Example #1:

Use of SUMIF and SUMIFS are explained with the help of the following example:

	A	B	C	D	E	F	G	H	I	J	K
50											
51		Item	Date	Cost							
52		Brakes	Jan	80							
53		Tyres	May	50							
54		Brakes	Feb	80							
55		Mirror	Mar	150							
56		Mirror	Jan	300							
57		Window	Jun	50							
58		Tyres	Apr	200							
59		Tyres	Mar	100							
60		Clutch	May	250							
61											
62		Total cost of all Brakes bought.				160	=SUMIF(B52:B60,"Brakes",D52:D60)				
63		Total cost of all Tyres bought.				350	=SUMIF(B52:B60,"Tyres",D52:D60)				
64		Total of items costing 100 or above.				1000	=SUMIF(D52:D60,">=100")				
65											
66		Total of item typed in following cell.			mirror	450	=SUMIF(B52:B60,E66,D52:D60)				
67											
68		Total cost Tyres bought costing above 100				200	=SUMIFS(D52:D60,B52:B60,"Tyres",D52:D60,">100")				
69											

Figure 3-27: Example of SUMIF, SUMIFS functions

Similar to COUNTIF(S) function, instead of counting the number of cells, the formulas in the preceding example are adding the values based on the criteria(s) specified. Again, note that the criteria can be a simple text or a formula or a reference to a cell

3.10.5 SUMPRODUCT

Multiplies corresponding components in the given arrays and returns the sum of those products.

Syntax is
"=SUMPRODUCT (array1, [array2], [array3], ...)"

Example # 1:

SUMPRODUCT is explained with the help of an example as shown below. SUMPRODUCT returns value 526 i.e., 5x100 + 2x10 + 3x2.

⧄	A	B	C	D	E	F	G	H
70								
71		Item	Sold	price				
72		Tyres	5	100				
73		Mirrors	2	10				
74		Bulbs	3	2				
75								
76		Total Sales Value :		526	=SUMPRODUCT(C72:C74,D72:D74)			
77								

Figure 3-28: *Example of SUMPRODUCT*

3.10.6 Calculations using SUM with OFFSET function

OFFSET together with the SUM function helps to create a dynamic function that can sum a variable number of cells. Limitation with the regular SUM formula is that it is a static calculation, but with OFFSET we can have the cell reference move around.

> Syntax is
>
> "= OFFSET (Reference to base offset, no. of rows, no. of cols, [no of rows in returned reference], [no of columns in returned reference])"

Note that the OFFSET function is also discussed in Chapter 3.12.3.

Example #1:

The following OFFSET function returns the 1 x 2 range, that is, 8 rows below from base offset B79 and 1 column to the right of cell B79. The SUM function calculates the sum of this range.

	A	B	C	D	E	F	G	H
78			**Sales**					
79		Region	North	South				
		Month						
80		Jan	100	1324				
81		Feb	506	789				
82		Mar	300	500				
83		Apr	928	1409		**SUM of August Sales**		
84		May	300	212		**776**		
85		Jun	815	983		=SUM(OFFSET(B79, 8, 1, 1, 2))		
86		Jul	919	1023				
87		Aug	241	535			1x 2 range	
88		Sep	1334	982				
89		Oct	452	645				
90		Nov	647	757				
91		Dec	322	346				

Figure 3-29: Example of OFFSET with values

Example #2:

In this example, the table has data for five months and based on the value entered for the Start and End month, the OFFSET function is used for cell range reference to SUM.

	A	B	C	D	E	F	G	H	I	J
93										
94		Type in the Start month.			Feb-18					
95		Type in the End month.			Mar-18					
96										
97		Total			Jan-18	Feb-18	Mar-18	Apr-18	May-18	
98		900			10	400	500	600	700	
99										
100		1020			15	20	1000	2000	3000	
101										
102		13			5	3	10	800	900	
103		=SUM(OFFSET(C102, 0, MONTH($E$94)) : OFFSET(C102, 0, MONTH($E$95)))								
104				*Returns value 2*				*Returns value 3*		

Figure 3-30: Example of OFFSET with reference

In the preceding example, the 'Total' value in cell B102 is calculated as 13 using the formula "=SUM(OFFSET(C102,0,MONTH($E$94)) : OFFSET(C102,0, MONTH($E$95)))".

3.10.7 SUBTOTAL

The SUBTOTAL function returns an aggregate result for supplied values. SUBTOTAL can return a SUM, AVERAGE, COUNT, MAX, and many others. When you type SUBTOTAL in a cell, Excel will show the complete list of functions, as given below.

Figure 3-31: SUBTOTOAL functions argument

As shown in the function list above, each function has been assigned a number that is used as the first argument in the SUBTOTAL function.

Syntax is
"=SUBTOTAL(function number, range 1, [range 2],...)"

If you choose function number between 1-11, all the manually hidden rows are included in the calculation, while 101-111 excludes them; filtered-out cells are always excluded. SUBTOTAL function is designed for columns of data, or vertical ranges. It is not designed for rows of data, or horizontal ranges.

Example #1:

	A	B	C
23			
24		2	
25		4	
26		6	
27		10	
28		8	
29		4	
30		6	
31		10	
32		2	
33	SUBTOTAL		
34	SUM	52	=SUBTOTAL(9,B24:B32)
35	COUNT	9	=SUBTOTAL(2,B24:B32)
36			

	A	B	C
23			
24		2	
25		4	
26		6	
30		6	
31		10	
32		2	
33	SUBTOTAL		
34	SUM	52	=SUBTOTAL(9,B24:B32)
35	COUNT	9	=SUBTOTAL(2,B24:B32)
36	SUM	30	=SUBTOTAL(109,B24:B32)
37	COUNT	6	=SUBTOTAL(102,B24:B32)
38			

Figure 3-32: Example of SUBTOTAL function

In the preceding example, see how the result changes when we used the different functions. In first case, the SUBTOTAL function returns 52 for function number 9 (SUM) and 9 for function number 2 (COUNT). In second case, we have hidden three rows, that is, rows 27, 28, and 29 are hidden. Now the SUBTOTAL function returns the same values for function numbers 9 and 2 but for function number 109 (SUM) it returns 30 versus 52 and for function number 102 (COUNT) it returns 6 versus 9.

Example #2:

When we need data based on different categories, SUBTOTALS help us to get the totals of several columns of data broken down into various categories. An apparel owner wants to know how many items of different colors (Red, Green, White, Blue, Orange) and sizes (2, 4, 6, 8, 10) are in the inventory of the two outlets. The raw data received for the two outlets is as given here:

	A	B	C	D
1	Color	Size	No in Shop#1	No in Shop#2
2	Red	2	10	12
3	Green	4	30	23
4	White	6	50	70
5	Blue	10	12	24
6	Orange	8	57	85
7	Red	4	35	36
8	Green	6	75	36
9	White	10	43	28
10	Blue	2	56	30
11	Orange	8	12	89
12	Red	6	62	67
13	Green	10	17	64
14	White	2	24	98
15	Blue	8	84	24
16	Orange	8	25	56
17	Red	10	88	34
18	Green	2	34	33
19	White	8	13	76
20	Blue	6	10	45
21	Orange	4	30	40

Before we use the SUBTOTAL function, we will have to sort the data for which we want to find the subtotal. Then, we can use the SUBTOTAL option from 'Data->Outline'.

In the Subtotal dialog box, we selected SUM as the function and selected checkbox for 'No in Shop#1' and 'No in Shop#2' as we want to get the subtotal of the different color items in both outlets.

Figure 3-33: SUBTOTAL with SUM example

By clicking on OK, Excel will show the subtotals as shown in the following screenshot. Note that subtotals are added in a new row below each color and the worksheet is now divided into different levels, that is, 1, 2, and 3 as seen in the top-left corner. Depending on the information you wish to display in the worksheet, you can switch between these levels.

	Color	Size	No in Shop#1	No in Shop#2
1	Color	Size	No in Shop#1	No in Shop#2
2	Blue	10	12	24
3	Blue	2	56	30
4	Blue	8	84	24
5	Blue	6	10	45
6	Blue Total		162	123
7	Green	4	30	23
8	Green	6	75	36
9	Green	10	17	64
10	Green	2	34	33
11	Green Total		156	156
12	Orange	8	57	85
13	Orange	8	12	89
14	Orange	8	25	56

Figure 3-34: SUBTOTAL with SUM result

Now if owner wants to see the count of each size for the outlets, to make sure that all sizes are available in either of them, SUBTOTAL for Size with COUNT function can be used as shown here:

	A	B	C	D	E	F	G	H	I
	Color								
1	Color	Size	No in Shop#1	No in Shop#2					
2	Blue	10	12	24	Subtotal		?	×	
3	Blue	2	56	30					
4	Blue	8	84	24	At each change in:				
5	Blue	6	10	45	Color				
6	Blue Total		162	123	Use function:				
7	Green	4	30	23	Count				
8	Green	6	75	36	Add subtotal to:				
9	Green	10	17	64	☐ Color				
10	Green	2	34	33	☑ Size				
11	Green Total		156	156	☐ No in Shop#1				
12	Orange	8	57	85	☐ No in Shop#2				
13	Orange	8	12	89					
14	Orange	8	25	56					
15	Orange	4	30	40	☐ Replace current subtotals				
16	Orange Total		124	270	☐ Page break between groups				
17	Red	2	10	12	☑ Summary below data				
18	Red	4	35	36	Remove All		OK	Cancel	
19	Red	6	62	67					
20	Red	10	88	34					
21	Red Total		195	149					

Figure 3-35: SUBTOTAL with COUNT example

Note that here we will uncheck the Replace current subtotals as we want to keep the previous subtotals.

	A	B	C	D
1	Color	Size	No in Shop#1	No in Shop#2
2	Blue	10	12	24
3	Blue	2	56	30
4	Blue	8	84	24
5	Blue	6	10	45
6	Blue Count	4		
7	Blue Total		162	123
8	Green	4	30	23
9	Green	6	75	36
10	Green	10	17	64
11	Green	2	34	33
12	Green Count	4		
13	Green Total		156	156
14	Orange	8	57	85

Figure 3-36: SUBTOTAL with COUNT result

Now, a new level has been added. You can switch between levels, click on the level for which you want to see data.

3.11 Text functions

3.11.1 TEXT

This function lets you change the way a number appears by applying formatting to it with format codes. It can be useful when you want to display numbers in a more readable format, or you want to combine numbers with text or symbols. Remember that once the numbers are changed to text format; it will be difficult to refer to them in calculations.

Syntax is

"=TEXT(Value to format, "Format code to apply")"

	A	B	C
10			
11		1,234.57	=TEXT(1234.567,"#,##0.00")
12		1:04 PM	=TEXT(NOW(),"H:MM AM/PM")
13		02/04/18	=TEXT(TODAY(),"MM/DD/YY")
14		Sun	=TEXT(TODAY(),"DDD")
15		56.5%	=TEXT(0.565,"0.0%")

Figure 3-37: Example of TEXT function

The preceding examples are some of the popular examples of the TEXT function usage. In the first one, it changes the number format by adding a thousand separator and two decimals. Note that it rounds the value to two decimal places in the process.

Another interesting use of the TEXT function is when you want to join the two strings, one being text and other, say a date.

	A	B	C	D	E
18		Text 1	Text 2	Result ⇩	Formula
19		Report on	02-05-2018	Report on : 43222	=B19&" : "&C19
20		Report on	02-05-2018	Report on : 05/02/18	=B20&" : "&TEXT(C20,"mm/dd/yy")
21					

Figure 3-38: Example of TEXT function to join strings

In the preceding example, result in row#19 shows a number instead of the date and in the next row by using the TEXT function we get the desired results.

3.11.2 FIND

This function returns the position of the first occurrence of a string of characters (which could be a single character) in a piece of text.

Syntax is "=FIND(find text, within text, [start no. to start search])"

In the following table, we will see how the return value of FIND function changes based on the input arguments.

	A	B	C
1			
2		Albert Einstein	
3			
4		3	=FIND("bert",B2)
5		3	=FIND("b",B2)
6		4	=FIND("e",B2)
7		13	=FIND("e",B2,5)
8		8	=FIND("E",B2)

Figure 3-39: Example of FIND function

Note that the return value is same, that is, 3 for first two formulas, reason being that function returns the start of the first occurrence of the search string "bert" or character "b". Similarly, it returns 4 for search string "e" and 13 only when the start number to search string was moved to 5. By default, the start number to search the string is 0. Also, it is case sensitive, hence, the return position of "e" and "E" is different, that is, 4 and 8 respectively.

3.11.3 LEN and TRIM

These functions are useful to know the length of your text and remove all spaces from the text except for single spaces between words.

	A	B	C	D
		Syntax is "=LEN (text)", "=TRIM(text)"		
1		The text length is	18	=LEN(B1)
2		Extra spaces in text	Extra spaces in text	=TRIM(" Extra spaces in text ")
3				

Figure 3-40: Example of LEN & TRIM functions

3.11.4 CONCATENATE

This text function is helpful to join two or more text strings into one string. You can also join strings using "&", the ampersand symbol. See the following example where we join text using both the methods.

Syntax is

"=CONCATENATE (text1, [text2], ...)"

where,

 ° text1 – Text item to be joined. The item can be a text value, number or cell reference
 ° text2 – Additional text items to join

C7	▼	⋮	× ✓ *fx*	=CONCATENATE(A5,B5)	

	A	B	C	D	E
4			Result	Formula used	
5	Na	Mo	NaMo	=A5&B5	
6			Na,Mo	=A5&","&B5	
7			NaMo	=CONCATENATE(A5,B5)	
8			Na,Mo	=CONCATENATE(A5,",",B5)	
9					

Figure 3-41: Example for CONCATENATE

Ampersand symbol does the same thing but when you do complex operations, CONCATENATE function is much easier and clean.

3.11.5 CONCAT

CONCAT is like the CONCATENATE function but shorter and easier to type. This function also supports range references, in addition to cell references.

Syntax is "=CONCAT (text1, [text2], ...)"

where,

- ° text1 – Text item to be joined. A string, or array of strings such as a range of cells
- ° text2 – Additional text items to join

	A	B	C	D
1	X	Y	Xa1a2a3a4Yb1b2b3b4	=CONCAT(A:A,B:B)
2	a1	b1	XYa1b1a2b2a3b3a4b4	=CONCAT(A1:B5)
3	a2	b2	X & Y	=CONCAT(A1," & ", B1)
4	a3	b3		
5	a4	b4		

Figure 3-42: Example for CONCAT

CONCAT function allows full column and row references, hence the function returns the results "Xa1a2a3a4Yb1b2b3b4" and "XYa1b1a2b2a3b3a4b4" in the preceding example.

Note: CONCAT is a new function introduced in Excel 2019. It is available on Windows or Mac if you have Office 2019 or Office 365 subscription with latest version of Office. This function replaces CONCATENATE function, however CONCATENATE function will stay available for compatibility with earlier version of Excel.

3.11.6 TEXTJOIN

This function combines the text from multiple ranges and/or strings and includes a delimiter you specify between each text value that will be combined.

Syntax is

"=TEXTJOIN(delimiter, ignore empty, text1, [text2], …)"

where,

- ° delimiter - A text string, either empty, or one or more characters enclosed by double quotes, or a reference to a valid text string. If a number is supplied, it will be treated as text.
- ° Ignore empty - If TRUE, ignores empty cells.
- ° text1 - Text item to be joined. A text string, or array of strings, such as a range of cells.
- ° [text2, …] (optional) - Additional text items to be joined. There can be a maximum of 252 text arguments, including text1.

	A	B	C	D	E	F
31	1	2	3	4	Result	Formula used
32	Mango	is		fruit	Mango is fruit	=TEXTJOIN(" ",TRUE,A32:D32)
33	Guava			Apples	Guava,,,Apples	=TEXTJOIN(",",FALSE,A33:D33)
34	Oranges	Pineapple	Banana		Oranges,Pineapple,Banana	=TEXTJOIN(",",TRUE,A34:D34)
35	Mango	Apple	Orange	Fruit	Mango,Apple,Orange;Fruit	=TEXTJOIN(A36:D36,TRUE,A35:D35)
36	,	,	;			

Figure 3-43: Example of TEXTJOIN

In the preceding example, the function "=TEXTJOIN(" ",TRUE,A32:D32)" combines the text from A32:D32 with delimiter as space and returns the string "Mango is fruit". Since we specified TRUE, the empty cells were ignored. In the next formula, that is, "=TEXTJOIN(",",FALSE,A33:D33)" we have specified FALSE hence the empty cells are not ignored, and the function returns the string "Guava,,,Apples". We can also specify cell range in the delimiter parameter, as given in "=TEXTJOIN(A36:D36,TRUE,A35:D35)". Here the delimiters are specified in cell range A36:D36 and the text to combine in cell range A35:D35.

Note: TEXTJOIN is a new function introduced in Excel 2019. It is available on Windows or Mac if you have Office 2019 or Office 365 subscription with latest version of Office.

3.11.7 LEFT, MID and RIGHT

These text functions are very helpful in extracting parts of the text:

- LEFT function: Returns text from the beginning of a cell (left to right)
- MID function: Returns text from any start point of the cell (left to right)
- RIGHT function: Returns text from the end of the cell (right to left)

Syntax is

"=LEFT (text, [no. of chars])

"=RIGHT (text, [no. of chars])

"=MID (text, start no., no. of chars)"

Example #1:

In the following example, we want to extract the Product ID (numerical value) that is embedded in the Product Description (text value). It would have been simple if the number of digits was the same but that is not the case below, both the text length and number of digits are different.

Using MID and FIND

	A	B	C	D	E	F	G	H	I
105									
106		Description	Product ID#	=MID (text, start_num, num_chars)					
107		TyresMRF(7283629)INDDL	7283629	=MID(B107, FIND("(",B107)+1, FIND(")",B107)-FIND("(",B107)-1)					
108		BrakesWLLKJD(1000290288)INDGGN	1000290288						
109					start no. =10			no. of chars =7	
110									

Figure 3-44: Example using MID and FIND

Let us understand the preceding example so that the usage is clear. The formula used is "=MID(B107,FIND("(",B107)+1,FIND(")",B107)-FIND("(",B107)-1)".

The first argument is B107, that is, the whole string "TyresMRF(7283629)INDDL" from which want to extract. The second argument "FIND("(",B107)+1", is used to find the start number to extract the string. The FIND function returns position number 9 for "(", but since we want the number between the brackets, we add 1 to get the start position as 10. The third argument is an arithmetic expression, FIND(")",B107) – FIND("(",B107)-1, for getting the number of characters (7) to extract from the start position (10). Now, FIND(")",B107) will return the position of ")", that is, 17. From 17, subtract 9 (return value of FIND("(",B107) function as seen before) and also 1 as we do not want the ")" that is, 17-9-1 =7.

Using MID, LEFT, and FIND

The formula used in example below is "=MID (LEFT(B115, FIND(")",B115) -1), FIND("(",B115)+1, LEN(B115))".

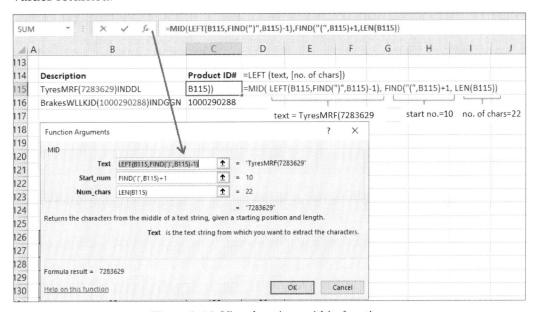

Figure 3-45: *Example using MID, LEFT & FIND*

In order to see the values returned by functions within a function, select the cell in which the formula has been written. Then go to the insert function icon next to the formula and click on it, the Function Arguments window gets launched showing the values returned.

Figure 3-46: *View functions within functions*

Example #2:

In the following example, we want to extract the Product Location (text after the numerical value) that is embedded in the Product Description (text value). We will use the RIGHT function.

The formula used in example below is "=RIGHT (B121, LEN(B121) - FIND(")", B121))".

▲	A	B	C	D	E	F	G
120		Description	Product Loc	=RiGHT (text, [no. of chars])			
121		TyresMRF(7283629)INDDL	INDDL	=RIGHT(B121,LEN(B121)-FIND(")",B121))			
122		BrakesWLLKJD(1000290288)INDGGN	INDGGN				

Figure 3-47: Example of RIGHT function

Figure 3-48: View function return value

3.12 Lookup and Reference functions

3.12.1 VLOOKUP, HLOOKUP

Use VLOOKUP when you need to find things in a table or a range by row. HLOOKUP searches for a value in the top row of a table or an array of values, and then returns a value in the same column from a row you specify in the table or array. VLOOKUP is more widely used function.

Syntax is

"=VLOOKUP (lookup value, table array,

column no in the range containing the return value,

Exact Match or Approximate Match – indicated as 0/FALSE or 1/TRUE)"

"= HLOOKUP (lookup value, table array, row index no., [range lookup])"

Example #1:

In this example, we are trying to look up the value in third column/row for the month of Mar that is, 69. In both cases, the same value is looked up, however, the difference is in the function used for the same, which explains when to use VLOOKUP and HLOOKUP. Reason is because of the different data structure.

	A	B	C	D	E	F	G	H	I	J
138										
139		Jan	15	20	50	34	60			
140		Feb	45	90	89	110	122			
141		Mar	90	**69**	50	51	80			
142										
143										
144				Specif month to look for :		Mar				
145				Which column to be picked :		3				
146										
147					Result is :	69				
148						=VLOOKUP(F144,B139:G141,F145,FALSE)				

Figure 3-49: Example of VLOOKUP function

In the preceding example, we are trying to lookup value for "Mar" from the table array starting B139 and ending G141 that is, all three rows and six columns. The third argument F145 (that is, 3) specifies the column from which we want the value to be returned corresponding to our lookup value, that is, Mar and FALSE indicates that we want an exact match to our lookup value that is, the value in column 1 should have text exactly as "Mar". So now the "69" value is returned, which is in third column and row matching lookup value "Mar" in column 1.

Note that in order for VLOOKUP to work correctly, the lookup value (that is, Mar in the preceding example) should be in the first column (that is, column B above) of the table array to be searched (range B139:G141).

Similar logic applies to HLOOKUP as you will see in the following example. Based on the structure of the data, we make a choice between VLOOKUP (vertical lookup) and HLOOKUP (horizontal lookup). VLOOKUP is more popular than HLOOKUP.

	A	B	C	D	E	F	G	H	I	J	K
125											
126		Jan	Feb	Mar							
127		15	45	90							
128		20	90	**69**							
129		50	89	50							
130		34	110	51							
131		60	122	80							
132											
133		Specify month to look for :				Mar					
134		Which row to be picked :				3					
135											
136		Result is :				69	=HLOOKUP(F133,B126:D131,F134,FALSE)				

Figure 3-50: Example of HLOOKUP function

3.12.2 MATCH, INDEX

Combination of the INDEX and MATCH functions is an advanced alternative to VLOOKUP or HLOOKUP, many times faster and more flexible.

> Syntax is
>
> "=INDEX (cell range, row no. in array from which to return a value,
> [column no. in array from which to return a value])"
>
> "= MATCH (match value, cell range, [match type -1, 0, or 1])"
>
> where,
> - ° -1: smallest value that is greater than or equal to lookup value
> - ° 0: first value that is exactly equal to lookup value
> - ° 1 or omitted: largest value that is less than or equal to lookup value

Example #1:

We have two tables below and correlating both we want to find out if the student passed or failed as per the scores. We will use the combination of the INDEX and MATCH functions for getting the student grade.

Figure 3-51: Example of INDEX & MATCH

In the preceding example, the first argument to the INDEX function is the cell range from where we want to return the value based on the match found, return of MATCH function (the row number) in second argument, and the column number 0 (column C) that is specified as the third argument. The MATCH function matches the student score (that is, 67) to the exam scores given in column B, and since we specified 1 as match type, it returns the row number as 2 because "65" is the largest value that is less than or equal to the lookup value.

In case you want to see the details of the MATCH function, select the cell in which formula is entered in column Grade, highlight the MATCH function and click the function icon on the menu bar.

Figure 3-52: Details of MATCH function

3.12.3 OFFSET

This function allows you to reference a range (or a single cell) relative to another cell. You can specify the number of rows and columns below (positive value) or above (negative value) the reference cell that you want to refer and the number of rows and columns to return. By default, the number of rows and columns returned is 1.

> Syntax is
>
> "OFFSET(reference to base the offset, rows, cols, [no of rows to return], [no of columns to return])"

In the following example, you can see how the values are returned based on the arguments, where a positive value of rows refers to a cell below the base offset and a negative value refers to a cell above the base offset.

Figure 3-53: Example of OFFSET

The OFFSET function can also be used in combination with summarizing functions like SUM, as discussed in chapter 3.10.6.

3.12.4 INDIRECT

The INDIRECT function returns the reference specified by a text string. This function converts a plain text which looks like a cell address, either on the same worksheet or on a different worksheet, into a usable cell reference. INDIRECT's usage is when you want to change the reference to a cell without changing the formula itself.

Syntax is

"= INDIRECT (reference text, [type of reference text])"

where,

   type of reference text if,

   ° TRUE or omitted: reference text is interpreted as an A1-style reference

   ° FALSE: reference text is interpreted as an R1C1-style reference

Example # 1:

In the following table, we have scores in column B and reference text in column D that is used in the INDIRECT function to get the value of the cell. First reference text, D10, is A1 style where it is a direct reference to the cell containing the value. In the next two, D12 and D14, the reference text is R1C1 style (a row number followed by a column number).

Figure 3-54: Example of INDIRECT with values

Example # 2:

In the following example, we will see how to create indirect references from cell value and text.

A	B	C	D	E	F	G
8						
9	Scores		Ref Text	Return Value	Formula Used	Ref Type
10	67		B12	99	=INDIRECT(D10)	A1 style
11	10					
12	99		R12C2	99	=INDIRECT(D12, FALSE)	R1C1 style
13	23					
14	92		R12C	99	=INDIRECT(D14, FALSE)	R1C1 style
15						
16	12	99	=INDIRECT("B"&B16)	Creating indirect reference from Text & Cell value		
17						

Figure 3-55: Example of INDIRECT using indirect reference to cell

In preceding example, the value in cell C16 is displayed using formula '=INDIRECT("B"&B16) that is, in the INDIRECT function the text 'B' is concatenated with the value in cell B16 (12) resulting in '=INDIRECT(B12)'.

Example #3:

In the following example, we will see the use of the INDRIECT function with named ranges:

named range B21:B29

Age   fx   12

A	B	C	D	E	F	G
19						
20	Age	Height				
21	12	5		Range Name	age	
22	34	2.5		Total :	410	=SUM(INDIRECT($F$21))
23	67	6.1		Average:	45.56	=AVERAGE(INDIRECT($F$21))
24	23	4.1		Max:	96	=MAX(INDIRECT($F$21))
25	96	3		Min:	6	=MIN(INDIRECT($F$21))
26	85	5.1				
27	77	4.2				
28	6	2.8				
29	10	4				
30						

Figure 3-56: Example of INDIRECT using Named Ranges

Example # 4:

In the following example, we will see the use of the INDRIECT function to dynamically refer to another worksheet. Using the same example as the previous one, now assume that the height data is in another sheet named "Student Details" and we want to copy the list in sheet that has student age list also.

Syntax is

"= INDIRECT ("'" & Sheet's name & "'!" & Cell to get data from)"

Figure 3-57: Example of INDIRECT referring another worksheet

In the preceding example, INDIRECT("'" & $D$32 & "'!" & C34) gets the sheet name, that is, 'Student Details' from cell D32, which is concatenated with C34 (of current sheet) that has the reference of the cell containing the actual data, that is, B3 of the other worksheet (Student Details). If we substitute the values, the above formula will result in INDIRECT ("'Students Details'!B3"), which returns the value 5.

3.13 Date and Time functions

Date and Time functions are very frequently used in formulas, but their calculation is sometimes tricky as Excel interprets according to the date system used by the local computer. We will try to cover different scenarios to help you in using these correctly in your formulas.

3.13.1 TIME

The TIME function returns the decimal number for a particular time.

> Syntax is "=TIME(hour, minute, second)"

For example, 12:00 PM is represented as 0.5 because it is half of a day, that is, "=TIME(12,0,0)"

3.13.2 DATE

The DATE function in Excel is categorized under the Date/Time Functions, returns the sequential serial number that represents a particular date.

Syntax is "=DATE(year,month,day)"

By default, Microsoft Excel for Windows uses the 1900 date system, which means the first date is January 1, 1900. January 1, 1900 is serial number 1, and January 1, 2008 is serial number 39448 because it is 39,447 days after January 1, 1900. Following are a few examples to help you see how results get calculated:

	A	B	C	D
1		Result	Resul formated as Date	Formula
2		42404	04-02-2016	=DATE(2016,1,35)
3			02-02-2018	=DATE(2017,14,2)
4			02-09-2015	=DATE(2016,-3,2)
5			05-05-2017	=DATE(2017, 5, 20)-15

Figure 3-58: *Example for DATE function*

In row#2 as mentioned earlier, the date function returns the sequential serial number '42404' (in cell B2) corresponding to the year, month, and day mentioned as given in D2 that is '=DATE(2016,1,35)'. When day is greater than the number of days in the specified month (1 to 31), day adds that number of days to the first day of the month. For example, DATE (2016,1,35) returns the serial number representing February 4, 2016 in C2, where the cell value is formatted as Date

Formula in D3 returns in cell C3 the serial number representing February 2, 2018. In case the month is greater than the number of months Excel takes as argument, that is, 1 to 12, then Excel will add the number of months to the first month of the specified year.

When the month is less than or equal to zero, like in D4, Excel will subtract the absolute value of month, plus 1, from the first month of the specified year. Hence in C4, Excel returns the serial number representing September 2, 2015.

In the last example, in cell C5, Excel returns the serial number representing May 5, 2017, that is, by Subtracting 15 days from May 20, 2017.

3.13.2.1 Same date format for different locale

As we mentioned earlier, Excel interprets date according to the date system used by the local computer. This becomes a problem when you have dates of different regions in the same worksheet, for example you have dates in US format i.e., mm/dd/yyyy and UK format i.e., dd/mm/yyyy. We will see how to work around this issue so that all dates are in consistent format.

	A	B	C	D	E	F	G	H	I	J	K	L
34												
35		Dates	Existing format	Converted format								
36		12/02/2018	dd/mm/yyyy	2018-02-12	=TEXT(YEAR(B36),"0000")&"-"&TEXT(MONTH(B36),"00")&"-"&TEXT(DAY(B36),"00")							
37		02/12/2018	mm/dd/yyyy	2018-02-12								
38												
39												

Figure 3-59: *Example of DATE formats in different locale*

In the preceding example, we have dates in two formats: US and UK and with our formula "=TEXT(YEAR(B36),"0000")&"-"&TEXT(MONTH(B36),"00")&"-"&TEXT(DAY(B36),"00")" we have converted the dates into the same format representing the date 12 Feb, 2018.

We have already discussed the TEXT function in earlier chapter (3.11.1) so we will not discuss those in details here. But to see what each function returns, YEAR, MONTH, and DAY, you can click on the cell with the formula, select the function you want to view and click on the insert function icon to launch the dialog as given here:

Dates	Existing format	Converted format
12/02/2018	dd/mm/yyyy	[EXT(DAY(B36),"00"]=TEXT(YEAR(B36),"0000")&"-"&TEXT(MONTH(B36),"00")&"-"&TEXT(DAY(B36),"00")
02/12/2018	mm/dd/yyyy	2018-02-12

Function Arguments ? ✕

DAY

Serial_number B36   ↥   = 43143

= 12

Returns the day of the month, a number from 1 to 31.

Serial_number is a number in the date-time code used by Microsoft Excel.

Formula result = 2018-02-12

Help on this function   OK   Cancel

Now that we have the concept of the date function, we will look at other related and commonly used functions.

3.13.3 TODAY

Syntax is "=TODAY()"

The TODAY function returns the serial number of the current date. For example, if it is 26th day of the month of January of year 2011, then "=TODAY()" will return 26-01-2011.

3.13.4 EOMONTH

Syntax is "=EOMONTH((start date, months)"

The EOMONTH function returns the serial number for the last day of the month that is the indicated number of months before or after start date. EOMONTH is most often used in financial calculations.

For example, "=EOMONTH("26-01-2011",1) will return 28-02-2011, that is, date of the last day of the month, which is one month after 26-01-2011. And if it was "=EOMONTH("26-01-2011",3), result would have been 30-04-2011.

3.13.5 NETWORKDAYS

Syntax is

"=NETWORKDAYS (start date, end date, [holidays])"

The NETWORKDAYS function returns the number of whole working days between start date and end date. Working days exclude weekends and any dates identified in holidays.

For example, "=NETWORKDAYS("04-02-2019","31-03-2019","14-02-2019")" will return the number of days as 39, where 04-02-2019 is the start date, 31-03-2019 the end date, and 14-02-2019 a holiday.

3.13.6 YEARFRAC

Syntax is

"=YEARFRAC (start date, end date, basis)"

The YEARFRAC function calculates the fraction of the year represented by the number of whole days between two dates (the start date and the end date). It also has an optional argument which specifies the type of day count basis to be used, that is, options 0,1,2,3, and 4 as given in the following table:

	A	B	C	D	E
1	Start date	End date	Result	Formula	Day count basis
2	01-01-2012	30-07-2012	0.580555556	=YEARFRAC(A2,B2,0)	US (NASD) 30/360
3	01-01-2012	30-07-2012	0.576502732	=YEARFRAC(A3,B3,1)	Actual/actual
4	01-01-2012	30-07-2012	0.586111111	=YEARFRAC(A4,B4,2)	Actual/360
5	01-01-2012	30-07-2012	0.578082192	=YEARFRAC(A5,B5,3)	Actual/365
6	01-01-2012	30-07-2012	0.580555556	=YEARFRAC(A6,B6,4)	European 30/360

As you see in the preceding screenshot, fraction between the same dates that is using the Actual/Actual day count basis, the result is the least because 2012 is a Leap year, it has a 366-day basis.

3.14 Math Functions

In the previous chapter (3.10), we already discussed few mathematical functions like SUM, SUMIF, SUMIFS, and SUMPRODUCT. In this section, we will cover other useful and commonly used mathematical functions.

3.14.1 INT

This is a very simple function that rounds a number down to the nearest integer.

Syntax is

"=INT (real number to round down to integer)"

Example #1:

In the following table, we will see how the real numbers are rounded by the function and their results.

◢	A	B	C	D	E
1	Real Number	-4.3	1.82	10	-7
2	**INT result**	-5	1	10	-7

Figure 3-60: Example of INT function

In this example, note that the negative number is rounded down away from 0, hence INT(-4.3) results in -5 and INT(1.82) is 1 as the function rounds down and does not round up to 2. Since the other two are integers, the same value is returned.

We will discuss the other functions in the subsequent sections that round up the numbers.

3.14.2 ROUND, ROUNDDOWN, ROUNDUP, MROUND

These functions round the numbers to the specified number of digits. We will see their usage using examples.

Syntax is

"=ROUND(number, number of digits to which you want to round)"

"=ROUNDDOWN(number, number of digits to which you want to round down)"

"=ROUNDUP(number, number of digits to which you want to round up)"

"=MROUND(number, multiple to which you want to round number)"

Example #1:

◢	A	B	C
3	**Number**	**Result**	**Function**
4	3.15	3.2	=ROUND(A4,1)
5	3.15	3	=ROUND(A5,0)
6	3.149	3.1	=ROUND(A5,1)
7	-1.481	-1.48	=ROUND(A6,2)
8	21.5	20	=ROUND(A7,-1)

Figure 3-61: Example of ROUND

In the preceding example, 3.15 is rounded to 3.2 because if the number of digits is greater than 0 (zero), then the ROUND function rounds the number to the specified number of decimal places. If the number of digits is 0, then the number is rounded to the nearest integer, that is, ROUND(3.15,0) which results in 3. If the number of digits is less than 0, the number is rounded to the left of the decimal point, that is, ROUND(21.5,-1) which results in 20, and ROUND(121.5,-2) which results in 100.

In case you want to always round up (away from zero) a number, ROUNDUP function should be used and similarly to always round down (toward zero), use the ROUNDDOWN function. In case you want to round a number to a specific multiple, use the MROUND function. We will see their usage in following examples.

Example #2:

In the following table, we have numbers and two sets of results, first if the numbers are rounded up and second if the numbers are rounded down. See how the results change based on the function used.

	A	B	C	D	E	F
10	Number	Result 1	Function ROUNDUP		Result 2	Function ROUNDDOWN
11	3.15	3.2	=ROUNDUP(A11,1)		3.1	=ROUNDDOWN(A11,1)
12	3.15	4	=ROUNDUP(A12,0)		3	=ROUNDDOWN(A12,0)
13	3.149	3.2	=ROUNDUP(A13,1)		3.1	=ROUNDDOWN(A13,1)
14	-1.481	-1.49	=ROUNDUP(A14,2)		-1.48	=ROUNDDOWN(A14,2)
15	21.5	30	=ROUNDUP(A15,-1)		20	=ROUNDDOWN(A15,-1)
16						

Figure 3-62: Example of ROUNDUP and ROUNDDOWN functions

Example #3:

MROUND(10,3) rounds 10 to the nearest multiple of 3, resulting in 9. Similarly, MROUND(8,3) results in 9 while MROUND(7,3) results in 6 as it rounds to the nearest multiple. MROUND(1.5, 0.2) will round 1.5 to the nearest multiple of 0.2, that is, 1.6 and MROUND(-1.5, -0.2) will result in -1.6. But MROUND(1.5, -0.2) will result in Error as the number and the multiple arguments must have the same sign.

3.14.3 CEILING, FLOOR

The CEILING function returns number rounded up, away from zero, to the nearest multiple of significance.

Syntax is

"=CEILING(number, significance or multiple to which you want to round)"

Example #1:

CEILING is a similar function to MROUND with a difference that CEILING always rounds up the number while MROUND finds the nearest multiple. In the following table, for the same arguments, the results differ for both the functions.

◢	A	B	C	D	E
17	Number	Result CEILING		Result MROUND	
18	3.15	4	=CEILING(A18,1)	3	=MROUND(A18,1)
19	3.149	3.2	=CEILING(A19,0.1)	3.1	=MROUND(A19,0.1)
20					

Figure 3-63: Example of CEILING function

FLOOR is like the CEILING function but with a difference that it always rounds number down, towards zero, to the nearest multiple of significance.

Syntax is

"=FLOOR(number, significance or multiple to which you want to round)"

Example #2:

In the following table, the results of the FLOOR function are given along with CEILING and MROUND to show how the results change for the same number and the given multiple.

◢	A	B	C	D	E
17	Number	Result CEILING		Result FLOOR / MROUND	
18	3.15	4	=CEILING(A18,1)	3	=FLOOR(A18,1)
19	3.149	3.2	=CEILING(A19,0.1)	3.1	=FLOOR(A19,0.1)
20	1.58	2	=CEILING(A20,2)	0	=FLOOR(A20,2)
21				2	=MROUND(A20,2)
22	2.58	4	=CEILING(A22,2)	2	=FLOOR(A22,2)
23				2	=MROUND(A22,2)
24					

Figure 3-64: Example of FLOOR function

Interesting results are of number 1.58 and 2.58. Since CEILING rounds up 1.58 to the multiple of 2, hence it returns 2 while FLOOR rounds down so returns 0 and MROUND finds the nearest multiple of 2 so returns 2. Now, in case of number 2.58, CEILING returns 4 while both FLOOR and MROUND return 2.

3.14.4 ABS, SQRT, SUMSQ

ABS returns the absolute value of the number. SQRT returns the positive square root of the number and SUMSQ returns the sum of the squares of the arguments.

Syntax is

"=ABS(real number of which you want the absolute value)"

"=SQRT(number for which you want the square root)"

"=SUMSQ(number1, [number2], ...)"

Note that the arguments can either be numbers, names, arrays, or references that contain numbers.

Example #1:

ABS function returns 2 for both ABS(2) and ABS(-2)

SQRT function returns 4 in both cases SQRT(16) and SQRT(ABS(-16)). Not that it returns error in case the number is negative.

SUMSQ function returns 25 for SUMSQ(3,4) that is, sum of squares of 3 (that is, 9) and 4 (that is, 16).

3.14.5 EXP, LN

The EXP function returns 'e' raised to the power of number. The constant e equals 2.71828182845904, the base of the natural logarithm. LN is the inverse of the EXP function that returns the natural logarithm of a number.

Syntax is

"=EXP(number i.e., exponent applied to the base e)"

"=LN(positive real number for which you want the natural logarithm)"

These functions are often used in working with non-linear trend lines or graphs and in many statistical calculations.

Example #1:

Assuming we have a population data of three regions for the year 2014, and the rate of growth of population in the given areas for five years was approximately 0.13%. Now, in order to know the latest population of the regions after five years, we can use the EXP function.

C26	▼	:	×	✓	*fx*	=B26*EXP($F$25*$F$26)		

◢	A	B	C	D	E	F
25	**Area**	**2014**	**2019**		**Rate of Growth**	0.13
26	R / North	4340	8313	=B26*EXP($F$25*$F$26)	**Time (yrs)**	5
27	R / Central	10321	19770	=B27*EXP($F$25*$F$26)		
28	R / South	1892	3624	=B28*EXP($F$25*$F$26)		
29						

Figure 3-65: Example of EXP function

Example # 2:

LN function, LN(2.7182818) return 1 as the number is the value of the constant e. And LN(EXP(3)) returns 3, as LN is inverse of EXP.

3.14.6 RAND, RANDBETWEEN

RAND returns an evenly distributed random real number which is greater than or equal to 0 and less than 1. A new random real number is returned every time the worksheet is calculated.

RANDBETWEEN is like RAND with a difference that it returns a random integer number between the numbers specified.

> Syntax is
>
> "=RAND()"
> "=RANDBETWEEN(bottom, top)"

Example # 1:

RAND and RANDBETWEEN returns a different number each time worksheet is recalculated by entering a formula or data in a different cell, or by manually recalculating (press F9).

◢	A	B	C
29			
30		0.8513784	=RAND()
31		1	=RANDBETWEEN(1,3)
32			
33		0.1600491	=RAND()
34		3	=RANDBETWEEN(1,3)

Figure 3-66: Example of RAND and RANDBETWEEN

3.15 Statistical Functions

In the previous chapter (3.10), we have already discussed few functions like AVERAGE, COUNT, COUTIF, and so on, that are categorized under statistical functions in Excel. In this section, we will discuss other functions that are frequently used and are helpful in calculations.

3.15.1 MIN, MAX

The MIN function returns the smallest number in a set of values and the MAX function returns the largest number in a set of values.

> Syntax is
>
> "=MIN(number1, [number2], ...)"
> "=MAX(number1, [number2], ...)"

Example #1:

In the following example, we have a list of customers loyalty program scores and we want to find the minimum and maximum achieved.

	A	B	G	H	I
39		Scores			
40		23	Lowest Score	3	=MIN(B40:B55)
41		45	Highest Score	121	=MAX(B40:B55)
42		3			
43		12			
44		56			
45		121			
46		78			
47		6			
48		33			
49		3			
50		41			
51		53			
52		10			
53		5			
54		27			
55		67			

Figure 3-67: Example of MIN and MAX

3.15.2 MINIFS, MAXIFS

The MINIFS function returns the minimum value and MAXIFS function returns the maximum value among cells specified by a given set of conditions or criteria.

Syntax is

"=MINIFS(min range, criteria range1, criteria1, [criteria range2, criteria2], ...)"

"=MAXIFS(max range, criteria range1, criteria1, [criteria range2, criteria2], ...)"

where,

- ° min range / max range - actual range of cells in which the minimum / maximum will be determined
- ° criteria range1 – set of cells to evaluate with the criteria
- ° criteria1 – the criteria in the form of a number, expression, or text that defines which cells will be evaluated as minimum / maximum
- ° criteria_range2, criteria2, ... - Additional ranges and their associated criteria. You can enter up to 126 range/criteria pairs

	A	B	C	D	E	F
14	School	Marks	Subject		Result	Formula used
15	X	97	Maths	Maximum marks in Maths	99	=MAXIFS(B15:B23,C15:C23,"Maths")
16	X	57	Maths	Maximum marks in Maths, School X	97	=MAXIFS(B15:B23,C15:C23,"Maths",A15:A23,"X")
17	X	75	Science	Maximum marks in Science, School Z	93	=MAXIFS(B15:B23,C15:C23,"Science",A15:A23,A21)
18	Y	99	Maths	Maximum marks in Science, Greater than 95	0	=MAXIFS(B15:B23,C15:C23,"Science",B15:B23,">95")
19	Y	75	Maths			
20	Y	89	Science	Minimum marks in Maths	56	=MINIFS(B15:B23,C15:C23,"Maths")
21	Z	85	Science	Minimum marks in Maths, School X	57	=MINIFS(B15:B23,C15:C23,"Maths",A15:A23,"X")
22	Z	56	Maths	Minimum marks in Science, School Z	85	=MINIFS(B15:B23,C15:C23,"Science",A15:A23,A21)
23	Z	93	Science	Minimum marks in Science, School Z, Greater than 85	93	=MINIFS(B15:B23,C15:C23,"Science",A15:A23,A21,B15:B23,">85")

Figure 3-68: Example of MINIFS & MAXIFS

In the preceding example, we are using the MAXIFS and MINIFS functions to find the maximum and minimum marks obtained based on different criterions.

The formula "=MINIFS(B15:B23,C15:C23,"Science",A15:A23,A21,B15:B23,">85")", returns the minimum value from the range of cells that satisfy the three given criterions. That is, this formula finds the minimum marks from the cell range B15:B23, where the marks are associated to, subject = Science (C15:C23,"Science"), school = Z (A15:A23, A21) and the marks are greater than 85 (B15:B23,">85").

The formula "=MAXIFS(B15:B23, C15:C23,"Science", B15:B23,">95")" returns a zero as there is no cell matching the giving criterions.

Note: MINIFS and MAXIFS functions are new functions introduced in Excel 2019. These functions are available on Windows or Mac if you have Office 2019 or Office 365 subscription with latest version of Office.

3.15.3 RANK.EQ, RANK.AVG

The RANK.EQ and RANK.AVG functions, both return the rank of a number in a list of numbers with a difference that if more than one value has the same rank, RANK. EQ returns the top rank of that set of values while RANK.AVG returns the average rank. Its size is relative to other values in the list.

Syntax is

"=RANK.EQ(number whose rank you want to find, list of numbers/ref, [order])"
"=RANK.AVG(number whose rank you want to find, list of numbers/ref, [order])"

where,
° order: 0 or omitted is descending & non-zero is ascending order

Example #1:

Using the same example of customer loyalty program scores, we now want to rank the customers based on the scores, without changing the sequence or data structure.

	A	B	C	D	E	F
39		Scores	RANK.EQ		RANK.AVG	
40		23	10	=RANK.EQ(B40, $B$40:$B$55)	10	=RANK.AVG(B40, $B$40:$B$55)
41		45	6		6	
42		3	15		15.5	
43		12	11		11	
44		56	4		4	
45		121	1		1	
46		78	2		2	
47		6	13		13	
48		33	8		8	
49		3	15		15.5	
50		41	7		7	
51		53	5		5	
52		10	12		12	
53		5	14		14	
54		27	9		9	
55		67	3		3	

Figure 3-69: Example of RANK.EQ and RANK.AVG (descending order)

Note that the highest number, 121, is given a rank of 1 because we did not specify the order. When the value for argument 'order' is omitted or specified as 0, it is descending order.

Example #2:

In this example, the rank is specified in ascending order as we specified a non-zero value, that is, 1 for argument 'order'. In this case, the lowest number, 3, is given a rank of 1 while 121 is the last rank.

A	B	C	D	E	F
39	Scores	RANK.EQ		RANK.AVG	
40	23	7	=RANK.EQ(B40, $B$40:$B$55,1)	7	=RANK.AVG(B40, $B$40:$B$55,1)
41	45	11		11	
42	3	1		1.5	
43	12	6		6	
44	56	13		13	
45	121	16		16	
46	78	15		15	
47	6	4		4	
48	33	9		9	
49	3	1		1.5	
50	41	10		10	
51	53	12		12	
52	10	5		5	
53	5	3		3	
54	27	8		8	
55	67	14		14	

Figure 3-70: Example of RANK.EQ and RANK.AVG function (ascending order)

3.15.4 FREQUENCY

The FREQUENCY function calculates how often values occur within a range of values, and then returns a vertical array of numbers. FREQUENCY ignores blank cells and text.

Syntax is

"=FREQUENCY(data array, bins array)"

where,

- ° data array - An array of or reference to a set of values for which you want to count frequencies.
- ° bins - array - An array of or reference to intervals into which you want to group the values in data array.

If data array or bin array contains no values, FREQUENCY returns an array of zeros.

The number of elements in the returned array is one more than the number of elements in bins array. The extra element in the returned array returns the count of any values above the highest interval.

Example #1:

From the scores given below we want to find how many scores are less than or equal to 60 and between 61 to 90.

Scores	97	57	75	99	75	89	85	56	93

So, in this example the scores list is the data array (cell range M2:U2) and in the bin array we will enter 60 and 90 (cell range M3:N3). Enter the formula '=FREQUENCY(M2:U2,M3:N3)' in cell M8 and press Enter. The results are returned in the cells M8:M10.

Note that in the bin array we had just entered two values that is 60 and 90 but the returned array has three values. The extra cell returns the number of values in data array that are greater than the second interval value.

3.15.5 MEDIAN, MODE.SNGL, MODE.MUTL

In statistics, the commonly used measures of central tendency are the mean, median, and mode. Mean, that is, the AVERAGE function in Excel, has been discussed in chapter 3.10. In this section, we will discuss median and mode. Median is the number in the middle of a set of numbers and Mode is the most frequently occurring, or repetitive value. For a small set of values, we can find the median and mode manually also but for huge complex data it becomes difficult. Excel has the MEDIAN and MODE functions that do it easily for us.

Syntax is

"=MEDIAN(number1, [number2], ...)"

"=MODE.SNGL(number1,[number2],...)"

"=MODE.MULT((number1,[number2],...)"

Excel defines two functions for mode, MODE.SNGL and MODE.MULT. MODE. SNGL returns the lowest mode value in case there are multiple repetitive values and MODE.MULT returns an array of the most frequently occurring or repetitive values. We will see their usage with an example in the following example:

Example #1:

For the given scores, the median is 30. Median is the middle number of the given set of numbers, that is, half the numbers are greater than the median, and half the numbers are less than the median.

	A	B	C	D	E	F	G	H	I	J	K	L	M	N	O	P	Q	R
56																		
57		Scores	23	45	3	6	56	121	78	6	33	3	41	53	10	5	27	67
58																		
59		Median	30	=MEDIAN(C57:R57)														

Figure 3-71: Example of Median function

Example #2:

For the given scores, MODE.SNGL returns 3, as it returns the lowest mode in case of multiple repetitive numbers. MODE.MULT returns both the repetitive numbers 3 and 6.

	A	B	C	D	E	F	G	H	I	J	K	L	M	N	O	P	Q	R
60																		
61		Scores	23	45	3	6	56	121	78	6	33	3	41	53	10	5	27	67
62		Single Mode	3	=MODE.SNGL(C61:R61)														
63																		
64		Multi Mode	3															
65			6	{=MODE.MULT(C61:R61)}														
66			#N/A															
67			#N/A															
68																		
69		Multi Mode	3	6	#N/A	#N/A												
70			{=TRANSPOSE(MODE.MULT(C61:R61))}															

Figure 3-72: Example of MODE function

Note that MODE.MULT returns an array of values, hence it must be entered as an array formula. If the formula was not entered as an array formula, the single result would have been 3, same result as using the MODE.SNGL function.

Array formula is entered by selecting the vertical range of cells, that is, C64 to C67, enter the formula '=MODE.MULT(C61:R61)' and confirm by pressing Control + Shift + Enter. In each selected cell, the function returns the mode value, if any. Since there are only two values and we selected four cells in range, it returns 3 and 6 in C64 and C65 cells and #N/A in C66 and C67 as there are no more mode values.

MODE.MULT returns result in a vertical array. In case we want to return the results in horizontal array then we will use the TRANSPOSE function of Excel along with MODE.MULT.

In this case, the array formula will be entered by selecting the horizontal range of cells, that is, C69 to F69, enter the same formula as before but inside the TRANSPOSE function '=TRANPOSE(MODE.MULT(C61:R61))' and confirm by pressing Control + Shift + Enter.

3.15.6 QUARTILE.INC(/.EXC), PERCENTILE.INC(/.EXC)

Quartiles in statistics are values that divide your data into quarters, that is, into four segments according to where the numbers fall on the number line; the lowest 25% of numbers, next lowest 25% of numbers (up to the median), second highest 25% of numbers (above the median), and the highest 25% of numbers.

A percentile is a measure used in statistics indicating the value below which a given percentage of observations in a group of observations falls. Median is the 50th percentile, that is, the point in the data where 50% of the data fall below that point, and 50% fall above it.

Excel defines two functions each for quartile and percentile, QUARTILE.INC and PERCENTILE.INC, meaning inclusive and QUARTILE.EXC and PERCENTILE.EXC meaning exclusive.

Syntax is

"=QUARTILE.INC(numeric values for which you want the quartile value, quart)"

where,

° quart value is 0 means minimum value, 1 is first quartile i.e., 25th percentile, 2 is median value i.e., 50th percentile, 3 is third quartile i.e., 75th percentile and 4 is maximum value

"=QUARTILE.EXC(numeric values for which you want the quartile value, quart)"

where,

  ° quart value 1 is first quartile i.e., 25th percentile, 2 is median value i.e., 50th percentile, 3 is third quartile i.e., 75th percentile

"=PERCENTILE.INC(range of data that defines relative standing, percentile value)"

"=PERCENTILE.EXC(range of data that defines relative standing, percentile value)"

Example #1:

Using the same Scores data, we will find the quartiles. Note that the median calculated in the previous example (Figure 3-71) was 30, which is returned by the QUARTILE.INC(B1:Q1,2) function.

▲	A	B	C	D	E	F	G	H	I	J	K	L	M	N	O	P	Q
1	Scores	23	45	3	6	56	121	78	6	33	3	41	53	10	5	27	67
2																	
3	Quartile Inclusive	3	=QUARTILE.INC(B1:Q1,0)														
4		6	=QUARTILE.INC(B1:Q1,1)														
5		30	=QUARTILE.INC(B1:Q1,2)														
6		54	=QUARTILE.INC(B1:Q1,3)														
7		121	=QUARTILE.INC(B1:Q1,4)														
8																	
9	Quartile Exclusive	6	=QUARTILE.EXC(B1:Q1,1)														
10		30	=QUARTILE.EXC(B1:Q1,2)														
11		55	=QUARTILE.EXC(B1:Q1,3)														

Figure 3-73: Example of Quartile function

QUARTILE.INC is like the older version of the QUARTILE function. QUARTILE. EXC has a slightly different algorithm for calculation, hence, the difference in the results for the 3rd quartile is 55 instead of 54 as returned by QUARTILE.INC.

Example #2:

In the following example, PERCENTILE.INC(B13:Q13,0.25) returns 6, which means that value 6 occupies the 25th percentile of the given set of scores. Similarly, 4 occupies the 10th percentile, returned by the PERCENTILE.INC(B13:Q13,10%) function. As there is a little difference in how PERCENTILE.EXC calculates the percentile, you see the difference in results for the same dataset and 10th percentile, PERCENTILE. EXC(B13:Q13,0.1), returns 3.

▲	A	B	C	D	E	F	G	H	I	J	K	L	M	N	O	P	Q
13	Scores	23	45	3	6	56	121	78	6	33	3	41	53	10	5	27	67
14																	
15	Percentile Inclusive	6	=PERCENTILE.INC(B13:Q13,0.25)														
16		4	=PERCENTILE.INC(B13:Q13,10%)														
17																	
18	Percentile Exclusive	3	=PERCENTILE.EXC(B13:Q13,0.1)														
19																	

Figure 3-74: *Example of Percentile function*

PERCENTILE.INC is similar to the older version of the PERCENTILE function, a slightly less accurate algorithm and works for percentile value between 0 and 1. On the other hand, PERCENTILE.EXE works for percentile value between $1/n$ and $1-1/n$, where n is the number of elements in the dataset or array.

Percentile is commonly used in salary surveys and by human resource department to compare employees' salary and see how they match to market compensation.

3.15.7 PERCENTRANK.INC, PERCENTRANK. EXC

PERCENTRANK.INC and PERCENTRANK.EXC return the percentile that a given data value has in relation to a set of data values. Basically, they are inverse functions of PERCENTILE.INC and PERCENTILE.EXC.

Syntax is

"=PERCENTRANK.INC(range of data that defines relative standing, value for which you want to know the rank, [significance])"

"=PERCENTRANK.EXC(range of data that defines relative standing, value for which you want to know the rank, [significance])"

where,

° significance: number of significant digits for the returned percentage value, default is three digits (0.xxx).

Example #1:

In the following example, for each of the cases the percentile is the 30th percentile.

◢	A	B	C	D	E	F	G	H	I	J	K
19											
20	1			3.6	=PERCENTILE.INC(A20:A24,0.3)						
21	3			0.3	=PERCENTRANK.INC(A20:A24,3.6)						
22	6										
23	12			2.6	=PERCENTILE.EXC(A20:A24,0.3)						
24	15			0.3	=PERCENTRANK.EXC(A20:A24,2.6)						
25											

Figure 3-75: Example of PERCENTRANK function

3.15.8 STDEV.P(/.S), VAR.P(./S)

Variance is a statistical measure that tells us how measured data vary from the average value of the set of data. Standard deviation is the square root of the variance. A low standard deviation indicates that the data points tend to be close to the mean of the set, while a high standard deviation indicates that the data points are spread out over a wider range of values.

Excel has two functions each for variance and standard deviation, indicating measure across the whole population, that is, STDEV.P, VAR.P and a sample, that is, STDEV.S, VAR.S of population respectively.

> Syntax is
>
> "=STDEV.P(number1, [number2],...)"
> "=STDEV.S(number1, [number2],...)"
>
> "=VAR.P(number1, [number2],...)"
> "=VAR.S(number1, [number2],...)"

Example #1:

For two groups Group 1 and Group 2 we have heights and we want to find the variance and standard deviation. Note that in case of sample, we have taken limited values for calculations and for population we have taken all values in consideration.

◢	A	B	C	D	E	F	G
26		Height (feet inches)					
27		Group 1	Group 2				
28		4.30	3.90		Population Variance	1.331	=VAR.P(B28:B32,C28:C32)
29		3.00	4.11		Standard Deviation	1.154	=STDEV.P(B28:B32,C28:C32)
30		5.20	5.12				
31		5.50	6.15		Sample Variance	0.331	=VAR.S(B28:B29,C28:C29)
32		6.10	7.00		Standard Deviation	0.575	=STDEV.S(B28:B29,C28:C29)

Figure 3-76: Example of Variance and Standard deviation functions

3.15.9 CORREL, COVARIANCE.P(/.S)

Correlation and covariance are two statistical concepts that are used to determine the relationship of two random variables.

Covariance measures the total variation of two random variables from their expected values, help to gauge the direction of the relationship, that is, whether the variables tend to move in tandem (positive covariance) or show an inverse (negative covariance) relationship.

On the other hand, correlation measures the strength of the relationship between variables, how change in one impacts the other. A correlation of +1 indicates that random variables have a direct and strong relationship, -1 indicates that there is a strong inverse relationship and an increase in one variable will lead to an equal and opposite decrease in the other variable and 0 indicates that the two numbers are independent.

Excel has two functions, COVARIANCE.P and COVARIANCE.S, for covariance of the whole population and a sample of the population, like variance and standard deviation functions.

Syntax is

"=CORREL(cell range of values, second cell range of values)"

"=COVARIANCE.P(first cell range of integers, second cell range of integers)"

"=COVARIANCE.S(first cell range of integers, second cell range of integers)"

Example #1:

We want to find correlation between the temperature and ice cream sales. From the following results, we can deduce that temperature and ice creams sales are directly and strongly correlated as the correlation is 0.9. And the positive covariance of population and sample indicate that as the temperature increases/ decreases, so does the ice creams sales increase/decrease, that is, they move in the same direction.

	A	B	C	D	E	F	G
34		Temp (C)	Ice Cream Sales				
35		22	420				
36		15	309		Correlation	0.9531	=CORREL(B35:B45,C35:C45)
37		26	432				
38		31	445		Covariance Population	1711.46	=COVARIANCE.P(B35:B45,C35:C45)
39		32	450		Covariance Sample	1084.00	=COVARIANCE.S(B35:B40,C35:C40)
40		10	101				
41		8	30				
42		29	445				
43		4	15				
44		17	312				
45		6	16				

Figure 3-77: *Example of Covariance and Correlation function*

3.16 Financial Functions

Excel formulas and functions are very helpful in performing financial analysis and building faster and efficient financial models. In the preceding sections, the functions discussed are generic, not very specific to a domain and are also used very often in financial analysis. Along with those, in this section we will discuss some useful functions that are more specific to financial analysis like calculating interest rates, monthly payments, or finding future value of investments.

3.16.1 PV and FV

PV function calculates the present value and FV function calculates the future value of a loan or an investment, based on a constant interest rate.

Syntax is

"=PV(rate, nper, pmt, [fv], [type])"

"=FV(rate, nper, pmt, [pv], [type])"

where,

- ◦ rate – interest rate
- ◦ nper – total no of payment periods
- ◦ pmt – payment paid each period
- ◦ fv – future value or cash balance you want to attain
- ◦ pv – present value
- ◦ type – when payment is due i.e., 0 = at the end & 1=at beginning

Example #1:

We want to calculate the present value of an annuity that pays 1,000 per month for a period of three years (3*12=36 months) at interest rate of 6% per year (that is, 0.50% per month) and each payment is made at the end of the month.

	A	B	C	D
1		Interest Rate (6% pa) = 6%/12	0.50%	
2		No of payment periods (3yrs) =3*12)	36	
3		Payment per month	1000	
4				
5		**Present Value (PV)**	-32871.02	=PV(C1, C2, C3)

Figure 3-78: Example of PV function

In the preceding example, the future value is omitted and hence it is considered as 0. Argument payment due has also not been specified, which by default is 0 meaning it is due at end of the period. If 1 is specified, it is considered that payment is due at the beginning of the period. Both are optional arguments. Note that since the unit for calculation is monthly, we have divided the interest rate by 12 to get rate per month 0.50% and multiplied by 12 to get number of payment periods as 36.

Example #2:

In this example, for an investment of 10,000 in 2017, paid yearly for interest rate of 10%, we want to know the future value of the investment in 2020, that is, after 3 years.

	A	B	C	D
8		Interest Rate 10%pa	10%	
9		No of payment periods 3yrs (2017-20)	3	
10		Present Value	10,000.00	
11		Type	1	
12				
13		**Future Value (FV)**	-13310.00	=FV(C8,C9,,C10,C11)

Figure 3-79: Example of FV function

In the preceding example, the payment for each period is omitted, hence it is mandatory to specify the present value, that is, the lump sum amount paid. Also, we have specified the type as 1, that is, the payments are due at the beginning of the period.

For both PV and FV functions to work correctly, you should be consistent about the units (yearly, monthly, weekly, and so on) you use for specifying rate and the total number of payment periods (nper).

Note that, in line with the general cash flow sign convention, cash outflows are represented by negative numbers and cash inflows are represented by positive numbers. Hence, the result in the preceding examples is negative, that is, cash outflow.

3.16.2 PMT, IPMT and PPMT

PMT function calculates the constant periodic payment required to pay off a loan or investment, with a constant interest rate, over a specified period.

Syntax is

"=PMT(rate, nper, pv, [fv], [type])"

where,

   °   rate – interest rate

   °   nper – total no of payment periods

   °   fv – future value or cash balance you want to attain

   °   pv – present value

   °   type – when payment is due i.e., 0 = at the end & 1=at beginning

Example #1:

The following example returns the annual payment on loan of 10,00,000 at an annual rate of 10%. The loan term is 20 years and all payments are made at the end of the period.

▲	A	B	C	D
15		Interest Rate 10%pa	10%	
16		No of payment periods 20yrs	20	
17		Amount of Loan / Present Value	10,00,000.00	
18		Type	0	
19				
20		PMT	-1,17,459.62	=PMT(C15,C16,C17,0,C18)
21				

Figure 3-80: Example of PMT function – annual payment

If for the same example we had to calculate the monthly payment, following will be the result:

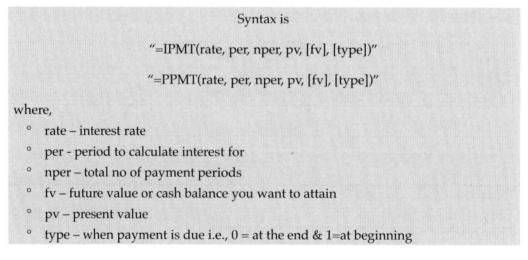

⊿	A	B	C	D
15		Interest Rate 10%pa	10%	
16		No of payment periods 20yrs	20	
17		Amount of Loan / Present Value	10,00,000.00	
18		Type	0	
19				
20		**PMT (annual)**	-1,17,459.62	=PMT(C15,C16,C17,0,C18)
21				
22		**PMT (monthly)**	-9,650.22	=PMT(C15/12,C16*12,C17,0,C18)

Figure 3-81: Example of PMT function – monthly payment

Note that, in line with the general cash flow sign convention, cash outflows are represented by negative numbers and cash inflows are represented by positive numbers.

Loan or Investment Payment has two components: Principal and the Interest Payment. PPMT and IPMT functions are related to these two components. IPMT and PPMT are similar functions to PMT with a difference that IPMT returns the interest payment for an investment while PPMT returns the payment on the principal amount for a given period for an investment based on periodic, constant payments, and a constant interest rate.

> Syntax is
>
> "=IPMT(rate, per, nper, pv, [fv], [type])"
>
> "=PPMT(rate, per, nper, pv, [fv], [type])"
>
> where,
> - ° rate – interest rate
> - ° per - period to calculate interest for
> - ° nper – total no of payment periods
> - ° fv – future value or cash balance you want to attain
> - ° pv – present value
> - ° type – when payment is due i.e., 0 = at the end & 1=at beginning

Example #2:

In this example, we want to know the interest and principal payments for the 4th year on a loan amount of 10,00,000 at an annual rate of 10%. The loan term is 20 years and all payments are made at the end of the period.

	A	B	C	D
24		Interest Rate 10%pa	10%	
25		Period (4th year)	4	
26		No of payment periods 20yrs	20	
27		Amount of Loan / Present Value	10,00,000.00	
28		Type	0	
29				
30		**IPMT**	-94,220.86	=IPMT(C24,C25,C26,C27,0,C28)
31		**PPMT**	-23,238.76	=PPMT(C24,C25,C26,C27,0,C28)

Figure 3-82: Example for PPMT and IPMT functions

3.16.3 NPV and XNPV

NPV calculates the net present value of an investment by using a discount rate (also called rate) and a series of future payments (negative values) and income (positive values). Basically, it is the difference between the present value of cash inflows and the present value of cash outflows over a period of time.

Example #1:

For example, the PV for 10,000 cash received after 5 years at a rate of 10% annual return compounded annually is 6,209. Now, if we want to calculate the NPV for an investment of 5,000 today that will result in 10,000 cash at the end of 5 years, at the rate of 10% annual return compounded annually, it will be the result of the present value of the cash inflow, that is, 6,209 minus the present value of the 5,000 cash outflow, 1,209. Note that 5,000 cash outflows occurred at the present time, its present value is 5,000.

The difference between NPV and PV (as discussed in section 3.16.1) is that NPV formula accounts for the initial investment required to fund, making it a net figure, while the PV calculation only accounts for cash inflows.

Now we will see how Excel function NPV works.

Syntax is

"=NPV(rate,value1,[value2],...) "

where,

° rate: rate of discount over the length of one period
° value1, [value2],... : payments and income equally spaced in time, in chronological order, occurring at end of each period

Note that negative payments represent outgoing payments and positive payments represent incoming payments.

Example #2:

In the following example, we will be calculating NPV with 10% rate of discount and the cash flow as given in the screenshot. If NPV is greater than zero, the series of cash flows returns something greater than 10%. If it's less than zero, the return is less than 10%.

	A	B	C	D
45		Rate	10%	
46		**Period**	**Cash Flow**	
47		0	-1000	Out-flow
48		1	200	In-flow
49		2	300	
50		3	400	
51		4	500	
52		5	600	
53				
54		**NPV**	**444.34**	=NPV(C45,C48:C52)+C47

Figure 3-83: *Example of NPV function*

Note that if the first cash flow occurs at the start of the first period, the first value must be added to the NPV result, not included in the values arguments.

Calculation can also be done manually which returns the same results using the following formula, however, we can see it is complex while Excel NVP function makes it very simple.

=C48/(1+0.1)^1+C49/(1+0.1)^2+C50/(1+0.1)^3+C51/(1+0.1)^4+C52/(1+0.1)^5+C47

Instead of (1+0.1)^2 and (1+0.1)^3 we could use Excel POWER function also, that is, POWER(1+0.1,2) and POWER(1+0.1,3) respectively.

C56 *fx* =(C48/(1+0.1))+(C49/POWER(1+0.1,2))+(C50/POWER(1+0.1,3))+(C51/POWER(1+0.1,4))+(C52/POWER(1+0.1,5))+C47

	A	B	C	D	E	F
45		Rate	10%			
46		**Period**	**Cash Flow**			
47		0	-1000	Out-flow		
48		1	200	In-flow		
49		2	300			
50		3	400			
51		4	500			
52		5	600			
53						
54		**NPV**	**444.34**	=NPV(C45,C48:C52)+C47		
55						
56			444.34			

Figure 3-84: *Example of NPV – Manual calculation*

In comparison, XNVP returns the net present value for a schedule of cash flows that is not necessarily periodic.

Syntax is

"=XNPV(rate,values,dates) "

where,
- ○ rate: rate of discount to apply to the cash flows
- ○ values: series of cash flows that corresponds to a schedule of payments in dates
- ○ dates: schedule of payment dates that corresponds to the cash flow payments

Example #3:

In the following example, we will calculate the XNPV and the NPV values to see the difference. The discount rate is 10%, start date is Jun 2008, and the first cash flow happens after 6 months. Subsequent cash flows are received on the corresponding dates as follows:

	A	B	C	D
58		Rate	10%	
59		**Period**	**Cash Flow**	
60		30-06-2008	0	
61		31-12-2008	200	
62		01-02-2009	300	
63		01-05-2009	400	
64		03-01-2010	500	
65		04-03-2011	600	
66				
67		**XNPV**	1741.32	=XNPV(C58,C60:C65,B60:B65)
68		NPV	1313.03	=NPV(C58,C60:C65)
69				

Figure 3-85: Example of XNPV function

In the preceding example for the same data, XNPV and NPV results are different. The reason being that XNPV takes the exact dates into consideration, NPV assumes that cash flow happens at the end of each period.

3.16.4 IRR and XIRR

The internal rate of return (IRR) is the interest rate received for an investment consisting of payments (negative values) and income (positive values) that occur at regular periods. The cash flows must occur at regular intervals, such as monthly or annually. XIRR returns the interest rate for an investment or cash flows occurring at irregular intervals.

> Syntax is
>
> "=IRR(values, [guess])"
> "=XIRR(values, dates, [guess])"
>
> where,
> - value: stream of cash flows
> - dates: schedule of payment dates that corresponds to the cash flow payments
> - guess: an initial guess at what the IRR might be. This is an optional argument, which, if omitted, takes on the default value of 0.1 (=10%).

Note that values must contain at least one positive value and one negative value to calculate the internal rate of return. Function works by calculating the present value of each cash flow based on the guessed rate (if given or default 10%). If the sum of those is greater than zero, it reduces the rate and tries again. Excel keeps iterating through rates and summing present values until the sum is zero. Once the present values sum to zero, it returns that rate.

Example #1:

The following example shows the difference between IRR and XIRR. The cash flow is the same in both cases but for IRR it assumes at regular interval while XIRR considers the actual dates at which the payments were made.

▲	A	B	C	D	E	F	G	H	I
70									
71		Period	1	2	3	4	5	6	
72		Cash Flow	-1000	200	300	400	500	600	
73									
74		IRR	23%	=IRR(C72:H72)					
75									
76		Dates	30-06-2008	31-12-2008	01-02-2009	01-05-2009	03-01-2010	04-03-2011	
77		Cash Flow	-1000	200	300	400	500	600	
78									
79		XIRR	70%	=XIRR(C77:H77,C76:H76)					
80									

Internal rate of return, both IRR and XIRR are good tools to evaluate the attractiveness of a project or investment using a percentage value. Helpful to compare the potential profitability of multiple prospective projects, and if the cost of investment is equal for all the projects, then the project with the highest IRR/XIRR would be the most attractive for investment.

NPV and XNVP can also be used as investment indicators, they use the actual money value for comparison while IRR and XIRR uses percentage value, which is preferable.

3.17 Error Handling

In case the formula has an error, Excel returns a value starting hash mark (#). There are different error values #N/A, #VALUE, #REF, #DIV/0!, #NUM, #NAME?, and #NULL!, which we will explain in this section and how to handle these errors.

To avoid errors, you should carefully review, check your data and values in the Excel sheet. Many times, the return value of functions is used in another formula or calculation and error values will mess those calculations. Excel has some built-in functions for error handling, under the 'Information' and 'Logical' function categories, such as ISERR, ISERROR, ISNA, ERROR.TYPE, IFERROR, and IFNA.

3.17.1 Error Types

3.17.1.1 #N/A

This error is returned when the function is unable to find the value it has been asked to look for or when the numbers you are referring to in your formula cannot be found. Simple example is when we try to see the exact match 'A' in array {B,C,D} using formula '=MATCH("A",{"B","C","D"},0)'. Another example could be if you are trying to look up a value using VLOOKUP/HLOOKUP and there are no matching values in the array, as shown here:

▲	A	B	C	D	E	F	G	H
1								
2		Group Name	Score					
3		Red	23		=VLOOKUP("White",B3:C6,2,FALSE)			
4		Green	56					
5		Yellow	41					
6		Blue	66					
7								
8								

Figure 3-86: Example of #N/A error

We can also handle this error using the ISNA (see 3.17.2.2) or IFNA (see 3.17.2.4) functions, so that instead of returning error #N/A, we return something meaningful that does not disrupt further calculations or just a message informing user of the error.

3.17.1.2 # VALUE!

This error is very general and can occur whenever the data type of a given function doesn't match what it is expecting or something is wrong with the way the formula is typed or there is something wrong with cells being referred to in formula.

For example, the '="A"+1' formula returns the #VALUE! as it is expecting number to calculate.

3.17.1.3 # REF!

Excel usually displays #REF! when a formula references a cell that is not valid.

For example, in the following example, we are adding numbers in columns NUM1, NUM2, and NUM3.

	A	B	C	D	E
1	Num1	Num2	Num3	Total	
2	1	5	3	9	=SUM(A2,B2,C2)
3	2	9	2	13	=SUM(A3,B3,C3)
4	3	7	1	11	=SUM(A4,B4,C4)
5	4	8	6	18	=SUM(A5,B5,C5)

Now what will happen if we delete column NUM2. Excel gives #REF! error in Total column.

C2			×	✓	f_x	=SUM(A2,#REF!,B2)	
	A	B	C	D	E	F
1	Num1	Num3	Total			
2	1		#REF!	=SUM(A2,B2,C2)		
3	2	2	#REF!	=SUM(A3,B3,C3)		
4	3	1	#REF!	=SUM(A4,B4,C4)		
5	4	6	#REF!	=SUM(A5,B5,C5)		
6						

3.17.1.4 # DIV/0!

This error occurs when you are asking Excel to divide a formula by zero or an empty cell.

For example, '=4/0', it types in the cell will return #DIV/0! Error.

3.17.1.5 # NUM!

Excel shows this error when a formula or function contains numeric values that aren't valid.

For example, '=SQRT(-9)' returns the #NUM! error as we entered a negative number.

3.17.1.6 #NAME?

The #NAME? error signifies that something needs to be corrected in the syntax.

For example, '=INT(a)' returns the #NAME? error as the INT function expects a number as value.

3.17.1.7 #NULL!

This error is shown when you use an incorrect range operator in a formula, or when you use an intersection operator (space character) between range references to specify an intersection of two ranges that don't intersect.

D2			×	✓	*fx*	=SUM(A2 C2)

◢	A	B	C	D	E
1	Num1	Num2	Num3	Total	
2	1	5	⚠	#NULL!	=SUM(A2 C2)
3	2	9	2		
4	3	7	1		
5	4	8	6		

3.17.2 Error Handling Functions

3.17.2.1 ISERR and ISERROR

Syntax is

"=ISERR(value to test except #N/A) "
"=ISERROR(value to test for any error value) "

The ISERR and ISERROR functions, checks the specified value and returns TRUE or FALSE depending on the outcome.

◢	A	B	C	D	E	F	G
13		Value	Result 1			Result 2	
14		#N/A	FALSE	=ISERR(B14)		TRUE	=ISERROR(B14)
15		#REF!	TRUE	=ISERR(B15)		TRUE	=ISERROR(B15)
16		0	FALSE	=ISERR(B16)		FALSE	=ISERROR(B16)
17							

Figure 3-87: Example of ISERR & ISERROR function

3.17.2.2 ISNA

ISNA function checks the value and returns TRUE if it is #N/A and FALSE otherwise.

> Syntax is
> "=ISNA(value to test for #N/A) "

As discussed in the example for error type #N/A in chapter 3.17.1.1, we will work further on that example to see how ISNA function helps in error handling and returning a meaningful information.

Example #1:

We have two schools participating in a competition and each school has four groups representing them. The scorer wanted to find the score of the 'White' group of School #2 but entered incorrect data range of School #1, hence, #N/A value was returned by the '=VLOOKUP(C8,B3:C6,2,FALSE)' formula. On correcting the data range in the '=VLOOKUP(C8,E3:F6,2,FALSE)' formula, correct value was returned, that is, 45. This is a tedious way to find scores by entering the correct data range. We can instead use the ISNA function to use the correct data range and get the correct value as given here:

⊿	A	B	C	D	E	F	G	H
2		School #1	Group Score		School #2	Group Score		
3		Red	23		White	45		
4		Green	56		Orange	50		
5		Yellow	41		Pink	32		
6		Blue	66		Black	18		
7								
8		Score of Group	White		#N/A	=VLOOKUP(C8,B3:C6,2,FALSE)		
9					45	=VLOOKUP(C8,E3:F6,2,FALSE)		
10								
11		Generic formula with Error Handling	White		45	=IF(ISNA(VLOOKUP(C11,$B$3:$C$6,2,FALSE)), VLOOKUP(C11,$E$3:$F$6,2,FALSE), VLOOKUP(C11,$B$3:$C$6,2,FALSE))		
12			Red		23	=IF(ISNA(VLOOKUP(C11,$B$3:$C$6,2,FALSE)), VLOOKUP(C11,$E$3:$F$6,2,FALSE), VLOOKUP(C11,$B$3:$C$6,2,FALSE))		

Figure 3-88: Example of ISNA function

Conditional function IF is used with ISNA in the preceding formula. The ISNA function has been first used to check if error is returned, that is, TRUE if VLOOKUP returns #N/A and FALSE otherwise. If TRUE, then the IF function returns the value of the second argument, VLOOKUP(C11,$E$3:$F$6,2,FALSE), else the value of the third argument, VLOOKUP(C11,$B$3:$C$6,2,FALSE), in case of row#11.

3.17.2.3 IFERROR

Syntax is
"=IFERROR(value to test, value to return if the formula evaluates to an error) "

The IFERROR function returns the value specified if the value to test returns error, else returns the result of the formula. For example, the formula '=IFERROR(MATCH("A",{"B","C","D"},0),"No Match")' returns 'No Match' as the MATCH function returns #N/A. On the other hand, the '=IFERROR(MATCH("C",{"B","C","D"},0),"No Match")' formula returns 2 as a match for C is found at the 2nd position in array {B,C,D}.

3.17.2.4 IFNA

The IFNA function tests if the value returns error #N/A and returns the value specified as the second argument value.

Syntax is
"=IFNA(value to test, value to return if the formula evaluates to the #N/A error value) "

Example #1:

In the following example, we are trying to lookup the score of the 'white' group using the VLOOKUP function. But since it does not exist, VLOOKUP will return error #N/A (see error description in chapter 3.17.1.1) and hence IFNA will return the text "Not Found", which was specified as second argument in the function.

	A	B	C	D	J	K	L	M	N	O	P
1											
2		School #1	Group Score								
3		Red	23		Not Found	=IFNA(VLOOKUP("White",B3:C6,2,FALSE),"Not Found")					
4		Green	56								
5		Yellow	41								
6		Blue	66								

Figure 3-89: Example of IFNA function

3.17.2.5 ERROR.TYPE

Returns a number corresponding to one of the error values in Microsoft Excel or returns its own #N/A error if no error exists, that is, returns a number from 1 through 8 that corresponds to the type of error in its input cell reference.

Syntax is
"=ERROR.TYPE(error value whose identifying number you want to find)"

If error value is	ERROR.TYPE returns
#NULL!	1
#DIV/0!	2
#VALUE!	3
#REF!	4
#NAME?	5
#NUM!	6
#N/A	7
#GETTING_DATA	8
Anything else	#N/A

As per the preceding table, the '=ERROR.TYPE(#NULL!)' formula will return 1 and '=ERROR.TYPE(MATCH("A",{"B","C"},0))' returns 7 as the MATCH function returns error #N/A.

3.18 Formula Auditing

Formula auditing in Excel allows you to display the relationship between formulas and cells. It gives the options to Trace Precedents, Trace Dependents, Show or display Formulas in the sheet, Error checking and Tracing Errors, Watch window to see change in cell values and Evaluate formula option to stepping in the formula. Formula Auditing are under the Formulas tab.

Figure 3-90: Formula Auditing

3.18.1 Show Formulas

The 'Formula Auditing -> Show Formulas' option can be used for displaying the formulas in the sheet rather than the results of the formulas.

| D15 | ▼ | : | ✕ | ✓ | f_x | =VLOOKUP(B15,A10:B13,2,FALSE) |

◢	A	B	C	D	E
8					
9	School #1	Group Score		School #2	Group Score
10	Red	23		White	45
11	Green	56		Orange	50
12	Yellow	41		Pink	32
13	Blue	66		Black	18
14					
15	Score of Group	White	!	=VLOOKUP(B15,A10:B13,2,FALSE)	
16					
17				=IFNA(D15,"Not Found")	
18					

Figure 3-91: Show Formulas example

In case you want to see the formulas in one window and results in another window, then before using the Show Formulas option, open a new window by going to the View tab 'Window->New Window' option.

3.18.2 Trace Precedents, Trace Dependents, and Remove Trace Arrows

The precedents of any cell that contains a formula are all cells referenced by the formula in that cell. The dependents of any cell are all cells with formulas that reference that cell. Excel allows us to trace the cell relationships. Select the cell that has an error #N/A, D15 in the following example. Click on the 'Formula Auditing->Trace Precedents' and 'Formula Auditing->Trace Dependents' options. In our example, Excel draws blue colored arrows to show precedents and red colored arrow to show dependents of the selected cell with error value, D15. Note that D15 is been referenced in the formula in cell D17, hence, it becomes the dependent.

D15		▼	⋮	×	✓	*fx*	=VLOOKUP(B15,A10:B13,2,FALSE)		

	A	B	C	D	E	F	G	H
8								
9	School #1	Group Score		School #2	Group Score			
10	Red	23		White	45			
11	Green	56		Orange	50			
12	Yellow	41		Pink	32			
13	Blue	66		Black	18			
14								
15	Score of Group	White	⚠	#N/A	=VLOOKUP(B15,A10:B13,2,FALSE)			
16								
17				Not Found	=IFNA(D15,"Not Found")			
18								

Figure 3-92: Trace Precedents and Dependents

Arrows can be removed by using the 'Remove Arrows' option from Formulas ->Formula Auditing. You can remove both arrows or either of them representing the precedents or dependents.

Figure 3-93: Remove Trace Arrows

3.18.3 Trace Error

The 'Formula Auditing->Trace Error' option helps in identifying the cell causing an error value to appear, activate the cell that contains the error, and then choose 'Formulas-> Formula Auditing -> Error Checking -> Trace Error'. Excel draws arrows to indicate which cell is the source of the error.

Figure 3-94: Trace Error Example

Arrows can be removed by using the 'Remove Arrows' option from Formulas ->Formula Auditing.

3.18.4 Error Checking, Evaluate Formula

The 'Formula Auditing->Error checking' dialog box gives an option to see help related to the error, step in the formula and see the calculation steps, ignore the error and edit the formula to make it correct.

Figure 3-95: Error Checking dialog box

The 'Show Calculation Steps…' option launches a window which allows you to step in the function and see the intermediate results. The same window is launched by using the 'Formula Auditing->Evaluate Formula' option.

Figure 3-96: Evaluate Formula window

The 'Evaluate Formula' helps you see the various parts of a nested formula evaluated in the order in which the formula is calculated. You can now use the 'Step In' button at each step to go in and see the calculation.

Figure 3-97: Evaluate Formula window – Step-in level 1

Figure 3-98: Evaluate Formula window – Step-in level 2

3.18.5 Watch Window

The Watch Window makes it easy to inspect, audit, or confirm formula calculations and results in large worksheets, avoiding repeatedly scroll or go to different parts of your worksheet.

Example #1:

In this example, we want to watch the result of VLOOKUP in cell D15 and of IFNA in cell D17. Go to the 'Formula Auditing ->Watch Window' option, launch the dialog box and click on the 'Add Watch…' button to lunch another dialog box to enter the cell D15 to watch. Again, click on 'Add Watch…' and select cell D17 to add in the watch window.

Figure 3-99: Watch window – Add watch dialog

Now we will change the look up value 'White' in cell B15 to 'Green' and see the change in values in the watch window.

Note that when we entered 'Green' in cell B15 the corresponding values for the D15 and D17 cells changed from '#N/A' and 'Not Found' to 56

CHAPTER 4

Data Visualization with New Chart types

Excel has many built-in chart types that existed in previous versions before Excel 2016, like Column, Line, Pie, Doughnut, Bar, Area, Scatter, Bubble, Stock, Surface, Radar, and Combo chart types. In Excel 2016 six new built-in chart types were introduced – Waterfall, Histogram, Pareto, Box & Whisker, Treemap and Sunburst; powerful charts which help you quickly visualize common financial, statistical and hierarchical data. The 3D Maps that were previously used as Excel add-in '3-D geospatial visualization' were fully integrated in Excel 2016. In latest version Excel 2019, two new charts have been introduced – Funnel Chart and Map Chart. Map chart is like 3D Map with a difference that Map charts are one-dimensional and do not support latitude/longitude or street address mapping. In this chapter we will see an overview of the older build-in chart types and discuss new chart types in detail, including 3D Maps and Sparkline charts, which are not new but are very helpful.

4.1 Chart types and when to use them

The following table gives an overview of different chart types and when to use which type.

Chart Type	When to Use
Column Chart	Compare values across a few categories, shown vertically.
Line Chart	Visualize trends over a period of time that is, months, days, years and so on.
Pie Chart	Quantify items and display them as percentages.
Doughnut Chart	Show the relationship of parts as a whole. Similar to a Pie Chart, however with the difference that it can contain more than one data series.
Bar Chart	Comparing values across a few categories, shown horizontally.
Area Chart	Illustrating the magnitude of change between two or more data points, using the sum of the plotted values to show the relationship of parts as a whole.
Scatter Chart	Show correlations between two sets of values.
Bubble Chart	Show correlations between two sets of values and the relative impact of a quantitative data item. It's a variation of an XY scatter plot with the addition of a third dimension that is represented by the size of each bubble in the chart.
Stock Chart	Show fluctuations in stock prices or other data, such as daily rainfall or annual temperatures.
Surface Chart	To find the optimum combinations between two sets of data, colors, and patterns indicating areas that are in the same range of values.
Radar Chart	Compare the aggregate values of several data series.
Combo Chart	A visualization that combines two or more chart types into a single chart. Commonly used to show the difference between targets versus the actual results.
3D Map	Compare values and show categories across geographical regions.
Waterfall	Visualize the impact of multiple data points (typically a series of positive and negative values) as a running total, commonly used when analyzing financial data.
Histogram	A variation of the bar chart that shows the frequencies within a distribution
Pareto	Similar to Histogram but including a sorted histogram chart with a line representing the cumulative total percentage
Box & Whisker	Show the distribution of data into quartiles, highlighting the mean and any outliers. Commonly used in statistics.
Treemap	A hierarchical view of data and a way to compare different levels of categorization. Also comparing proportions within the hierarchy.

Sunburst	A hierarchical visualization of data, in the form of concentric circles and show how outer rings relate to inner rings
Funnel Charts	Visualize the progressive reduction of data as it passes from one phase to another. Typically, the values decrease gradually, allowing the bars to resemble a funnel.
Map Charts	Compare values and show categories across geographical regions. *Note:* Map charts can only plot high-level geographic details, so latitude/longitude, and street address mapping isn't supported. Map charts also support one-dimensional display only, for multi-dimensional detail use Excel's 3D Map feature.

4.2 Waterfall Chart

Waterfall charts are helpful in visualizing the impact of multiple data points—series of positive and negative values—as a running total. Commonly used to the track monetary performance over time like analyzing financial data, for example an income statement. Waterfall charts are also helpful in scenarios like analyzing inventory or sales, comparing product earnings, showing product value over time and so on.

We will create a Waterfall chart for the data mentioned in the following screenshot:

Gross Revenue	3,45,621
Rev Adjustments	(3,050)
Net Revenue	**3,42,571**
Inventory	(1,24,900)
Merchandise	(16,700)
Other costs	(6,333)
Gross Income	**1,94,638**
Staff	(50,750)
Marketing	(12,579)
Facilities	(46,000)
Operating Income	**85,309**
Taxes	(5,400)
Net Income	**79,909**

Figure 4-1: Waterfall chart example data

Select the data cell range A1 to B13 and on the 'Insert' tab select the 'Waterfall' option from the 'Charts' group. You can also select 'Recommended Charts' and under the 'Insert Chart' dialogue box, go to the 'All Charts' tab and select 'Waterfall Chart' from the listed chart type options.

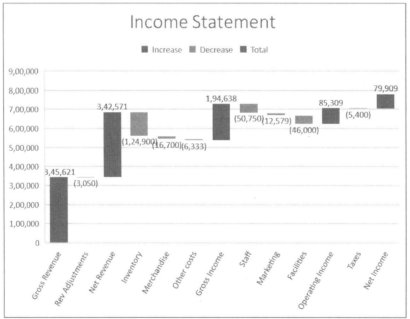

Figure 4-2: Waterfall Chart

It's useful for understanding how an initial value (for example, net income) is affected by a series of positive and negative values. The columns are color coded so you can quickly tell positive from negative numbers. The initial and final value columns often start on the horizontal axis, while the intermediate values are floating columns.

In the preceding example, we have values that are considered Subtotals or Totals, such as Net Revenue, Gross Income, Operating Income, and Net Income; and we want to set those values so they begin on the horizontal axis at zero and don't "float". For Excel to identify the bar as a total or sum value, right-click on the bar and select option "Set as Total".

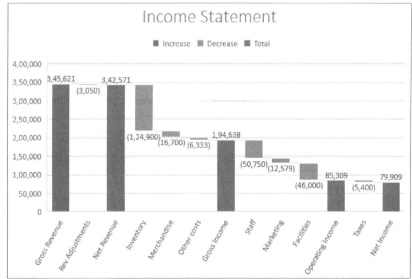

As you see in the above screenshot, each step in the waterfall takes you to the result that is the net income and demonstrates how you got there.

4.3 Histogram

Commonly used in statistics, a Histogram automatically displays the frequencies within a distribution. Consider an example that a survey was done in a restaurant for knowing the popular age group in order to revise the menu card, ages being: 13 ,10 ,6 ,22 ,20 ,13 ,12 ,25 ,43 ,29 ,31 ,23 ,5 ,6 ,7 ,15 ,23 ,47 ,9 ,50 ,39 ,40 ,63 ,5 ,36 ,57 ,63.

To create a Histogram, copy these values in a column of a sheet. Select the cell range, go to the 'Insert' tab and choose 'Histogram' (the left-side chart type) from the 'Charts' group.

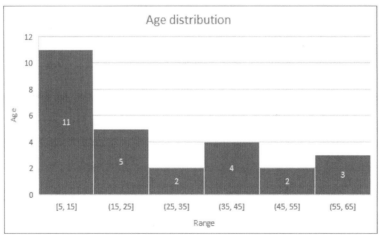

Figure 4-3: Histogram Chart

Histogram clearly shows that the most popular age group is 5-15.

4.4 Pareto Chart

The Pareto chart is used to find the largest impact. It is a variation of a bar chart with a combination of a line chart. The bars of the chart represent data values in a descending order while the line chart represents the progression of the cumulative percentage of the total. Using similar data as used while creating the Histogram, we will create a Pareto chart.

To create a Pareto, copy the age values as given in Histogram chapter (4.3) in a column of a sheet. Select the cell range, go to the 'Insert' tab and choose 'Histogram' (the right-side chart type) from the 'Charts' group.

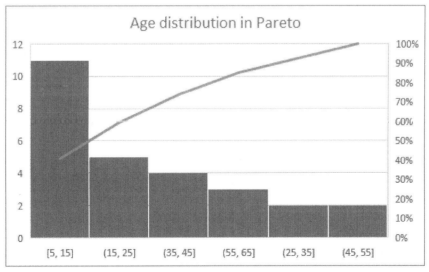

Figure 4-4: *Pareto Chart*

This chart shows the age groups in the order of its highest popularity to the lowest and shows that the top three age categories are 5-15, 15-25, and 35-45 that make up for around 75% of the population coming to the restaurant.

4.5 Box & Whisker Chart

The Box and Whisker chart show how your data is spread out. It is also used in statistics to show the distribution of data into quartiles, also highlighting the mean and outliers, if any. Quartiles are indicated as the following:

- First quartile: The horizontal line on the lower whisker (minimum value) up to the bottom line of the box.

- Second quartile: The lower line of the box to the Mean

- Third quartile: From the Mean to the top of the box

- Last quartile: The top of the box up to the length of the upper whisker (maximum value)

- Outliers: Are plotted as points above or below the length of either of the whiskers. They are suspected to be anomalies, that is, the values that are very high or very low and fall far outside the other values of the data set.

For creating the Box & Whisker chart we will use the data as seen in the following screenshot, with many more data points for plotting the graph.

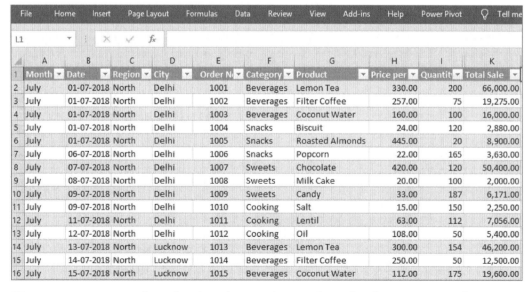

Here we want to see the sales distribution for products by their Category, hence we will only consider the 'Total Sales' values for the Categories. Select the data from the columns named 'Category' and 'Total Sale', go to the 'Insert' tab and select 'Box and Whisker' from the 'Charts' group.

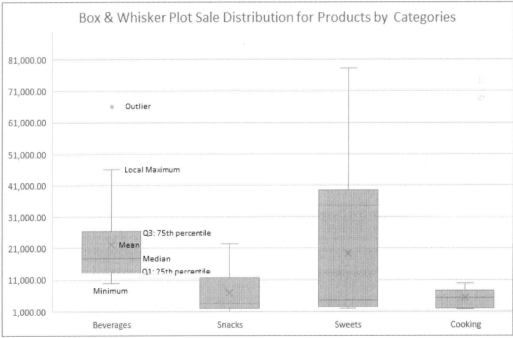

Figure 4-5: Box & Whisker chart

In our example, the 'Box and Whisker' chart allows us to visualize the variation in sale for each product category as well as where details like the mean and any outliers fall in relation to that variation. There is one outlier for Beverages, whose value is very high and hence it is showing far away from the other values in the data set.

4.6 Treemap Chart

The Treemap Chart is great for visualizing hierarchical data within categories, as compared to other categories. For the data given in the following table, we will create the Treemap chart.

Category	Product	Total Sale
Beverages	Coconut Water	1,22,100.00
	Filter Coffee	1,29,250.00
	Lemon Tea	2,77,329.00
Cooking	Lentil	63,770.00
	Oil	48,268.00
	Salt	15,740.00
Snacks	Biscuit	26,146.00
	Popcorn	15,528.00
	Roasted Almonds	1,23,400.00
Sweets	Candy	34,378.00
	Chocolate	4,10,440.00
	Milk Cake	18,520.00

Looking at the data in the above table, even though grouped by category, the best or worst sales volume or trend is not evident immediately. While if we create a Treemap chart for this data, we can clearly see that Beverages has the best sales at category level.

To create a Treemap, go to the 'Insert' tab and select 'Treemap' from the 'Charts' group

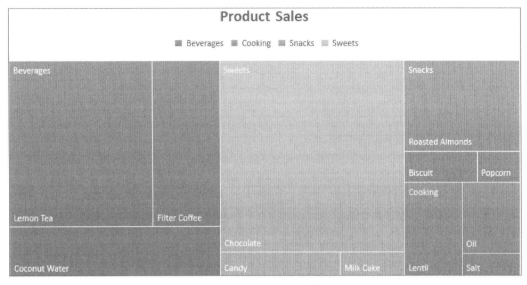

Figure 4-6: Treemap Chart

4.7 Sunburst Chart

The Sunburst Chart provides a hierarchical visualization of data which represents data in the form of concentric circles. When visualizing data that is organized into multiple levels of categories, the Sunburst chart shows how outer rings relate to inner rings.

We will create the Sunburst chart using the same data set used for the Treemap chart. To create, go to the 'Insert' tab and select 'Sunburst' from the 'Charts' group.

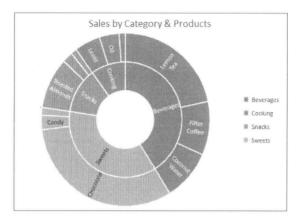

Figure 4-7: Sunburst Chart

4.8 Sparkline Chart

Sparklines are not new in Excel but are very helpful inline charts that we will discuss. They are tiny charts placed in single cells, each representing a row of data in your selection and provide a quick way to see trends. Sparklines are of three types: Line, Column, and Win/Loss.

Select the data for which the Sparklines are to be created. Preferably, position a sparkline near its data for greatest impact which is, in the next empty cell. A Quick Analysis button appears on the right bottom corner of the selected data, click on sparklines and then the type you want to create, for example Column in this case.

Category	Product	Q1'17	Q2'17	Q3'17	Q4'17	Q1'18	Q2'18	Q3'18	Q4'18	
		Sale per Quarter								
Beverages	Lemon Tea	90	500	400	23	200	700	200	50	
Beverages	Filter Coffee	88	300	700	900	150	450	790	1,050	
Beverages	Coconut Water	-10%	20%	32%	-40%	15%	55%	5%	-5%	

Formatting   Charts   Totals   Tables   **Sparklines**

Line   Column   Win/Loss

Sparklines are mini charts placed in single cells, each representing a row of data in your selection.

Sparklines are mini charts placed in single cells.

Figure 4-8: Sparkline Chart

You can change the sparkline design with existing styles by specifying what to show: High / Low / First / Last / Negative Point and change the sparkline / marker colors.

In the Design tab, under the group 'Show', tick the checkboxes for High Point, Low Point, First Point, Last Point and Negative Points so that they are visible in the Sparkline chart.

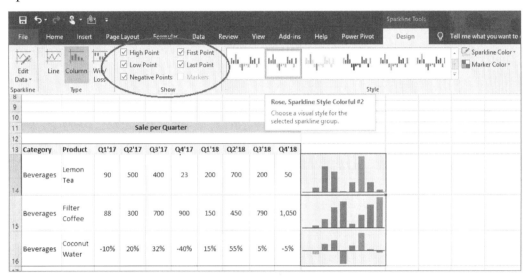

To change the Sparkline colors, in the Design tab go to group 'Style' and for each marker point under 'Marker Color' select the theme color of your choice.

Figure 4-9: Sparkline Designs

Similarly, we can create Line and Win/Loss Sparklines. Each row can have a different type as shown below by selecting the row data and then inserting the required sparkline.

Figure 4-10: Different Sparklines on each row

4.9 3D Map

3D Map is a three-dimensional data visualization tool that lets you look at information in new ways. In earlier versions of Excel 2013, this was an add-in '3-D geospatial visualization' but it got fully integrated in Excel 2016. For creating a 3D map, your data should have geographic properties like the names of cities, countries, zip codes, longitude or latitude coordinates and so on. which can be mapped to the 3D map. It requires data to be in an Excel table format, where each row is a unique record and each column has a heading.

4.9.1 Create a Tour

We will create a 3D Map using sample data with a list of states and their estimated population. Note that the sample data we are using is in an Excel table format as required and has a column 'State' that has a geographic property. To insert the 3D

Maps, click on any cell within the table and go to the 'Insert' tab '3D Map' option under Tours. Click on 'Open 3D Maps' and a new window is launched. 3D Maps uses Bing to geocode your data based on its geographic properties. After a few seconds, the globe will appear next to the first screen of the Layer Pane. When you start 3D Maps from a workbook that doesn't already contain a tour, a new tour with a single scene is automatically created. Tours and scenes are the basic way to save the 3D Maps visualizations of your data. You can have multiple Tours in a workbook and multiple Scenes in a Tour.

Figure 4-11: 3D Map sample data

In the Layer pane, on the right-hand side, Layer 1 is shown by default. Since we want to depict the state wise population estimate, under 'Location' select 'State'. Now we will add fields in other parameters like 'Population Estimates' for 'Height' and 'State' for 'Category'. The data is plotted on the map that is, population estimates are shown as columns on the map region identified by the state name. Color legend is also shown for Layer 1.

We can customize the look and feel of the map like; change the size or move the Layer 1 legend, Zoom in and out of the map using the plus and minus sign, Rotate left/right, tilt up and down using the arrows, change Chart Type from column to a bubble chart using the option under Data in layer pane, change the Theme and add Map Labels.

Figure 4-12: 3D Map - Tour

Close the 3D Map window to Save. This is saved as a Tour named 'Tour 1', which can be opened again by going to 'Insert->3D Map-> Open 3D Maps'.

4.9.2 Create a New Scene

We can add a 'New Scene' to 'Tour 1' by using the 'New Scene' option in the 3D Maps window. Using the same process as before we created the 3D Map, except that here we are using columns for data and filtered this data (using the Add Filter option) to display only those states in a specified population range.

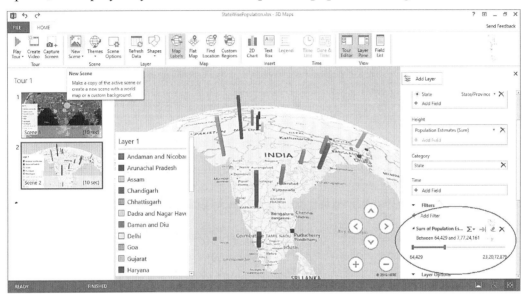

Figure 4-13: *3D Map - Scene*

Multiple scenes can be created for different views of the same data. For each scene you can have a different setting, like the time duration for how long the scene will play, name of the scene preferable describing the data visualization, transition duration, effect and the speed of the effect, and the map type. 'Scene Options' is available on the main menu's 'Home' tab and available on each Scene under the Tour pane on the left-hand side. The Tour name can also be changed by a single click on the name and typing the new name.

Figure 4-14: 3D Map – Scene options

4.9.3 Play Tour/Scene, Create Video

After the Tours and Scenes are created, you can play them using 'Play Tour' option or create a video for your presentations using the 'Create Video' option in the 3D Map window.

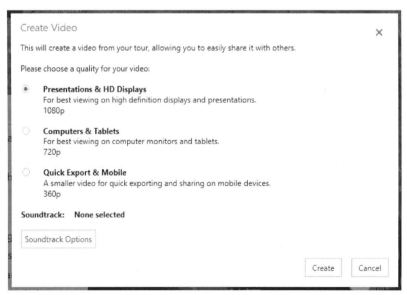

Figure 4-15: 3D Map: Create Video

You can choose the quality of the video by selecting any of the available options. It also gives an option to add a Soundtrack with the Video.

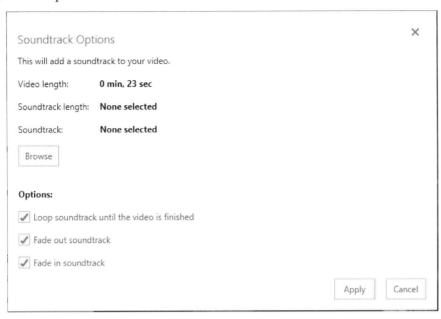

Figure 4-16: 3D Map: Add Soundtrack to Video

Browse the audio file and click 'Apply' to add the soundtrack. Then click 'Create' on the 'Create Video' dialog box to save the video in the selected location. The video is saved as an '.MP4' file. You can share your tour with people who don't have a version of Excel that supports 3D Maps, when you want to show it on the web through a media player, or run it on a large monitor as a video file without using Excel.

4.10 Funnel Chart

Funnel charts show values across multiple stages in a process. Typically, it starts at 100% and the values decrease gradually, allowing the bars to resemble a funnel. For example, you could use a funnel chart to show the number of projects at each stage in the projects pipeline, as given in screenshot below. In column "Stage" (column B), we have the different project stages or phases, Feasibility, Initiation, Planning, Execution, Validation, Deployment and Acceptance. In column "No of projects" (column C), we have the number of projects which are currently in that stage.

	A	B	C
1			
2		**Project Pipeline**	
3		**Stage**	**No of projects**
4		Feasibility	50
5		Initiation	35
6		Planning	23
7		Execution	21
8		Validation	10
9		Deployment	5
10		Acceptance	2
11			

To create a Funnel chart, select the cell range B3:C10 and click "Insert-> Insert Waterfall, Funnel, Stock, Surface or Radar chart -> Funnel.

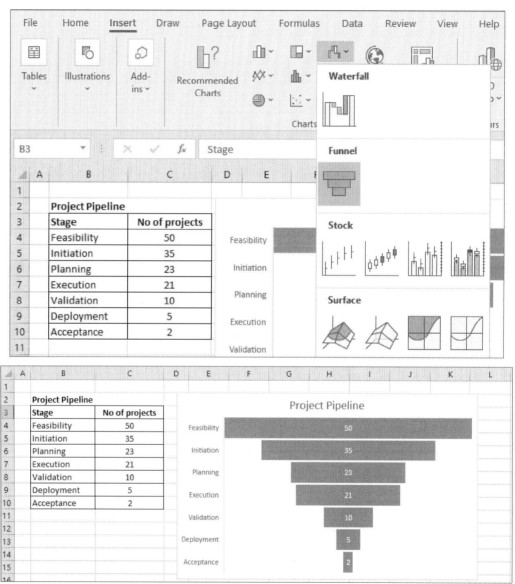

Figure 4-17: Example of Funnel chart

Funnel chart in preceding example gives a good view of the projects pipeline, where the number of projects at each stage are shown as bars in decreasing order.

Note: Funnel chart is a new chart type introduced in Excel 2019. It is available on Windows or Mac if you have Office 2019 or Office 365 subscription with latest version of Office.

4.11 Map Chart

You can create a map chart to compare values and show categories across geographical regions, like 3D Map (see 4.9) but with limitations. Map chart support one-dimensional display only and you can only plot high-level geographic details, so latitude/longitude, and street address mapping isn't supported. For example, we can create a Map chart for depicting country wise population distribution as given in table[1] below.

Country	% of World Population
China	18.500%
India	17.500%
United States	4.340%
Brazil	2.770%
Russia	1.960%
Mexico	1.640%
France	0.900%
Argentina	0.590%
Australia	0.325%
Sweden	0.134%
United Arab Emirates	0.130%
Namibia	0.031%

To create a Map chart, select the cell range (i.e., B19:C31) and click "Insert->Maps->Filled Map".

Figure 4-18: *Example of Map chart*

Excel creates a 2-color Map chart using a gradient spectrum of two colors. The color for each country is dictated by where along the spectrum its population value falls. By default, the higher the value is, the darker its corresponding color will be. We

---

1 data is just a representation and not a reflection of actual numbers.

can change the design from 2-color to 3-color Map chart by clicking on the map and then choose from the Chart Design or Format tabs in the Ribbon. It can also be done by double-clicking on the chart to launch the Format Object Task Pane, which will appear on the right-hand side of the Excel window. This will also expose the map chart specific Series options, as shown in screenshot below.

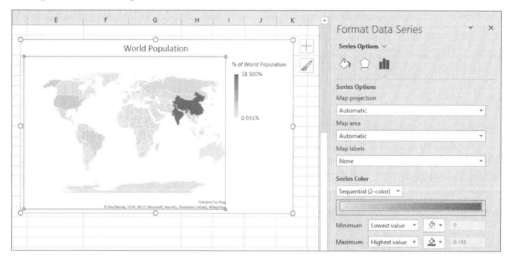

Figure 4-19: Map chart – Format Data Series option

In the "Format Data Series" options window, change the "Series color" from Sequential (2-color) to Diverging (3-color) and select different colors for Minimum, Midpoint and Maximum values as per your choice. You can also add Map labels by selecting options under Series options->Map labels, like "Best fit only" in our example.

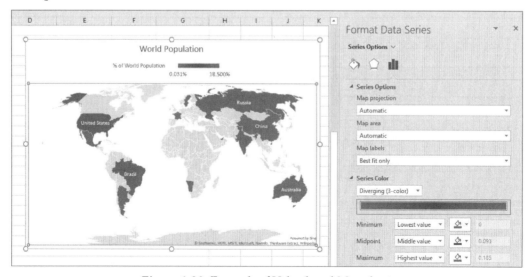

Figure 4-20: Example of Value based Map chart

The Map chart created in preceding example used values to plot data on the world map. We can also create category-based Map chart, as in below screenshot.

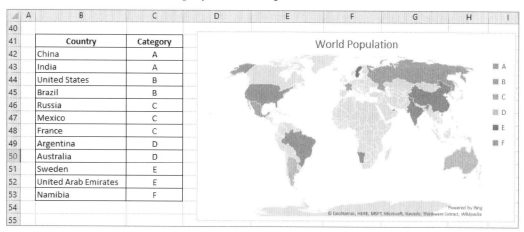

Figure 4-21: Example of Category based Map chart

In preceding example, each country falls under a specific category based on its population size. We have used country and category data to create the Map chart, where each category has been assigned a specific color.

CHAPTER 5

Gantt and Milestone Chart

A Gantt chart is a very important and popular tool of project management that helps you in planning and scheduling project activities or tasks required to achieve the project objective/goal and then helps in tracking its progress against time. Gantt includes details for each activity, like the duration of the activity, timeline of the activity, (which are its start and finish dates), resources attached to the activity (man power, hardware or software), relationship with other activities (dependencies), and so on.

You can create a Gantt to whatever detailed level required, it can have activities broken down to a 2-day duration or even less. It can thus have multiple line items, sometimes going up to 20, 50 or even a couple of hundred lines. Which is good for tracking details but not easy to monitor the overall project progress. Hence in project schedules, Milestones are identified.

A Milestone is an activity with a fixed date but no duration, indicating a point in the project (noting down the start or finish of an activity or set of activities) marking the completion of a major phase of work or a branching decision point within a project. The Milestone Chart is a very helpful visual or graphical tool for monitoring the overall project health using milestones and good indicators or measures for reporting progress.

5.1 Creating a Gantt Chart in Excel

A Gantt Chart in Excel can be created either by typing data in a sheet, writing formulas, and creating bar charts and so on, or by using the existing templates. Using templates is not only easier, its faster and efficient. Launch Microsoft Excel, go to the 'File' menu and click on 'New'. On the right-hand pane a list of the existing templates is seen. Type 'Gantt' in the search box and you will see the available templates.

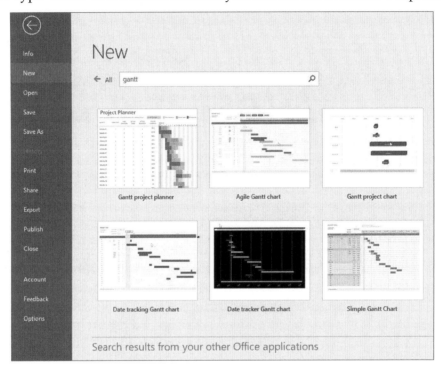

Select 'Simple Gantt Chart' and click 'Create' in the dialog box to start the process.

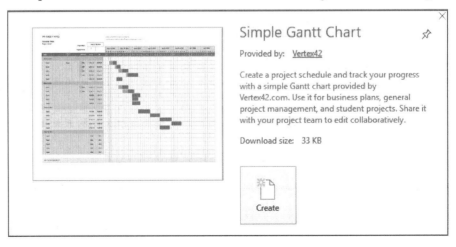

Excel will download the template and create a new workbook for you to use for your project.

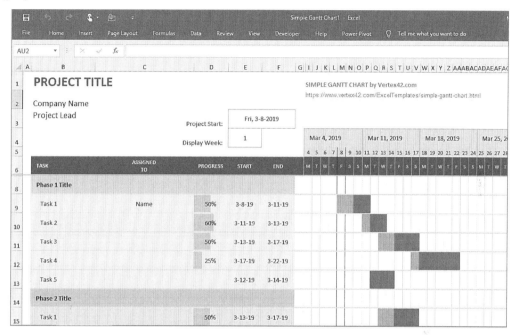

You can modify the project details like, Company Name, Project Lead, Project Start date, and Display timeline. Type your activities, owners of those activities, start and end date and percentage of completion of the activities. Based on the input data on the left-hand side the horizontal bars change on the right-hand side, as seen in the following screenshot. Save the file at the desired location for future tracking.

Figure 5-1: *Gantt Chart in Excel*

You can try the different templates available in Excel or via partners and modify them as per your requirements. Even complex Gantt charts can be created in Excel, but it is not an easy task. Microsoft also has a standalone 'Microsoft Project' software, a full fledge project management tool that is used by many organizations for project planning. Since both are from Microsoft, Gantt in Excel can be imported into Microsoft Project and the schedules made in Microsoft Project can be exported in Excel format.

5.2 Creating a Milestone Chart in Excel

We want to create a Milestone chart for a project in Excel as per the details given below, in the Project Milestones Table (including dates, name and owners) and the desired output that is the Milestone Chart. X-Axis is the timeline and the different Milestones are plotted on the Y-axis.

Date	Activity	Owner
Mar-19	Inputs	Mktng
Mar-19	Kick-off Mtng	Engr
Apr-19	Final SRS	Engr
May-19	Final Design	Engr
Jul-19	Final Code	Engr
Aug-19	Final Testing	Val
Sep-19	Deliver	Val
Nov-19	Deploy	Field
Dec-19	Feedback	QA

Figure 5-2: Project Milestones Table

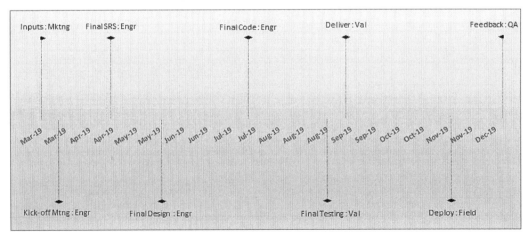

Figure 5-3: Milestone Chart

Following are the steps for creating the Milestones chart:

Step 1: Consolidate the Milestone data in a sheet and prepare data for creating the chart.

	A	B	C	D	E	F
1						
2		Date	Activity	Owner	Milestone + Owner	Text Placement
3		Mar-19	Inputs	Mktng	Inputs : Mktng	10
4		Mar-19	Kick-off Mtng	Engr	Kick-off Mtng : Engr	-10
5		Apr-19	Final SRS	Engr	Final SRS : Engr	10
6		May-19	Final Design	Engr	Final Design : Engr	-10
7		Jul-19	Final Code	Engr	Final Code : Engr	10
8		Aug-19	Final Testing	Val	Final Testing : Val	-10
9		Sep-19	Deliver	Val	Deliver : Val	10
10		Nov-19	Deploy	Field	Deploy : Field	-10
11		Dec-19	Feedback	QA	Feedback : QA	10
12						-10
13						10
14						-10
15						

Columns for Date, Activity, and Owner are as per the original data (as seen in Figure 5-2). The added two columns will be used later. Since we want to show Activity with its Owner in the chart, we have CONCATENATED the texts from both the columns in column E.

E3			✕ ✓ f_x	=CONCATENATE(C3," : ",D3)		
	A	B	C	D	E	F
1						
2		Date	Activity	Owner	Milestone + Owner	Text Placement
3		Mar-19	Inputs	Mktng	Inputs : Mktng	10
4		Mar-19	Kick-off Mtng	Engr	Kick-off Mtng : Engr	-10

Column F which are the 'Text Placement' values, will be used to plot the Milestones alternatively in the upper and lower halves of the timeline axis, for the display to be clear and neat.

Step 2: Go to the 'Insert' tab and in the 'Charts' group select 'Line Chart with Markers'.

It will create a blank chart. Now to add data, go to the 'Design' tab and click on 'Select Data'.

Step 3: In the Select Data Source dialog box, click on 'Add' to insert a series and enter the following:

Series Name = Date

Series Values = E3:E11 *(i.e., milestone + owner name)*

This inserts a line chart with its X-axis values as 1,2,3, …,9 and Y-axis values as 0.

Now in the Select Data Source dialog box, click on 'Edit' from the 'Horizontal (Category) Axis Labels' and select the cell range B3:B11 that is the milestone dates.

Now the X-axis displays the dates instead of numbers 1,2,3 …. 9.

<u>Step 4</u>: In the Select Data Source dialog box, click on 'Add' and in the 'Edit Series' dialog box, enter the following:

Series Name = Activity

Series Values = F3:F11 (*i.e., text placement values*)

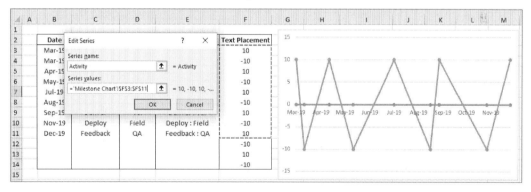

This creates a haphazard line chart.

<u>Step 5</u>: Now we will change the haphazard line to a column chart. Select the 'Activity' series and right click on 'Change Series chart type…' and select the Column chart.

This creates a column chart.

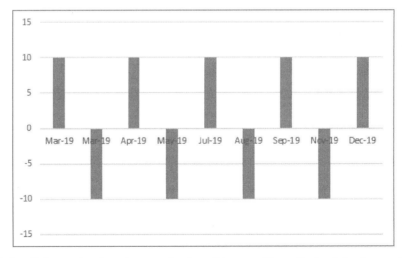

Step 6: Right click on the data bar and select 'Format Data Series'. In the series option pane, select 'Secondary Axis' in the 'Plot Series on' option. A new secondary vertical axis on the right of the chart is inserted. But we do not want to see that, hence click on it and delete it.

Step 7: Go to the 'Design' tab and click on 'Select Data'. For the 'Activity' series, click on 'Edit' from the 'Horizontal (Category) Axis Labels' and select the cell range E3:E11.

Now we will format the data bars. Select the data bars and right-click to select the option 'Format Data Labels'. Uncheck all options and only select the 'Category Name' check box and 'Inside End' for the label position.

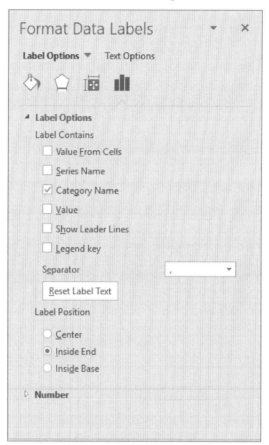

Step 8: Again, select the data bars. Go to the 'Design' tab, in the 'Chart Layouts' group select the option 'Add Chart Element' and click on 'Error Bars-> More Error Bar Options'. In the 'Error Bar Options' pane select the options; Vertical Error Bar: Minus, End Style: No Cap and Error Amount: Percentage – 100%

Right click on bars and select Format Data Series. In Format Data Series Pane (in Fill and Line) select 'No Fill' and 'No Border'.

There are many options on changing the look and feel that can be tried for example you can change the background of the chart area as gradient fill as in our example or solid fill etc.

CHAPTER 6

SmartArt & Organization Chart

SmartArt graphic helps to quickly and easily make a visual representation of your information as well as construct fancy graphical lists and diagrams in your worksheet. Organization charts are very often created using the SmartArt. In this section we will look at different SmartArt Layouts and create a simple Organization chart to understand how to insert a SmartArt graphic and then modify it.

6.1 SmartArt graphics

SmartArt option is available in the 'Insert' tab, in the 'Illustrations' group.

SmartArt has multiple layouts like List, Hierarchy, Picture and so on, each having multiple graphics as seen in the following screenshot:

Figure 6-1: SmartArt Graphic

You can also view the different graphics based on the different types or categories. The table below has the list of different layouts along with some information to help choose which layout to consider for use.

SmartArt type	Used to
List	Show nonsequential information.
Process	Show steps in a process or timeline; creating a flow chart.
Cycle	Show a continual process.
Hierarchy	Create an organization chart.
Hierarchy	Show a decision tree.
Relationship	Illustrate connections.
Matrix	Show how various parts relate as a whole.
Pyramid	Show proportional relationships with the largest component on the top or bottom.
Picture	Use pictures prominently to convey or accent content.
Office.com	Show additional layouts available on Office.com

After you have inserted your SmartArt graphic, you will see contextual tabs 'SmartArt Design' and 'Format'. Using the settings under these tabs you can modify the look and feel of the graphic added and add information.

6.2 Organization Chart

Organization chart portrays the reporting structure or relationships in an organization, which can be easily represented using the graphics in the Hierarchy layout.

6.2.1 Insert Graphic

Select the worksheet in which you want to insert the SmartArt and go to the 'Insert' tab, under the 'Illustrations' group and select the 'SmartArt' option. Under the layout 'Hierarchy', select any of the graphics that you think is a good representation as per your requirements.

For our example we will use the Picture Organization chart and click OK. This inserts graphics in the sheet as seen in the following screenshot.

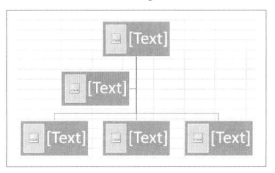

6.2.2 Change Layout, Color & Text

Click [Text] in the SmartArt Text pane, and then type your text. Click on the picture icon to insert pictures from either a file on your system, a Bing image search, or OneDrive.

Using the 'SmartArt Design->Change Colors' option we changed the graphics to have different colors for the head of the organization and the team below.

We can also change the layout using any of the options available; we changed it from picture to 'Name and Tile' organization. You will see that the text remains the same even on change.

Figure 6-2: Picture organization chart and Name and Title organization chart

6.2.3 Add/Delete boxes

You can add new boxes before, after, below, or above the selected box and add an assistant to the selected box using the options under 'Add Shape'.

Select the VP box and go to 'SmartArt Design->Add Shape' or right-click and select 'Add Shape' and click on 'Add Shape Above'. Similarly select the VP box each time and click on the other options to add the box before, above, and so on.

Figure 6-3: Add boxes

For the second assistant added, we will change the shape. Select the box, right-click and select the option 'Change Shape' and click on the desired shape, we selected oval. Also, to change the color, right click and select 'Format Shape' and use 'Fill' to change the color to orange.

You can also Delete a box by selecting the new assistant box that was added, then right-click and click on 'Cut' or press the Delete button on keyboard.

6.2.4 Move boxes

We can move the boxes within the chart using options 'Promote', 'Demote', 'Move Up' and 'Move Down' under the 'SmartArt Design->Create Graphics' options. We have the organization chart as seen in the following screenshot and using this we will see how to use these options.

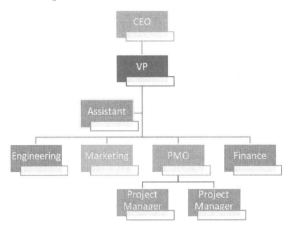

Following are the changes we want to make and the options we will use.

- Move the 'Finance' box close to the 'Marketing' box. Select the Finance box and use the 'Move Up' option to move towards the left side. Similarly, 'Move Down' moves the box to the right.

- There is a change in the organization and now PMO must go under CEO. Select the PMO box and use the option 'Promote'. PMO comes under the CEO, in alignment with the VP.

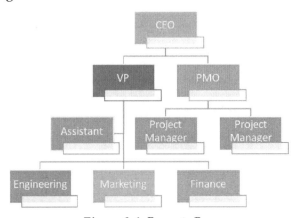

Figure 6-4: Promote Box

Note, when we promoted the PMO hierarchy the structure remained the same. But now if you want to bring the PMO structure down under VP again, you will need to select the PMO box as along with the two Project Manager boxes and click 'Demote'.

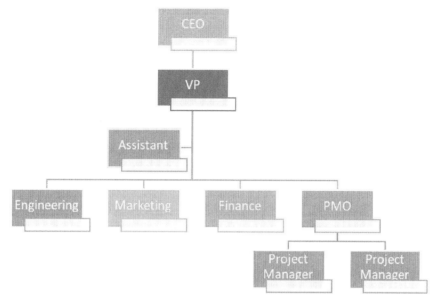

If we only select the PMO box as shown in Figure 6-4 and click 'Demote', all the three boxes that is the PMO and the two Project Managers will come under the VP box.

CHAPTER 7

Get creative with Icons, 3D models, Digital Inking

In Excel 2019, multiple new features have been introduced to enhance the visual presentation like inserting Icons, Scalable Vector Graphics (SVG) and 3D models in Microsoft documents, workbooks, presentations, emails. Digital Inking features have also got some new improvements and new features added in the latest version.

7.1 Insert Icons

You can insert an Icon into your Microsoft Office documents, workbooks, emails and presentations to visually communicate using symbols. To insert an Icon in Excel, open the worksheet in which you want to insert an Icon. Go to "Insert" tab, in the "Illustrations" group select "Icons".

Figure 7-1: Insert Icon menu option

Microsoft Excel application has around 500 built in Icons, under thirty-five different categories.

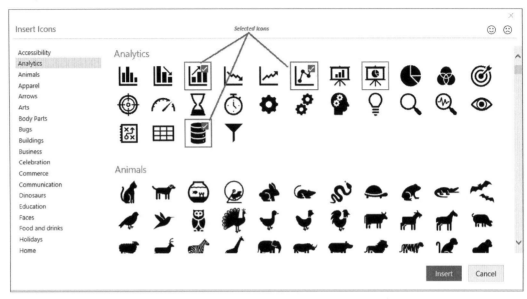

Figure 7-2: Icons list category wise

Select one or more Icons by clicking the Icon and press "Insert" to insert the selected Icons in the active worksheet. You can move the Icons in the worksheet as required and resize, change color or rotate them using options under "Graphics Format" contextual menu.

In the preceding screenshot we inserted three Icons, two under Dashboards and one under Database. We resized the first Icon, changed color of the second / third Icon to orange / blue and rotated the third Icon to the left by 90 degrees using the Graphics Format options.

7.2 Insert / Edit Scalable Vector Graphics

You can insert and edit Scalable Vector Graphics (SVG) files in your Microsoft Office documents, workbooks, emails and presentations. To insert the SVG file in Excel, open the worksheet in which you want to insert the file. Go to "Insert" tab, in the "Illustrations" group select "Pictures" to browse your SVG file.

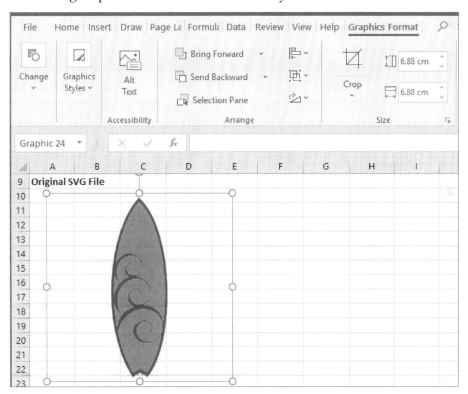

Figure 7-3: Scalable Vector Graphics file (SVG) inserted in worksheet

Select the SVG file inserted in the worksheet to view the contextual menu "Graphics Format" that gives multiple options to customize how the SVG image looks like in your document. Graphics Format has options that allow you to Change Graphic i.e., replace the current image with a different one, Graphics Styles tool to change the appearance of the image, Arrange tool to align the image and Size to resize or crop the image.

You can also convert an SVG image or icon to an Office shape, that is, you can disassemble the SVG file and edit individual pieces of it, using the option "Graphics Format->Change-> Convert to Shape". Microsoft Excel will ask for confirmation, click "Yes" to continue.

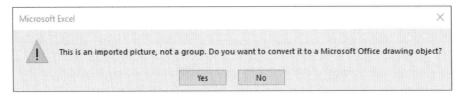

You will be able to select the different pieces of the image and modify using options under the contextual menu "Shape Format".

Figure 7-4: Edit SVG image - Convert to Shape

In the preceding screenshot the first image is the original SVG image that was inserted. The second image is the image that we converted to Microsoft drawing object and changed the fill color of one piece within the image using "Shape Format->Shape Styles" option. We can change the other pieces of the image as well using different options and completely change the original image appearance as shown in screenshot below.

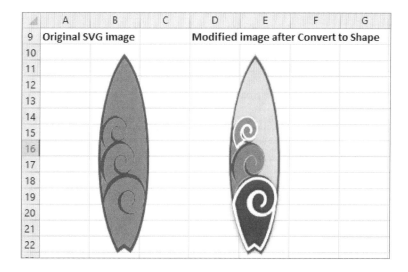

7.3 Insert 3D Models

You can insert 3D models in your Microsoft Office documents, workbooks, presentations to illustrate a point. You can rotate models 360 degrees or tilt up and down to show a specific feature of an object. To insert 3D model in Excel, open the worksheet in which you want to insert the model. Go to "Insert" tab, in the "Illustrations" group select "3D Models". You can select a 3D model from a file or from online sources.

Figure 7-5: Insert 3D Models

After the 3D model is inserted, you can play with the appearance of the model using the 3D Model contextual menu.

As shown in preceding screenshot, you can Pan & Zoom and control of how your 3D image fits within the frame.

7.4 Digital Inking

Digital Inking features have been there since Excel 2013/2016. In Excel 2019, Microsoft has added some new improvements and features, as we will discuss in this chapter. The different Inking options are available in the 'Draw' tab as shown in screenshot below.

Figure 7-6: Digital Inking options in Excel

You can draw, write and highlight text using the different pen, pencil and highlighter options available in Excel. You can also define new pens using the "Add Pen" option, and they will then be available in Word, Excel and PowerPoint. Microsoft has made the new pen set customizable and portable. There is also a new "Ink Replay" feature that allows you to replay or rewind your Ink to better understand the flow of it. Anyone other than you, can also use this option to replay and get step by step instructions.

You can write your own equation from scratch using the new "Ink to Math" feature in case the Office built-in equations don't meet your needs. Excel also allows you to convert your Ink drawings to standard shapes using "Ink to Shape" feature. Other improvements include new ink effects, pencil texture, Lasso select - a free form tool for selecting Ink.

Excel also gives you the option to correct or erase your Ink strokes using the "Eraser" under the "Tools" group. Select the "Eraser" and drag the eraser over the ink you want to remove.

7.4.1 Define new pen – Add Pen

To define a new pen, go to "Draw" tab, click "Add Pen" and tap the down arrow to select one of the three options, that is, Pencil, Pen or Highlighter. In the example below we selected the first option to add a new Pencil.

Figure 7-7: Draw - Add Pen option

Excel adds a new pencil on the right of the existing pens and opens the menu of Thickness and Color options of the pencil.

Figure 7-8: *New Pencil - Thickness, Colour options*

You can customize the pencil as per your choice. There are five pen thickness settings ranging from .25 mm to 3.5 mm. Select a thickness or use the plus or minus sign to make your pen thicker or thinner. Sixteen solid colors are available on the menu, with more available when you tap More Colors. A pencil texture is also available. When you draw with the Pencil texture while using a supported digital stylus, you can tilt the stylus to get a "shading" effect, just like you would get with a real pencil.

Figure 7-9: *New Pen - Thickness, Colour and Effects options*

In case you add a new Pen, new ink effects have been added like Rainbow, Galaxy, Lava, Ocean, Gold, Silver, and more. Office remembers your pen set in Word, Excel, and PowerPoint across all your Windows devices. Note that if your device is touch-enabled, you can draw with your finger, a digital pen, or a mouse.

7.4.2 Modify, Move or Delete Existing Pens

Excel gives you options to modify, move or delete existing pens as shown in snapshot below.

Figure 7-10: *Modify, Move or Delete Exiting Pens*

7.4.2.1 Modify Pen

To edit the exiting pen, highlight the pen and on right click select "Modify Pen" option. This opens the menu with Thickness, Color and Effects options as shown in Figure 7-8 and Figure 7-9.

7.4.2.2 Move Pen Left / Right

You can change the position of the pens based on your preferences. To move the pen right, highlight the pen and on right click select "Move Right". The pen will be moved one place to the right.

Figure 7-11: *Move pen to the right*

To move the pen left, highlight the pen and on right click select "Move Left". The pen will be moved one place to the left.

Figure 7-12: Move pen to the left

7.4.2.3 Delete Pen

You can also delete an existing or a newly added pen. To delete a pen, highlight the pen and on right click select "Delete". The pen will be removed from the list.

Figure 7-13: Delete existing pen

In the preceding example, we selected the highlighter pen and deleted the pen using the "Delete Pen" option. Excel removed the highlighter pen from the list of pens as shown in snapshot above.

7.4.3 Rewind your Ink – Ink Replay

You can replay or rewind the ink strokes as they were drawn. The "Ink Replay" option is available in the "Draw" tab, under the "Replay" group. To see how it works, open a worksheet where you want to draw your Ink and go to "Draw" tab. Select a pen to draw, change the thickness or color or effects as per your needs. As you select a pen, the "Draw" option under "Tools" group gets highlighted.

In case the "Draw" option doesn't get highlighted for some reason, click on "Draw". As you start drawing your design, Excel starts recording the ink strokes. Once you complete the design, click on "Draw" option again to stop Inking. In the example below we wrote "Good Day" using a highlighter pen of black color. On clicking the "Ink Replay", you can rewind or replay the ink strokes as they occurred.

Figure 7-14: *Example of Ink to Replay*

Excel enables the Rewind, Play and Forward buttons for you to go through the ink strokes step by step. You can also pause the replay and select a point anywhere in between to start replay from.

You can delete your design using the "Eraser" option. Note that on clicking "Ink Replay", the deleted action is not replayed. If your design consists of multiple drawings and you delete one of it, then "Ink Replay" will only show the ink strokes that were drawn.

7.4.4 Write your equation – Ink to Math

Office has built-in equations that you can readily use and insert in your documents. In case the built-in equations don't meet your needs, you can write your own equation from scratch using the new "Ink to Math" feature. Go to "Draw" tab, in the group "convert" click on "Ink to Math". This will launch a "Math Input Control" window for you to write your equation.

Figure 7-15: Ink to Math - Math Input Control window

You can also launch the "Math Input Control" window by going to "Insert" tab, "Symbols" group and selecting "Equations->Ink Equation".

On touch devices, you can use your finger or a touch stylus to write math equations by hand, and Excel will convert it to text. On non-touch devices, you can use a mouse to write your equations. You can also erase, select and correct or clear what you've written as you go, using the options available at the bottom pane in the Math Input Control window. You can view your equation as you write in the preview box and make sure that Excel is correctly interpreting your handwriting. After you have correctly written you equation, click "Insert" to convert the ink equation to an equation in your document.

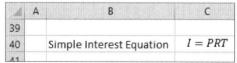

Figure 7-16: Example for Ink to Math

In the preceding example, we wrote the simple interest equation, that is, I=PRT and inserted in the Excel worksheet.

7.4.5 Convert drawing to shape – Ink to Shape

You convert your ink drawings to standard shapes using "Ink to Shape" feature. Open the worksheet in which you want to draw your design. Go to "Draw" tab and select "Ink to Shape". Draw the shape of your choice by selecting the desired pen. It automatically gets converted to the equivalent Office graphic shape. Once you are satisfied and done, select "Ink to Shape" again to stop having your drawings automatically converted to shapes.

Figure 7-17: *Example of Ink to Shape*

In the preceding example, we drew two circles and connected them with lines. Excel automatically converted the drawing to Office graphic shape. Table below lists the Ink shapes that can be converted to Office shapes.

Ink drawing	Corresponding shape
Rectangle	Rectangle
Square	Square

Contd…

Diamond	Diamond
Parallelogram	Parallelogram
Trapezoid	Trapezoid
Irregular quadrilateral	Irregular quadrilateral
Pentagon	Pentagon
Hexagon	Hexagon
Ellipse	Ellipse

Contd…

Circle	Circle
Single-headed arrow	Arrow
Double-headed arrow	Double arrow
Connector between two shapes	Connector
Right triangle	Right triangle
Equilateral triangle	Equilateral triangle
Isosceles triangle	Isosceles triangle

Contd…

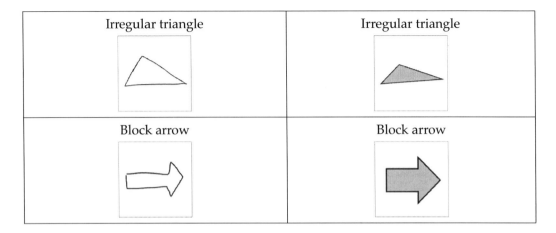

7.4.6 Use Lasso Select for selecting Ink

Lasso Select is an ink selection tool, specifically for selecting objects drawn with ink. This tool cannot select non-ink objects, that is, shapes, pictures, etc. It's most useful when you have a mixture of standard and ink objects and you only want to select an ink object.

Go to "Draw -> Tools" on the Ribbon, tap "Lasso Select". With your mouse, pen or finger (in case of touch display), drag to draw a circle around the part of the drawing or word that you want to select. A faded, dashed selection region appears around it, and when you're done, the portion you lassoed is selected.

Figure 7-18: Select ink using Lasso Select

In the preceding example, we changed the color of the selected region from black to blue. Similarly, we can select different regions using "Lasso Select" and change color or thickness etc. as shown in snapshot below.

Figure 7-19: *Changed colour and thickness of different drawing regions*

CHAPTER 8

Putting Data in perspective with Pivots

PivotTable is a simple but very powerful tool to summarize and analyze data and helps in making decisions based on it. Generally, the problem is not the lack of data; instead, it's making sense out of the huge amount of data collected overtime. And many users avoid using Pivots because they think it is too complicated. With the help of examples, this chapter will demonstrate the use of advanced PivotTable techniques and how easily it can be mastered.

8.1 Understanding the Terminology

Getting familiar with the terminology associated with the PivotTable is an important aspect in mastering this feature. PivotTable is a view and is created from the source data, which is the original data residing in a worksheet or an external database. Changes in source data are not automatically reflected but can be seen by refreshing the PivotTable. PivotTable consists of Table Filter, Column Labels, Row Labels, Sub Totals, Grand Totals, Items, Groups and Values as shown in snapshot below.

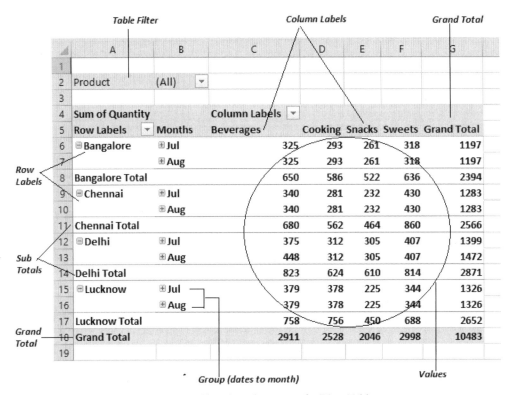

Figure 8-1: *Showing elements of a PivotTable*

Table Filter – Filters allow you to manage or limit what data is summarized in the PivotTable. In the preceding example the "Product" field is used as a filter. Since the condition is "All", there is no limit and all data is shown.

Column Labels – A field that has a column orientation in the PivotTable. "Beverages", "Cooking", "Sweets" etc. are the column labels in the preceding example.

Row Labels – A field that has a row orientation in the PivotTable. In our example "Bangalore"," Delhi" etc. are row labels

Sub / Grand Totals – You can have row or column subtotals, like the "Chennai Total", "Delhi Total" etc. shown in preceding example. Grand Totals are totals of all cells in a row or column of a PivotTable.

Item – An element in a field that appears as a row or column header in a PivotTable. For example, the City field has items as "Bangalore", "Delhi" etc.

Values – The cells that contain the summary data (as sum, average, count and so on)

Groups – A collection of items treated as a single item. In the preceding example, Excel automatically grouped the dates to month. This will be discussed in more details later in this chapter.

A graphical or visual representation of the PivotTable is the PivotChart. They are both connected to each other. To create a PivotChart, select any cell in the PivotTable for which you want to create a chart and go to "Insert" tab, select "PivotChart" from the "Charts" group.

Figure 8-2: *PivotChart option from Insert tab*

The "PivotChart" option is also available in the contextual menu "PivotTable Analyze" tab under the "Tools" group.

Figure 8-3: *PivotChart option from PivotTable Analyze tab in Excel 2019*

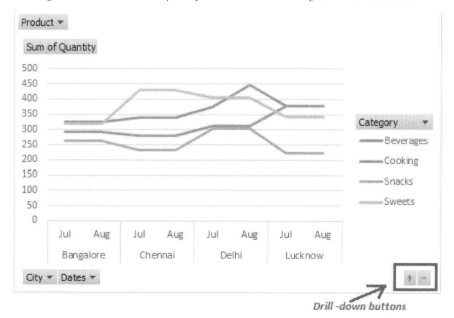

Drill -down buttons

Figure 8-4: *PivotChart*

A PivotChart gets created for the PivotTable shown in Figure 8-1. PivotChart have a set of drill-down buttons in the bottom right corner as shown in the chart above. These drill-down buttons allow you to zoom in and out across groupings of time, and other hierarchical structures within your data. For example, if you click the "-" (minus) drill-down button in the PivotChart above, it will collapse the field and the PivotTable and PivotChart view will change as shown below.

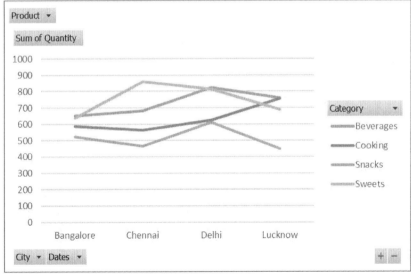

Figure 8-5: *PivotChart drill-down buttons*

Again, on clicking the "+" (plus) drill-down button the view in PivotTable and PivotChart gets expanded as shown in Figure 8-1 and Figure 8-4.

Note: In the previous versions of Excel i.e., Excel 2016 and earlier, there was 'PivotTable Tools' menu that had two sub-tabs as 'Analyze' and 'Design'. All the PivotTable options were under these two sub-menus. In the latest version of Excel 2019, it has been replaced by two separate menu options i.e., 'PivotTable Analyze' &

'Design'. Pivot functionalities have got more enhanced in Excel 2019 as we will see in this chapter.

8.2 Verify the Source

First step before starting to use a Pivot is to <u>scrub and organize your raw data</u> that will be the source for creating the Pivot. The source data should be verified for the following:

- no blank rows or columns.
- no missing data (preferably add an estimated value based on similar data in table if the actual is not available).
- unique column headers and only on one row.
- no duplicates.
- data organized in a tabular format that is into rows and columns.

8.3 Format data for sync

The best practice is to <u>format the data as Excel Table,</u> so that the data range becomes dynamic. A dynamic range will automatically expand and shrink the table as you add or remove data, and the corresponding PivotTable will always be in sync with your source data. Hence no data will get missed from your analysis and the changes will be reflected immediately in your Pivot.

To format data as Excel Table, select any cell in the dataset and use the shortcut key CTRL+T to create the table.

	A	B	C	D	E	F	G	H	I	J
1	Month	Date	Region	City	Category	Product	Price per	Quantity	Returned	Total Sale
2	July	01-07-2018	North	Delhi	Beverages	Lemon Tea	330.00	200	10	66,000.00
3	July	01-07-2018	North	Delhi	Beverages	Filter Coffe	257.00	75	4	19,275.00
4	July	01-07-2018	North	Delhi	Beverages	Coconu			5	16,000.00
5	July	01 07 2018	North	Delhi	Snacks	Biscuit				2,000.00
6	July	01-07-2018	North	Delhi	Snacks	Roaste				8,900.00
7	July	06-07-2018	North	Delhi	Snacks	Popcor				3,630.00
8	July	07-07-2018	North	Delhi	Sweets	Chocol				50,400.00
9	July	08-07-2018	North	Delhi	Sweets	Milk Ca				2,000.00
10	July	09-07-2018	North	Delhi	Sweets	Candy				6,171.00
11	July	09-07-2018	North	Delhi	Cooking	Salt				2,250.00
12	July	11-07-2018	North	Delhi	Cooking	Lentil	63.00	112	6	7,056.00
13	July	12-07-2018	North	Delhi	Cooking	Oil	108.00	50	3	5,400.00
14	July	13-07-2018	North	Lucknow	Beverages	Lemon Tea	300.00	154	8	46,200.00
15	July	14-07-2018	North	Lucknow	Beverages	Filter Coffe	250.00	50	3	12,500.00
16	July	15-07-2018	North	Lucknow	Beverages	Coconut Wa	112.00	175	9	19,600.00

Create Table   ?   ×

Where is the data for your table?

=$A$1:$J$97

☑ My table has headers

OK   Cancel

Figure 8-6: Format data as table

Click the checkbox 'My table has headers' if your selected data set has column headers in the first row. Excel will then use the first row as column header in the Excel Table.

If you do not have column headers in the data set, as shown in screenshot below, then leave the checkbox unchecked and Excel will automatically insert column headers as 'Column1', 'Column2' and so on as the first row in the data set.

Figure 8-7: Table with Excel inserted column headers

You can rename the columns as per need, like the 'Column4' has been renamed as 'Quantity' in the preceding example.

8.4 Recommended PivotTables

You can create the PivotTable using the option 'Summarize with PivotTable' in 'Table Design' tab, under 'Tools' group. In previous versions of Excel i.e., versions earlier to Excel 2019, users will find 'Summarize with PivotTable' option in the 'Table Tools -> Design' menu.

Figure 8-8: Create Pivot

Excel also gives the option of 'Recommended PivotTables' under the 'Insert' tab. Based on the source data, Excel creates multiple PivotTables for you to choose from. This is a faster, time saving option and a good start point to work on Pivots.

You can start by selecting any one of the recommended PivotTables and modify it. Or you can choose a Blank PivotTable and add columns, rows, and values as required.

Figure 8-9: Recommended PivotTables

8.5 Setting PivotTable default layout

This is a new feature introduced in Excel 2019. It is available on Windows if you have Office 2019 or Office 365 subscription with latest version of Office.

You can personalize and save the default PivotTable layout options. Next time when a new PivotTable is created in any workbook, it is created with the default layout settings. The existing PivotTables are not impacted by the changes in the default layout settings. To personalize the PivotTable layout options, go to 'File->Options->Data' and under the 'Data options' click on 'Edit Default Layout…' to show the 'Edit Default Layout' dialog box.

Figure 8-10: PivotTable - Edit Default Layout dialog box

In the 'Edit Default Layout' dialog box, as shown in figure above, you can set certain options that all new PivotTables will inherit.

Layout Import – To automatically import layout settings from an existing PivotTable, select any cell in an existing PivotTable and click the "Import" button. You can reset, import new settings or edit the settings at any time in future.

Subtotals – You can select any one of the three options; Do Not Show Subtotals or Show all Subtotals at Top of Group or Show all Subtotals at Bottom of Group.

Grand Totals - You can select any one of the four options: Off for Rows and Columns or On for Rows and Columns or On for Rows Only or On for Columns Only.

Report Layout – You can pick the report layout from Show in Compact Form or Outline Form or Tabular Form.

Blank Rows – On checking the 'Insert Blank Line after Each Item' box, PivotTable will automatically insert a blank row after each item.

Reset to Excel Default – This restores the Excel's default PivotTable settings.

PivotTable Options – This launches the standard PivotTable dialog box as shown in snapshot below.

Figure 8-11: PivotTable options dialog box

In the PivotTable options dialog, you can edit the settings like specify 'zero' for empty cells etc. and save them as part of default layout.

8.6 Adding Slicers & Timelines

Slicers, introduced in Excel 2010, are a powerful tool to filter and refine data included in the Pivot. Timelines are special type of slicers, using which you can view information based on dates or for specific time periods. Note that you can use Timelines only if the original data has the date formatted as Date in the Excel.

To insert a Slicer, click anywhere within the PivotTable that you created and go to 'PivotTable Analyze->Insert Slicer' option. In previous Excel versions i.e., versions earlier to Excel 2019, the option to add slicers 'Insert Slicer' is under "PivotTable Tools-> Analyze' tab.

Figure 8-12: Inserting Slicer

To select or deselect multiple items in the Slicer, you can use the 'Multi Select' button that is next to the 'Clear Filter' button. This is a toggle button, activate multi selection by clicking on the button or using keys Alt+S and then select the items in the slicer. To deactivate, again click the button or press keys Alt+S.

Figure 8-13: Multi-select button

If the multi-select button is deactivated, then also you can select multiple items by holding the Ctrl key and selecting each item. This approach is little tedious than multi-select. To clear all selections made, you can use the 'Clear filter' option.

In case you want to exclude filter items that have no data from showing up in the Slicer, you can use the 'Slicer Settings' dialog box to do it. Right click on the Slicer, go to option 'Slicer Settings' to launch the settings dialog box and click on the 'Hide items with no data' check box as shown below.

Figure 8-14: Slicer Settings dialog box

To add a timeline, click anywhere within the PivotTable that you created and go to 'PivotTable Analyze->Insert Timeline' option. In previous Excel versions i.e., versions earlier to Excel 2019, the option to add timelines 'Insert Timeline' is under "PivotTable Tools-> Analyze' tab.

Figure 8-15: Inserting Timeline

Note that in case the Insert Slicer / Timeline options are greyed out, try the keyboard shortcut keys 'CTRL + 6'.

With the help of different scenarios, we will understand the usefulness and usage of slicers and timelines.

Scenario Qs.: In the PivotTable shown below, how can we view the total quantity of Filter Coffee sold in Bangalore and Delhi in different months on the click of a button?

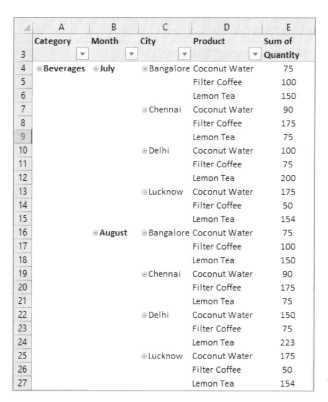

Answer: Insert a Slicer and select the City and Product checkboxes and click OK. Select Bangalore and Delhi in City slicer (hold the Ctrl key for multiple selections or use multi-select button) and Filter Coffee in Product slicer.

The data in Pivot is filtered as per the selection in the City and Product slicers. The Grand Total also corresponds to the filtered data.

Scenario Qs.: Again, using the same PivotTable as shown in previous scenario, how can we view the total quantity of Products for duration from 6th Jul to 10th July with the click of a button?

Answer: Insert a Timeline using 'PivotTable Analyze -> Insert Timeline' and select the Date option..

You can view data via Timelines for Years, Quarters, Months, or Days based on the selection made. For our example we will select 'Days'.

Now, if we want to view data for the duration from 6th Jul to 10th July, then we will select the month and the dates in the Timeline using the slider

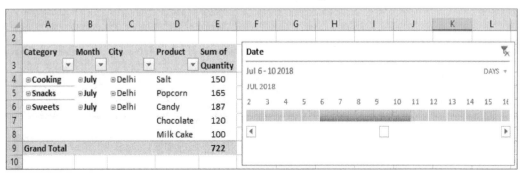

If we want to see the month total then first select MONTH instead of DAYS from the upper right options and then select the desired month to view data

	A	B	C	D	E	F	G	H	I	J	K	L
3	Category ▾	Month ▾	City ▾	Product	Sum of Quantity ▾	Date						🏷
4	⊟Beverages	⊟August	⊟Bangalore	Coconut Water	75	Aug 2018					MONTHS ▾	
5				Filter Coffee	100	2018						
6				Lemon Tea	150	MAR	APR	MAY	JUN	JUL	AUG	SEP	OCT	NOV
7			⊟Chennai	Coconut Water	90							
8				Filter Coffee	175	◀						▶
9				Lemon Tea	75							
10			⊟Delhi	Coconut Water	150							
11				Filter Coffee	75							
12				Lemon Tea	223							
13			⊟Lucknow	Coconut Water	175							
14				Filter Coffee	50							

In the preceding example, we selected the month of August to view all the items sold in different cities.

8.7 Adding Calculated Fields in Pivot

Calculated fields allow you to add additional information in your PivotTable that was not in the original data but derived from it. Calculated Fields can refer to other fields in the PivotTable and always uses the SUM of other values. They get added in the PivotTable Field list on creation and users can add them in the PivotTable Values.

For understanding, we will use the original data as shown below.

	A	B	C	D	E	F	G	H	I	J
1	Month	Date	Region	City	Category	Product	Price per Uni	Quantity	Returned Units	Total Sale
2	July	01-07-2018	North	Delhi	Beverages	Lemon Tea	330	200	10	66,000.00
3	July	01-07-2018	North	Delhi	Beverages	Filter Coffee	257	75	4	19,275.00
4	July	01-07-2018	North	Delhi	Beverages	Coconut Water	160	100	5	16,000.00
5	July	01-07-2018	North	Delhi	Snacks	Biscuit	24	120	6	2,880.00
6	July	01-07-2018	North	Delhi	Snacks	Roasted Almor	445	20	1	8,900.00
7	July	06-07-2018	North	Delhi	Snacks	Popcorn	22	165	8	3,630.00
8	July	07-07-2018	North	Delhi	Sweets	Chocolate	420	120	6	50,400.00
9	July	08-07-2018	North	Delhi	Sweets	Milk Cake	20	100	5	2,000.00
10	July	09-07-2018	North	Delhi	Sweets	Candy	33	187	9	6,171.00
11	July	09-07-2018	North	Delhi	Cooking	Salt	15	150	8	2,250.00
12	July	11-07-2018	North	Delhi	Cooking	Lentil	63	112	6	7,056.00
13	July	12-07-2018	North	Delhi	Cooking	Oil	108	50	3	5,400.00

We have Product information related to the Price per Unit and number of Returned Units and now we want to see what the loss is due to returned units is in the PivotTable, which is NOT there in the original data.

First create a PivotTable as shown below for the original data set, with row fields as City, Product, Price per Unit and values as Sum of Returned Units.

	A	B	C	D
3	City	Product	Price per Unit	Sum of Returned Units
4	⊟ Bangalore	⊟ Biscuit	24	14
5		⊟ Candy	33	10
6		⊟ Chocolate	415	10
7		⊟ Coconut Water	154	8
8		⊟ Filter Coffee	150	10
9		⊟ Lemon Tea	200	16
10		⊟ Lentil	63	16
11		⊟ Milk Cake	20	12
12		⊟ Oil	118	4
13		⊟ Popcorn	22	8
14		⊟ Roasted Almond	450	6
15		⊟ Salt	20	10
16	⊟ Chennai	⊟ Biscuit	24	18
17		⊟ Candy	20	5
18			50	5
19		⊟ Chocolate	410	20
20		Coconut Water	110	10

To create a Calculated field, go to 'PivotTable Analyze -> Fields, Items & Sets -> Calculated Fields'. In the 'Insert Calculated Field' window, enter the new field name, say "Return Loss" in our case, and in the Formula field enter the formula (='Price per Unit'*'Returned Units') constituting the existing fields by clicking the "Insert Field" button; then add the new calculated field by clicking ADD button. On clicking OK in the 'Insert Calculated field' window, Excel adds this new field in the PivotTable Fields list. .

Figure 8-16: *Insert Calculated field in Pivot*

To view the new calculated field in the PivotTable, select the field from the PivotTable Field list and add to Values.

| | A | B | C | Sum of | Sum of |
	City	Product	Price per Unit	Returned Units	Return Loss
4	⊟Bangalore	⊟Biscuit	24	14	672
5		⊟Candy	33	10	660
6		⊟Chocolate	415	10	8300
7		⊟Coconut Water	154	8	2464
8		⊟Filter Coffee	150	10	3000
9		⊟Lemon Tea	200	16	6400
10		⊟Lentil	63	16	2016
11		⊟Milk Cake	20	12	480
12		⊟Oil	118	4	944
13		⊟Popcorn	22	8	352

— New calculated field

The calculated fields do not get added in the original data, they are just inserted in the PivotTable for data analysis or summarizing the data.

8.8 Deleting Calculated Fields from Pivot

To remove the calculated field from the PivotTable, go to 'PivotTable Analyze-> Fields, Items & Sets -> Calculated Fields'. In the 'Insert Calculated Field' window, select the field to be deleted from the Name list and click 'Delete'.

The calculated field will be removed from the PivotTable and will no longer be available in the PivotTable Fields list.

8.9 Adding Calculated Items in Pivot

Calculated Items are formulas that can refer to other items within a specific Pivot field. Calculated Items are not shown in the PivotTable Fields list like Calculated Fields but are listed with other items in the Row or Column area of the PivotTable.

For the original data given below, we will create a PivotTable and show how to add calculated items

	A	B	C	D	E	F	G	H
1	Month	Date	City	Category	Product	Price per Uni	Quantity	Total Sale
2	July	01-07-2018	Delhi	Beverages	Filter Coffee	257	75	19,275.00
3	July	01-07-2018	Delhi	Snacks	Biscuit	24	120	2,880.00
4	July	14-07-2018	Lucknow	Beverages	Filter Coffee	250	50	12,500.00
5	July	16-07-2018	Lucknow	Snacks	Biscuit	25	113	2,825.00
6	July	26-07-2018	Bangalore	Beverages	Filter Coffee	150	100	15,000.00
7	July	28-07-2018	Bangalore	Snacks	Biscuit	24	134	3,216.00
8	July	19-07-2018	Chennai	Beverages	Filter Coffee	102	175	17,850.00
9	July	21-07-2018	Chennai	Snacks	Biscuit	24	173	4,152.00
10	August	19-08-2018	Delhi	Beverages	Filter Coffee	257	75	19,275.00
11	August	19-08-2018	Delhi	Snacks	Biscuit	24	120	2,880.00
12	August	31-08-2018	Lucknow	Beverages	Filter Coffee	250	50	12,500.00
13	August	02-08-2018	Lucknow	Snacks	Biscuit	25	113	2,825.00
14	August	04-08-2018	Bangalore	Beverages	Filter Coffee	150	100	15,000.00
15	August	06-08-2018	Bangalore	Snacks	Biscuit	24	134	3,216.00
16	August	08-08-2018	Chennai	Beverages	Filter Coffee	102	175	17,850.00
17	August	18-08-2018	Chennai	Snacks	Biscuit	24	173	4,152.00

As the first step we will create a PivotTable for the data set with row fields as City, Product and Sum of Quantity as Values.

	A	B	C
21			
22	City	Product	Sum of Quantity
23	⊟Bangalore		468
24		Biscuit	268
25		Filter Coffee	200
26	⊟Chennai		696
27		Biscuit	346
28		Filter Coffee	350
29	⊟Delhi		390
30		Biscuit	240
31		Filter Coffee	150
32	⊟Lucknow		326
33		Biscuit	226
34		Filter Coffee	100

Next we will add calculated items to show the total quantity that is sold in South i.e., including total of Bangalore and Chennai and North i.e., including total of Delhi and Lucknow. To do so, click on the last empty cell where you want to add the calculated item i.e., A34 in our example and go to 'PivotTable Analyze -> Fields, Items & Sets -> Calculated Items'.

In the 'Insert Calculated Item' window, enter 'South' in the Name field. Now add the formula, start by typing '=' in the Formula field and then select 'City' in Fields list. Select 'Bangalore' from Items list and click 'Insert Item' to add it in the formula. Since we want the total quantity sold in these two cities, we will add a plus sign in the formula. After the plus sign, again go to Items, select 'Chennai' and click 'Insert Item' to add it in the formula. The formula we entered is '=Bangalore+ Chennai'. Click OK and the calculated item 'South' gets added in the Pivot table as shown below.

	A	B	C	
21				
22	City ⯆	Product ⯆	Sum of Quantity	
23	⊟Bangalore		468	
24		Biscuit	268	
25		Filter Coffee	200	
26	⊟Chennai		696	
27		Biscuit	346	
28		Filter Coffee	350	
29	⊟Delhi		390	
30		Biscuit	240	
31		Filter Coffee	150	
32	⊟Lucknow		326	
33		Biscuit	226	
34		Filter Coffee	100	
35	⊟South		1164	*Calculated Item*
36		Biscuit	614	
37		Filter Coffee	550	

Similarly, we can add the calculated item 'North' with the Formula as '=Delhi + Lucknow' as shown below. Note that the calculated item 'South' that we created before this, is now shown in the Items list.

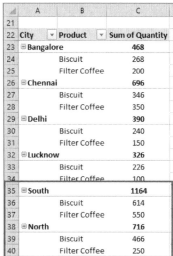

8.10 Deleting Calculated Items from Pivot

To remove the inserted Calculated Items, select the item in the PivotTable and go to 'PivotTable Analyze -> Fields, Items & Sets -> Calculated Items'. In the 'Insert Calculated Item' window, select the item from the Name list and click 'Delete'.

The Calculated Item will be deleted from the PivotTable and will no longer be visible in the Items list.

8.11 Group Field in Pivot

We can group similar items in Pivot, without adding any new field in the original data, by using the 'Group Field' option from "PivotTable Analyse -> Group". Grouping is another useful tool for analyzing data from perspectives by viewing data based on criteria, range, and so on. What you have grouped can be ungrouped using the Ungroup option at any time.

Scenario Qs.: The following PivotTable and chart depict the sale done on a specific date. We want to know in which price range products have the maximum sale. Currently it's not easy as both table and chart do not give us any meaningful information for any discussion or decision making.

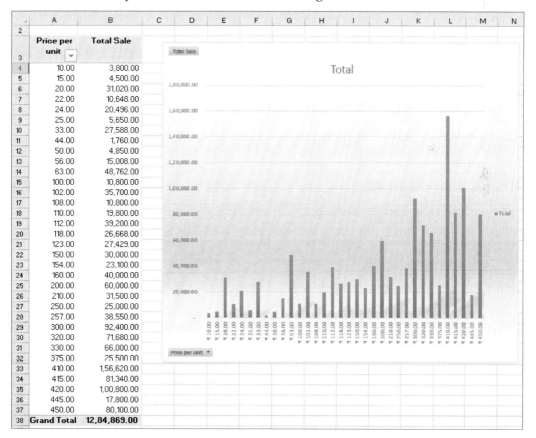

Price per unit	Total Sale
10.00	3,800.00
15.00	4,500.00
20.00	31,020.00
22.00	10,648.00
24.00	20,496.00
25.00	5,650.00
33.00	27,588.00
44.00	1,760.00
50.00	4,850.00
56.00	15,008.00
63.00	48,762.00
100.00	10,800.00
102.00	35,700.00
108.00	10,800.00
110.00	19,800.00
112.00	39,200.00
118.00	26,668.00
123.00	27,429.00
150.00	30,000.00
154.00	23,100.00
160.00	40,000.00
200.00	60,000.00
210.00	31,500.00
250.00	25,000.00
257.00	38,550.00
300.00	92,400.00
320.00	71,680.00
330.00	66,000.00
375.00	25,500.00
410.00	1,56,620.00
415.00	81,340.00
420.00	1,00,800.00
445.00	17,800.00
450.00	80,100.00
Grand Total	**12,84,869.00**

Answer: Use the 'Group Field' option for grouping the 'Price per Unit' in a range, such that we get total sale for a range. The range can be decided by the user, although by default, based on the minimum and maximum values, Excel recommends a range.

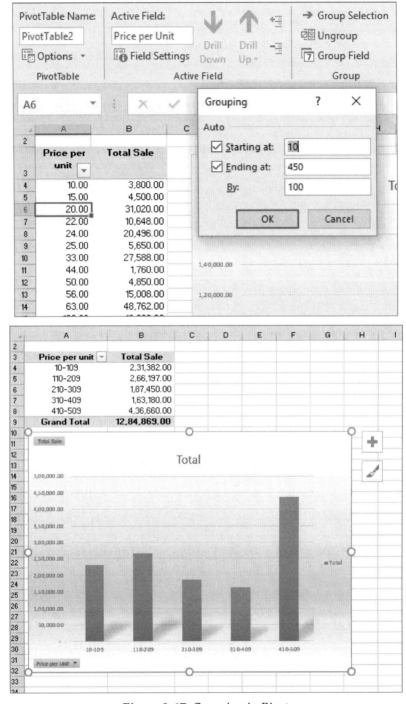

Figure 8-17: Grouping in Pivot

What you have grouped can be ungrouped using the Ungroup option

Figure 8-18: Ungroup in Pivot

8.11.1 Automatic time grouping

Automatic time grouping is a new feature in Excel 2019. If your PivotTable has time-related fields, it automatically detects and groups them on your behalf. You can add the group by simply dragging it to your PivotTable in one action, and immediately begin your analysis across the different levels of time with drill-down capabilities.

For example, create a PivotTable for the sample source data as shown in snapshot below.

	A	B	C	D	E	F	G
1	City	Category	Product	ice pe	uar	Dates	
2	Bangalore	Beverages	Filter Coffee	150	100	26-07-2018	
3	Bangalore	Snacks	Biscuit	24	134	28-07-2018	⟶ Jul
4	Bangalore	Cooking	Oil	118	37	30-07-2018	
5	Bangalore	Beverages	Filter Coffee	150	100	04-08-2018	
6	Bangalore	Snacks	Biscuit	24	134	06-08-2018	
7	Bangalore	Cooking	Oil	118	37	06-08-2018	
8	Delhi	Beverages	Filter Coffee	257	75	01-07-2018	
9	Delhi	Snacks	Biscuit	24	120	01-07-2018	
10	Delhi	Cooking	Oil	108	50	12-07-2018	
11	Delhi	Beverages	Filter Coffee	257	75	19-08-2018	
12	Delhi	Snacks	Biscuit	24	120	19-08-2018	⟶ Aug
13	Delhi	Cooking	Oil	108	50	19-08-2018	

Excel automatically groups the dates into month and shows in the PivotTable.

	A	B	C	D	E
2					
3	Sum of Quantity	Column Labe ▾			
4	Row Labels ▾	Biscuit	Filter Coffee	Oil	Grand Total
5	⊟ Bangalore	268	200	74	542
6	⊞ Jul	134	100	37	271
7	⊞ Aug	134	100	37	271
8	⊟ Delhi	240	150	100	490
9	⊞ Jul	120	75	50	245
10	⊞ Aug	120	75	50	245
11	Grand Total	508	350	174	1032

Figure 8-19: PivotTable created with grouping

In case you do not want Excel to automatically group time-related fields, you can disable the option. To disable, go to "File->Options->Data" and select the checkbox to disable automatic grouping as shown in snapshot below.

Figure 8-20: *Disable automatic time grouping in Pivot*

8.12 Interactive Dashboard with PivotTables, Charts and Slicers

In above sections we discussed the different Pivot features. In this section however we will discuss interactive dashboards that is, PivotTables and PivotCharts connected to Slicers that give different perspectives based on selection. For the same data used in previous examples in this chapter, first we will create different PivotTables/Charts and Slicers, and then compile them in a dashboard.

PivotTable/Chart #1 – City Wise - Total Sale (as percentage):

Create the PivotTable as explained in earlier sections, with City in Rows and Total Sale in the Values field. To convert your Total Sale to a percentage, click on any cell in Total Sale and right-click to select the option Show Value as -> % of Grand Total. Select the Pivot and add a Pie chart and Slicer for city and region as seen in the following screenshot.

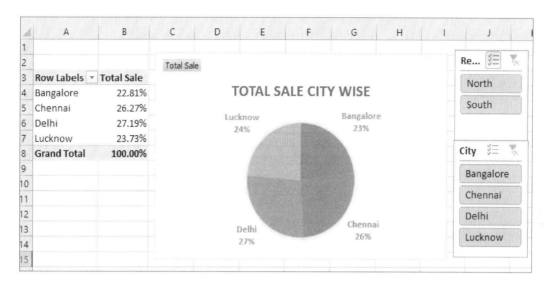

PivotTable / Chart #2 – Product Wise - Total Sale:

Create a Pivot with Product in Rows and Total Sale in the Value fields. Then create a Column chart as seen in the following screenshot.

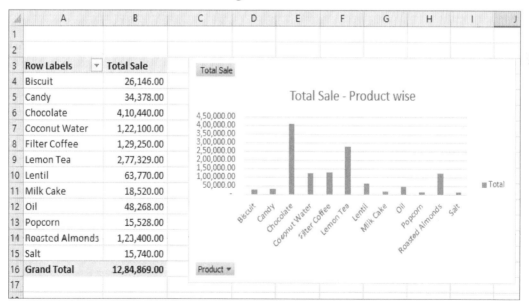

Create a new sheet and name it as 'Dashboard'. Copy the PivotCharts and Slicers that we just created, in the new sheet as seen in the following screenshot.

Now we also want a Slicer for month so that we can view data based on the month of sale. In the Dashboard sheet, we will create a Slicer by selecting the PivotChart. Note that you can create a Slicer by selecting any one of the PivotTable or Chart. Select the PivotChart 'PivotTable / Chart #2' and select from the menu options "PivotChart Analyze -> Insert Slicer" and click on Month.

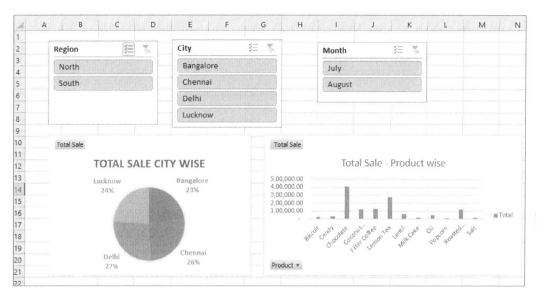

In above Dashboard, currently Slicers are associated with their respective graphs. Next step is to connect the Charts and the Slicers such that we can see the changes in both graphs based on a selection in any of the Slicers.

Firstly, note the PivotTables names that are associated with the Slicers. In this case they are Pivot 1 and Pivot 4. On each Slicer, right-click and select the menu option 'Report Connections' and check the Pivot names to connect.

After the connections are made, the Dashboard has become interactive which means, the graphs will change based on the selection in the Slicers.

8.13 Consolidate data from different sources in Pivot

8.13.1 Method #1: Data with identical column structure using Pivot Wizard

PivotTables can be used to consolidate data from different sources, be it different sheets of the same workbook or sheets from different workbooks. Only condition is that the sheets should have identical column structure that is, the number and name of columns should be the same in all sheets to be consolidated, while the number of rows can be different.

In the previous sections the data used was for year 2018. Now we will also add similar data of year 2017 for consolidation and yearly comparison purposes. In the workbook we have two sheets named Yr 2017 and Yr 2018. We will use the PivotTable and PivotChart Wizard for consolidating the data from these two sheets.

Note: There is no option available directly on the main menu so we will use the keyboard shortcut keys. Select any cell on a worksheet and **press Alt + D, and then press P** that will open the wizard. On the wizard select Multiple consolidation ranges and click Next.

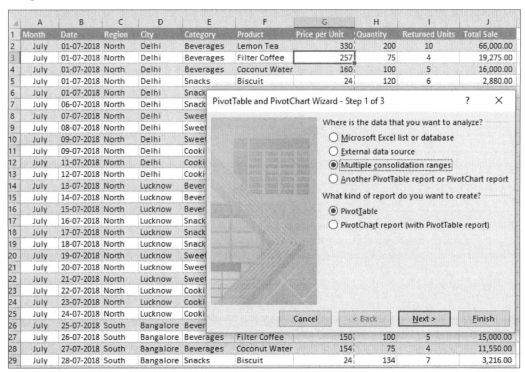

On the next screen select the option "I will create the page fields" and press Next

Select the ranges from the different sheets (Yr 2017 and Yr 2018) and press Add. Click 1 as the number of Page Fields, select each range, add the item labels, and then press Next.

In the next window select the Pivot location and click on Finish. A PivotTable is created on the worksheet, with the first field in the Row area, and all the other fields from the source data in the Values area, showing a Count.

	A	B	C	D	E	F	G	H	I	J	K
1	Page1	(All) ▼									
2											
3	Count of Value	Column ▼									
4	Row Labels ▼	Category	City	Date	Price per Unit	Product	Quantity	Region	Return	Total Sa	Grand Total
5	July	96	96	96	96	96	96	96	96	96	864
6	August	96	96	96	96	96	96	96	96	96	864
7	Grand Total	192	192	192	192	192	192	192	192	192	1728
8											

In the preceding format the Month is the first column in the data source and hence the Pivot table row heading shows the months (July, August) while remaining fields (Category, City and so on) are shown in the column area. In case the first column in the data source was the Product, the PivotTable would have made more sense as shown in below screenshot.

	A	B	C	D	E
1	Page1	(All) ▼			
2					
3	Sum of Value	Column Labels ▼	Page1 ≡ ▼		
4	Row Labels ▼	Total Sale			
5	Biscuit	39,624.04	Yr 2017		
6	Candy	52,321.67	Yr 2018		
7	Chocolate	6,18,807.80			
8	Coconut Water	1,87,300.80			
9	Filter Coffee	1,97,401.09			
10	Lemon Tea	4,29,871.12			
11	Lentil	97,578.59			
12	Milk Cake	28,114.77			
13	Oil	72,594.81			
14	Popcorn	24,242.07			
15	Roasted Almonds	1,87,817.03			
16	Salt	24,126.49			
17					

To get the best results, rearrange your columns such that the most important column is to the far left. That column of data will become the Row values in the PivotTable. Columns that you don't want in the PivotTable, move those to the far right in the source data. Do not include those columns when selecting the data ranges for the PivotTable.

8.13.2 Method #2: Data with identical column structure using Microsoft Query

There was a limitation in using the Pivot wizard, which is solved using the Microsoft Query method. Points to remember again are that the sheets should have identical column structure, the data should be in a table format and it's better to give a name to your tables such that they are clearly identifiable in the query. We will use the same data sheets as in previous example that is, sheets named 'Yr 2018' and 'Yr 2017'. Insert a new sheet for consolidating the data of the query. Click on any cell and go to option "Data -> Get Data -> From Other Sources -> From Microsoft Query"

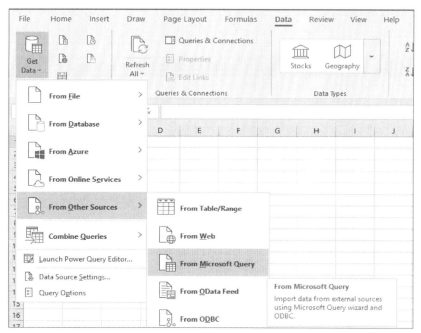

Select Excel files in the next window and click OK. In the Select Workbook window browse to your Excel file.

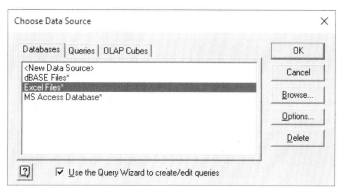

In the Query Wizard select the columns from one of the sheets that you want in the query, add them one by one and then click Next.

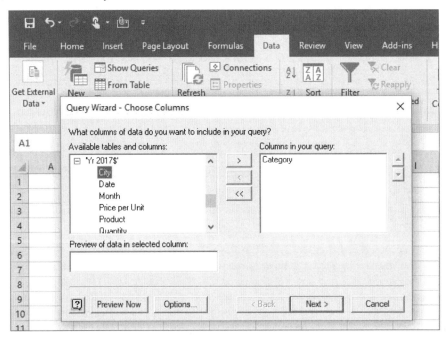

Click Next on the "Filter data" and "Sort by" windows. On the last window select the check box "View data or edit query in Microsoft query" and click on Finish.

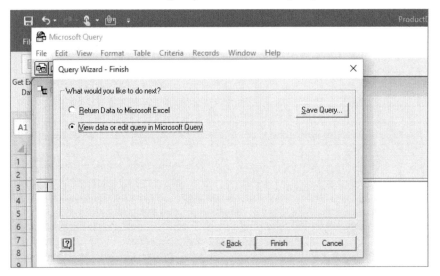

Select the SQL option and edit the SQL query to connect data from all the sheets, using the UNION ALL option. The format of the query will be as given below,

SELECT * FROM <<Sheet #1>>

UNION ALL

SELECT * FROM <<Sheet #2>>

Click OK and now the Microsoft Query window will have data of all the sheets. Close the window and wait for few seconds for the next 'Import Data' dialog box to come up.

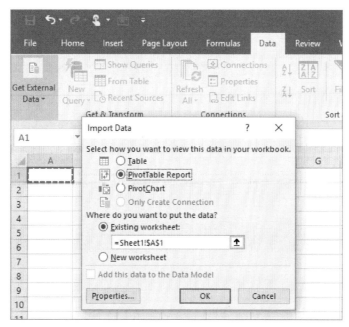

Create the PivotTable with the required fields. As we connect the data of the two sheets the Pivot shows the consolidated data.

▲	A	B	C	D	E	F	G	H
1	Row Labels ▼	Product	Years	City	Quantity	Price per Unit	Total Sale	
2	⊟Beverages	⊟Coconut Water	⊟2017	Bangalore	135	204.96	13,834.71	
3				Chennai	162	97.90	7,929.90	
4				Delhi	225	218.00	24,228.00	
5				Lucknow	315	121.96	19,208.20	
6			⊟2018	Bangalore	150	308.00	23,100.00	
7				Chennai	180	220.00	19,800.00	
8				Delhi	250	320.00	40,000.00	
9				Lucknow	350	224.00	39,200.00	
10		⊟Filter Coffee	⊟2017	Bangalore	180	199.64	17,967.15	
11				Chennai	315	90.78	14,297.85	
12				Delhi	135	350.16	23,635.97	
13				Lucknow	90	272.23	12,250.13	
14			⊟2018	Bangalore	200	300.00	30,000.00	
15				Chennai	350	204.00	35,700.00	
16				Delhi	150	514.00	38,550.00	
17				Lucknow	100	500.00	25,000.00	

8.13.3 Method #3: Data with different column structure using Pivot

In this section we will combine data from two sheets that have different column structures but have some common columns to show the relationship between them. As in previous examples, modify the data in Table format and give a relevant name to the table. In this example the two data sheets have 'SalesInfo' and 'VendorInfo' tables and 'Order No'. is the common column between the two that will help in creating a relationship between the two datasets.

▲	A	B	C	D	E	F	G	H	I	K
1	Mont▼	Date ▼	Region▼	City ▼	Order N▼	Category▼	Product ▼	Price per▼	Quantit▼	Total Sale ▼
2	July	01-07-2018	North	Delhi	1001	Beverages	Lemon Tea	330.00	200	66,000.00
3	July	01-07-2018	North	Delhi	1002	Beverages	Filter Coffee	257.00	75	19,275.00
4	July	01-07-2018	North	Delhi	1003	Beverages	Coconut Water	160.00	100	16,000.00
5	July	01-07-2018	North	Delhi	1004	Snacks	Biscuit	24.00	120	2,880.00
6	July	01-07-2018	North	Delhi	1005	Snacks	Roasted Almonds	445.00	20	8,900.00
7	July	06-07-2018	North	Delhi	1006	Snacks	Popcorn	22.00	165	3,630.00
8	July	07-07-2018	North	Delhi	1007	Sweets	Chocolate	420.00	120	50,400.00
9	July	08-07-2018	North	Delhi	1008	Sweets	Milk Cake	20.00	100	2,000.00
10	July	09-07-2018	North	Delhi	1009	Sweets	Candy	33.00	187	6,171.00
11	July	09-07-2018	North	Delhi	1010	Cooking	Salt	15.00	150	2,250.00
12	July	11-07-2018	North	Delhi	1011	Cooking	Lentil	63.00	112	7,056.00
13	July	12-07-2018	North	Delhi	1012	Cooking	Oil	108.00	50	5,400.00
14	July	13-07-2018	North	Lucknow	1013	Beverages	Lemon Tea	300.00	154	46,200.00
15	July	14-07-2018	North	Lucknow	1014	Beverages	Filter Coffee	250.00	50	12,500.00
16	July	15-07-2018	North	Lucknow	1015	Beverages	Coconut Water	112.00	175	19,600.00
17	July	16-07-2018	North	Lucknow	1016	Snacks	Biscuit	25.00	113	2,825.00
18	July	17-07-2018	North	Lucknow	1017	Snacks	Roasted Almonds	375.00	34	12,750.00
19	July	18-07-2018	North	Lucknow	1018	Snacks	Popcorn	20.00	78	1,560.00
20	July	19-07-2018	North	Lucknow	1019	Sweets	Chocolate	320.00	112	35,840.00
21	July	20-07-2018	North	Lucknow	1020	Sweets	Milk Cake	20.00	98	1,960.00
22	July	21-07-2018	North	Lucknow	1021	Sweets	Candy	33.00	134	4,422.00

Figure 8-21: SalesInfo Table

◢	A	B	C	D	E
1	Order N▾	City ▾	Product ▾	Vendor Info ▾	
2	1001	Delhi	Lemon Tea	Taj Tea	
3	1002	Delhi	Filter Coffee	Narasus	
4	1003	Delhi	Coconut Water	Narasus	
5	1004	Delhi	Biscuit	Sunfeast	
6	1005	Delhi	Roasted Almonds	Kabila	
7	1006	Delhi	Popcorn	Kabila	
8	1007	Delhi	Chocolate	Dairy Milk	
9	1008	Delhi	Milk Cake	Kabila	
10	1009	Delhi	Candy	Dairy Milk	
11	1010	Delhi	Salt	Tata Sampann	
12	1011	Delhi	Lentil	Tata Sampann	
13	1012	Delhi	Oil	Tata Sampann	
14	1013	Lucknow	Lemon Tea	Taj Tea	
15	1014	Lucknow	Filter Coffee	Narasus	

Figure 8-22: VendorInfo Table

Click on the first sheet that is, the 'SalesInfo' sheet and create a PivotTable, click the check box for 'Add this data to the Data Model' and then click OK.

A new PivotTable is created in a new sheet. In the PivotTable Fields task pane click ALL to see all existing tables. But now the tables are not connected, which can be done by navigating to the option "PivotTable Analyze -> Relationships". On the "Manage Relationship" dialog click on "New". In the Create Relationship dialog box, select the two tables that are to be combined and specify the Primary key which is the 'Order No.' in this example.

Now that the tables are connected, insert the required fields from the connected data sets in the PivotTable.

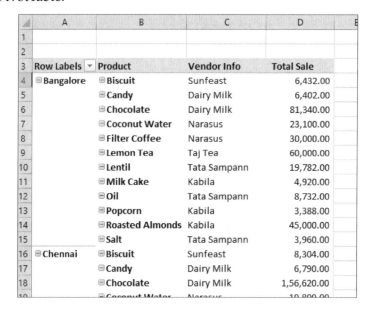

8.14 Using Power Pivot Add-in

Power Pivot is an Excel add-in for powerful data analysis and data modelling. As seen in previous section, in Excel also we can create a Data Model, a collection of tables with relationships. The basic difference between Power Pivot and Excel is that we can create a more sophisticated data model by working on it in the Power

Pivot window. It can work on large volumes of data from various sources, perform information analysis rapidly, and share insights easily. The data model we see in a workbook in Excel is the same data model we see in the Power Pivot window. Any data we import into Excel is available in Power Pivot, and vice versa.

Power Pivot is an Excel add-in that can be installed by navigating to "File -> Options -> Add-Ins". In the Manage box select COM Add-Ins and click Go. Check the 'Microsoft Power Pivot for Excel' box, and then click OK.

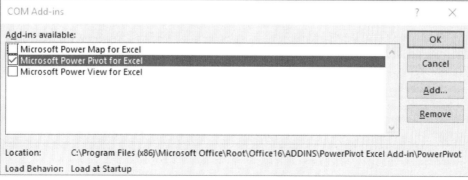

Power Pivot Tab with different options can be seen once the Power Pivot is enabled.

***Figure 8-23:** Power Pivot tab*

To demonstrate the usage of Power Pivot, we will use the same example as in the previous section where we had two data sheets having 'SalesInfo' (Figure 8-21) and 'VendorInfo' (Figure 8-22) tables; and the 'Order No.' being the common column between the two will help in creating a relationship between the two data sets.

8.14.1 Add to Data Model

First, we will add the two tables into the data model. Select the range of data from the sheet that has the 'SalesInfo' table and then navigate to the option "Power Pivot -> Add to Data Model". A new pop up window "Power Pivot" opens and you will notice it has several options to edit, modify, and update the data model. Notice that a new tab is created with the table name.

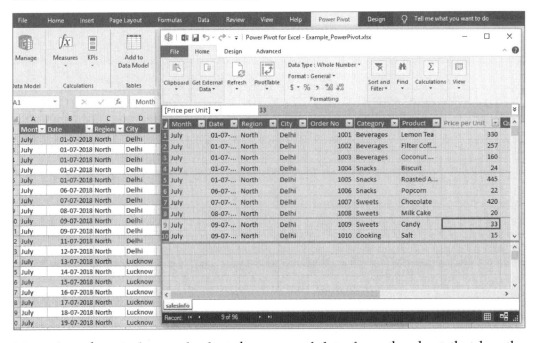

Now close the window and select the range of data from the sheet that has the 'VendorInfo' table and add it to the data model.

In the Power Pivot tab, for each data added onto the Data Model a new tab is created. As shown in the screenshot below, for our example the PowerPivot tab has 'SalesInfo' and 'VendorInfo' tabs.

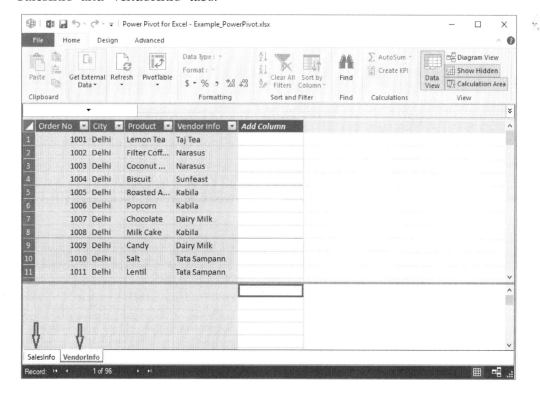

8.14.2 Create a Relationship between datasets

The common field between the two datasets added to the data model (in this case the Order No.), will be used to create the relationship between them. To see the existing data models, navigate to the Power Pivot tab and select "Manage" option under Data Model group. This launches the Power Pivot Window for you to continue working on the datasets.

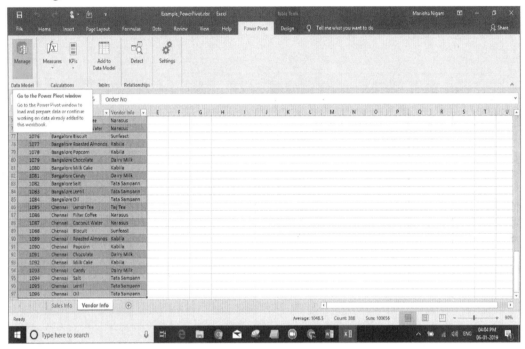

In the Power Pivot Window's Design tab select the "Create Relationship" option. Select the two tables 'SalesInfo', 'VendorInfo' and the common field 'Order No' for creating the relationship and click OK.

Figure 8-24: PowerPivot Create Relationship

You will notice that after selecting the first table i.e., 'VendorInfo' and the column 'Order No', the 'Order No' column in the second table i.e., 'SalesInfo' gets auto selected, as it is a common column between the two tables. Auto column suggestion for same column name in both tables, is a new enhancement in Excel 2019 that will not be visible to users in previous versions of Excel.

Another enhancement in Excel 2019 is that for each table, Excel displays up to five rows of sample data that helps create faster and more accurate relationships, without the need to go back and forth to the data view every time you wish to create or edit a table relationship.

To verify that the relationship between the two datasets have been created correctly, go to the Power Pivot Window's Home tab and select the option 'Diagram View'. Hover your mouse over the link and the common fields get highlighted in both tables.

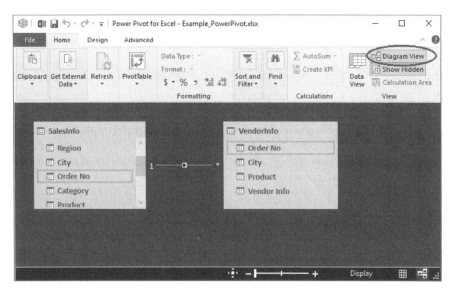

You can go back to the columnar view by selecting **Data View** in the Power Pivot window

8.14.3 Save Relationship Diagram View as Picture

Excel allows you to save the data model diagram view as a high-resolution image file. The image file can then be used for sharing, printing or analyzing the data model. To create the image file, in the Power Pivot window, click 'File > Save View as Picture'.

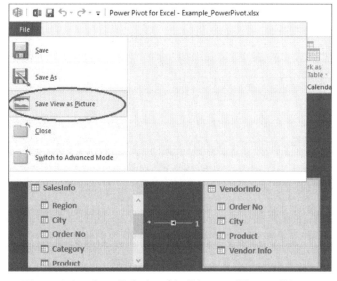

Figure 8-25: Save Relationship Diagram View as Picture

This feature is a new enhancement in Excel 2019 and is not available in older versions of Excel i.e., Excel 2016 and earlier.

8.14.4 Edit / Delete Relationship between data sets

You can also edit the existing relationships between the data sets. To edit or delete a relationship, click on 'Manage Relationships' in the Power Pivot window.

Manage Relationships dialog box allows user to 'Create', 'Edit' or 'Delete' relationships between tables. We have already discussed creating relationships in previous section 8.14.2 and in this section we will discuss deleting and editing relationship.

Figure 8-26: Delete Relationship between data sets

To delete a relationship, select the relationship row you want to delete and click 'Delete'. Excel will ask for confirmation before deleting the selected relationship. On confirmation the relationship will no longer be shown in 'Manage Relationships' dialog.

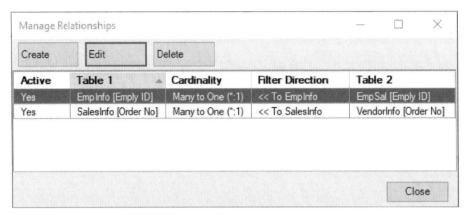

Figure 8-27: Edit Relationship between data sets

To edit a relationship, select the relationship row you want to edit and click 'Edit'. The Edit Relationship dialog box is launched. It shows the two data sets and the common field that was used for creating the relationship between them is highlighted.

Figure 8-28: Edit Relationship dialog box

In the above screenshot the two data sets "EmpInfo" and "EmpSal" are connected by the common field "EmplyID". But now we want to edit this relationship and connect the two data sets by field "Employee Name". We can do this by selecting the columns "Employee Name" in both the data sets, in the Edit Relationship dialog box and click OK.

This takes you back to the Manage Relationships dialog box, which now reflects the changes that you made in Edit Relationship dialog box. That is, now the two data sets "EpmInfo" and "EmpSal" are connected by the common field "Employee Name" instead of "EmplID".

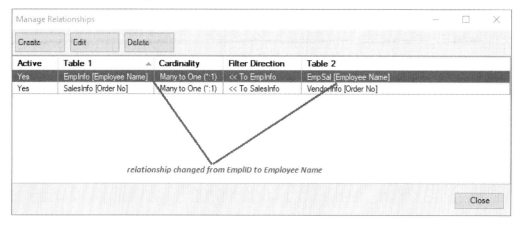

8.14.5 Adding Calculated Column

We can also add a calculated column in the Power Pivot data model. Using the same example as in section 8.14.1, we will see how to add calculated columns in Power Pivot.

In the Power Pivot window, select the tab "SalesInfo" and scroll right till the last column named "Add Column". In the first cell of the column named 'Add Column', enter your formula. In this example we will calculate the cost of the returned units, which is the 'Returned Unit' multiplied by the 'Price per Unit'. Enter the formula in the first cell of the column "Add Column" and press Enter.

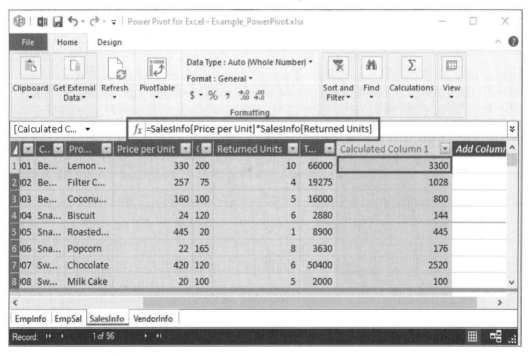

A new column is created by the name of 'Calculated Column 1' with the desired results for all rows, as shown in screenshot above. Also, one additional column gets added by name of "Add Column" on right.

We will rename this column to 'Returned Unit Cost' by right-clicking and selecting the 'Rename Column' option.

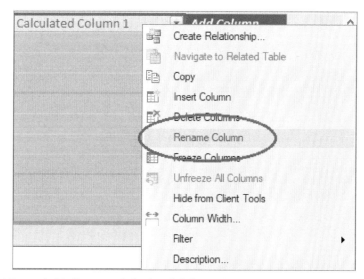

Figure 8-29: Rename Calculated Column in Power Pivot Data Model

8.14.6 Creating Perspectives in Power Pivot

Using the Power Pivot add-in, we can add perspectives, which enable users to create custom views for a user group or business scenario; making it easier to navigate through large datasets. In the Advanced tab of the Power Pivot Window, select 'Create and Manage' under 'Perspectives' group.

Note: In case the "Advance" tab is not visible in the window, go to "File" tab and click "Switch to Advanced Mode". You can toggle back to normal mode by clicking "Switch to Normal Mode".

Click on 'New Perspective' button at the top in the Perspectives window as shown in screenshot below, that will add a new column named "New Perspective" with a check box against each field.

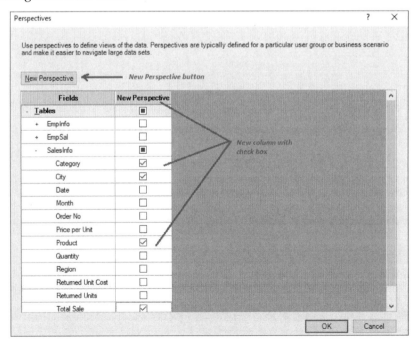

Select the check boxes to include the desired fields and click on OK to create the new perspective. User is taken back to the Power Pivot window with the <Default> view. To see the newly created perspective in the Power Pivot window, click "New Perspective" in the Select drop down list..

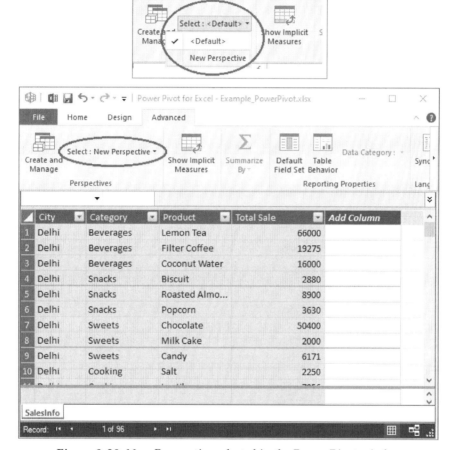

Figure 8-30: New Perspective selected in the Power Pivot window

8.14.7 Adding Measures / Calculated Fields

Measures (also known as calculated fields) are one of the most powerful features in Power Pivot, used frequently for data analysis.

Some measures are easy to create, using a standard aggregation such as SUM, AVERAGE, COUNT, MIN, MAX etc. and created by using the AutoSum feature in the Power Pivot window, or implicit measures created in Excel by simply dragging a field into the Values area. More complex and advanced calculations, such as those following relationships, or filtering results, are created using a Data Analysis Expressions (DAX) formula.

8.14.7.1 Implicit & Explicit Measures

Measures are either implicit or explicit, which affects how you use them in a PivotTable or PivotChart, and in other applications that use a Power Pivot Data Model as a data source.

An implicit measure or calculated field is created by Excel when you drag a field, such as Total Sales, to the VALUES area of the PivotTable Fields list. Implicit measures can only use a standard aggregation (SUM, COUNT, AVG etc.) and can only be used by the PivotTable or chart for which they were created.

An explicit measure or explicit calculated field is created when you type or select a formula in a cell in the Calculation Area, or by using the AutoSum feature in the Power Pivot window. Enter a formula in this format <measure name>:<formula>. Explicit measures can be used by any PivotTable or PivotChart in the workbook and by Power View reports.

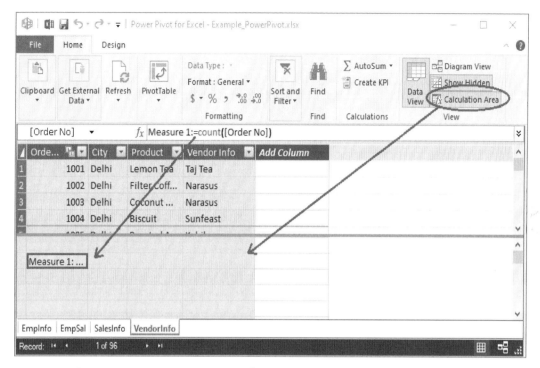

You can also create a measure using the Measure dialog box. Go to 'Power Pivot->Measures->New Measure…'

In the Measure dialog box, type the measure name, description and enter the formula in the formula text box. You can validate the formula using 'Check formula' option.

After formula is validated, click OK. Measures created are stored in the table selected. You can view and edit the measure in the Manage Measures dialog box in Excel or in the Calculation Area for the table in the Power Pivot window.

Note that while measures and calculated columns are similar in that both are based on a formula, they differ in how they are used. Measures are most often used in the VALUES area of a PivotTable or PivotChart. Calculated columns are used when you want to place calculated results in a different area of a PivotTable (such as a column or row in a PivotTable, or on an axis in PivotChart).

8.14.7.2 Data Analysis Expressions (DAX)

More complex and advanced calculations are created using DAX formulas. DAX is a formula language to define custom calculations for Calculated Columns and Measures or Calculated Fields in Power Pivot. DAX formulas include functions, operators, and values to perform advanced calculations and queries on data in related tables and columns in tabular data models.

DAX includes some of the functions used in Excel formulas, and additional functions designed to work with relational data and perform dynamic aggregation. The functions are categorized as; Date and Time, Time-intelligence, Filter, Information, Logical, Math and Trig, Parent and Child, Statistical and Text functions.

For example, DAX can be used to create a PivotTable with Text in Values area. Traditionally you can only summarize fields in Values area of a PivotTable using the different aggregation methods like taking the sum, average, minimum, maximum or standard deviation. Detailed example is listed in Chapter 14 Get help for your problem, Qs 5.

8.15 Get and Transform Data / Power Query tool

Get and Transform Data or Power Query tool in Excel enables you to connect, combine, and refine (that is remove a column, change a data type, or merge tables) data sources to meet analysis needs. It can link to external data from different sources, link them into an internal data model, or present data in form of tables. Get and Transform Data tool options are available under the "Data" tab as shown in screenshot below.

Figure 8-31: Get and Transform Data / Power Query Tool options

Using the Get & Transform Data, you can import data into Excel from a variety of data sources such as Text/CSV files, Excel table / range, databases, Azure and Online services, and more. It also allows easy to perform transformations of data.

Excel has added the top three popular connectors i.e., From Text/CSV, From Web, and From Table/Range on the ribbon itself so that they are easily accessible to users who want to import data.

Note that in older versions of Excel, that is Excel 2016 and earlier, the options are different where the legacy data import wizards are available under "Data->Get External Data". Also, the legacy wizards have got replaced in Excel 2019 with the new connectors that are based on Power Query technology.

In addition to the "Get & Transform Data" options there is "Queries & Connections", as shown in screenshot below, which lets you manage queries and connections easily.

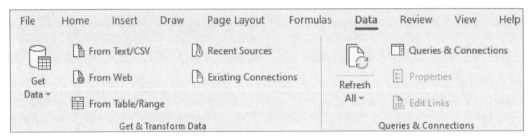

Figure 8-32: *Queries & Connections*

Note that in older versions of Excel, that is Excel 2016 and earlier, "Query & Connections" group is not available. This is a new improvement in Excel 2019.

The Power Query data import tool in Excel 2013 was renamed Get & Transform in Excel 2016, but the name has reverted to Power Query in Excel 2019, bringing it in line with the name conventions used by the related Microsoft products Power Pivot, Power Map, and Power BI.

8.15.1 Import data from Text/CSV

This connector is used for importing data from your text (*.txt), comma-separated values (*.csv) or formatted text (*.prn) files.

To start importing data, click "Data->From Text/CSV". In the "Import Data" dialog box, select the source file and click "Import". The import window is launched with the pre-analyzed settings. The connector analyses the structure of the input file, and automatically applies the relevant import settings like split columns by delimiter, define first row as column headers, and more. In the example below, a CSV file is imported, and the connector automatically used the "Comma" delimiter to split the columns and the first row gets promoted as column headers.

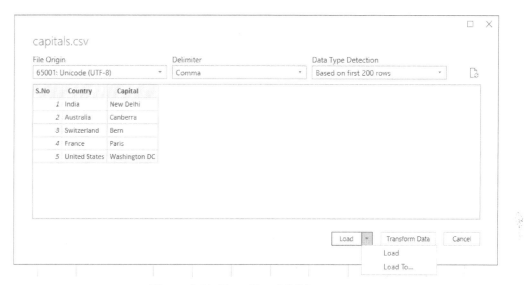

Figure 8-33: From Text / CSV connector

User can modify the automatically applied import settings such as File Origin, Delimiter, or Data Type detection logic right there. The preview of data gets automatically updated based on new import settings. After you are satisfied with the data preview, click on 'Load' to directly load the data into the worksheet.

You can also load the data into your Data Model. Click 'Load To…' as shown in Figure 8-33 and in the Import Data dialog box tick the checkbox 'Add this to the Data Model' and click OK to load the data into your Data Model.

If you want to apply additional data transformations in the Query Editor, click 'Transform Data' as shown in Figure 8-33. Power Query editor is launched with the imported data from the Text/CSV file.

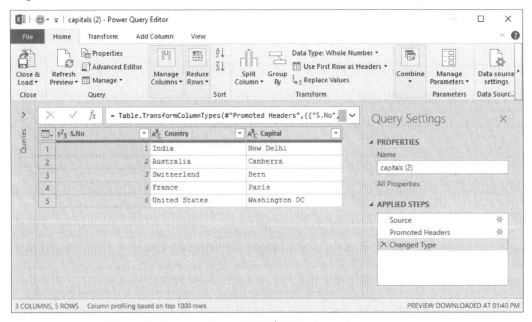

Figure 8-34: Import from TEXT/CSV – Transform data option

8.15.2 Import data from Web

This connector is used for importing data from HTML pages. Click 'Data > From Web', specify the target page URL, and then click OK. In the example below, the URL specified is 'https://www.weather-forecast.com/'.

A list of all the tables on the page is shown in the Navigator dialog. Excel allows you to see the web page in table view and the web view. You can select multiple tables in either view by ticking the check box 'Select multiple items'

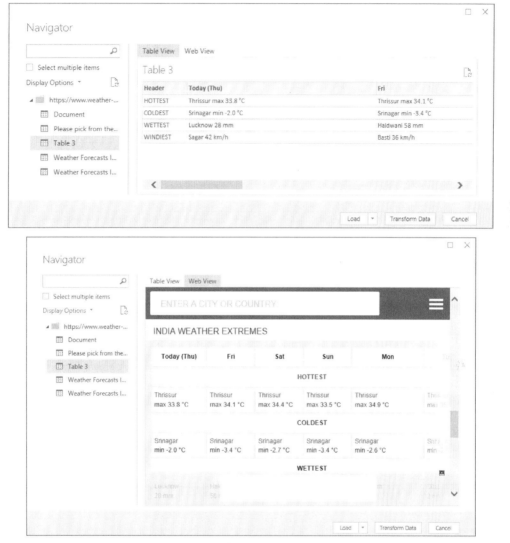

Figure 8-35: Import from Web – Navigator window

You can load the data directly into your worksheet or load it in the data model using the 'Load' and 'Load To…' options. In order to apply additional data transformations, click 'Transform Data' as shown in preceding example.

8.15.3 Import data from Table / Range

This connector can be used to create a new query that is linked to a table or named range in your Excel worksheet. Select the table or the named range in your worksheet and click 'Data->From Table/Range', the Power Query Editor window is launched with the imported data.

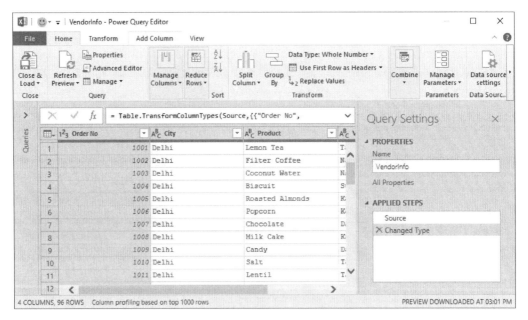

You can then refine your data and apply additional transformations to it in the Query Editor window.

8.15.4 Import data from Other sources

You can import data into Excel from a wide variety of data sources like JSON, XML, MS Access database, MS SQL Server database, Azure services, online services like SharePoint, and a wide variety of other sources like OData or ODBC. Click on 'Data > Get Data', the available data source options are organized in categories and presented to you in a drop-down menu as shown in screenshot below.

Figure 8-36: *Import data from other sources*

8.15.5 Refine data using Power Query Editor

Get and Transform lets you refine your data, that is, clean and shape data for a better analysis. You can remove columns, filter rows, change column data types, replace values and more. This is done through the dedicated Power Query Editor window that facilitates and displays all your data transformations.

The Power Query Editor records each step that is executed that is, whenever we connect to, transform, or combine data with other data sources and allows the user to undo, redo, change the order, or modify any step. The original data source remains unchanged after transformation, only the view changes.

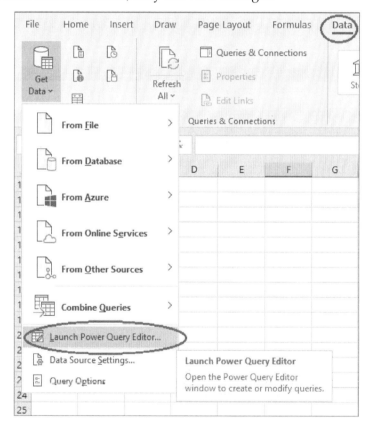

***Figure 8-37:** Launch Power Query Editor*

We will use a simple example to understand this feature. In a new workbook we will create a new query or import data from an existing Excel workbook that has the Sales data for the year 2018.

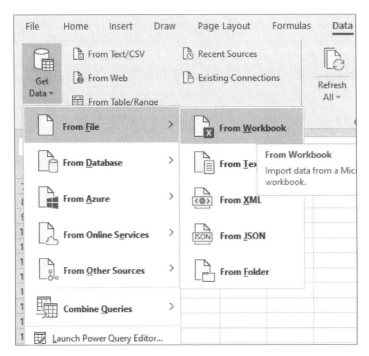

Select the workbook that has the source data and click Import.

From the Navigator Window, select the sheet that has the Sales data for the year 2018 and click on the option 'Load or Load To', this gives an option to view data as a table or only a connection.

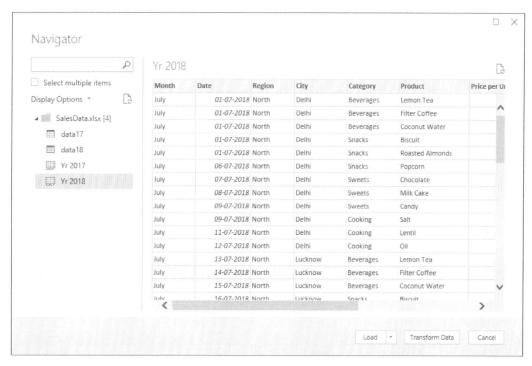

As shown in the preceding screenshot, select the sheet 'Yr 2018' to import the sales data for year 2018. Now select 'Load ->Load To' and in the Import Data dialog box click option 'Only Create Connection'. Click OK to create connection to the data.

Similarly, we will load the Sales data for the year 2017 by selecting the sheet 'Yr 2017' and import data with option of 'Only Create Connection'. On right hand side the workbook queries are displayed.

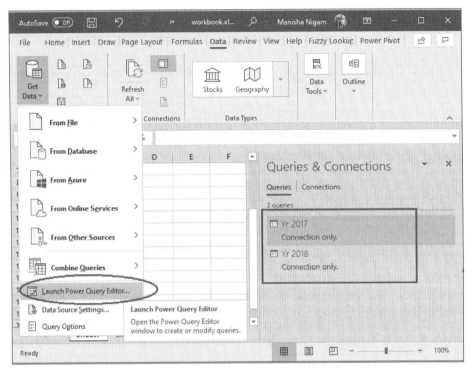

Now we will Launch the Power Query Editor and try to transform and merge the queries using the editor. Go to Data tab, under 'Get & Transform Data' group, select 'Get Data-> Launch Power Query Editor…' as shown in preceding screenshot.

The Query Editor has four tabs namely, Home, Transform, Add Column and View and Query Settings on the right-hand side of the window. Query Editor tracks each operation in the 'Applied Steps' section of the Query Settings pane. Transform tab has different options to change the view, Add column tab enables users to add new columns and View allows to change data preview

It's important to know that the actions we define in Query Editor don't change the original source data. Instead, Excel records each step and after we have finished shaping the data, takes a snapshot of the refined dataset and brings it into the workbook.

8.15.5.1 Remove Other Columns

In the example below, we will first remove columns that we do not want to see so that we have a clear view and then see how to merge the queries.

Select the columns that you want to view that is, Month, Date, Product & Total Sales; and go to option 'Home -> Remove Columns -> Remove Other Columns'.

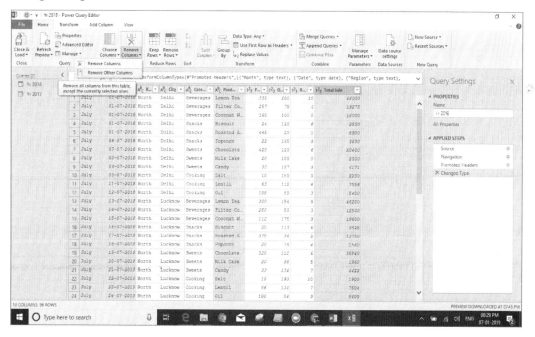

Note that in the 'Applied Steps' this operation has been recorded and in case we want to go back we can either Delete it (using the right-click option) or Click on the previous step.

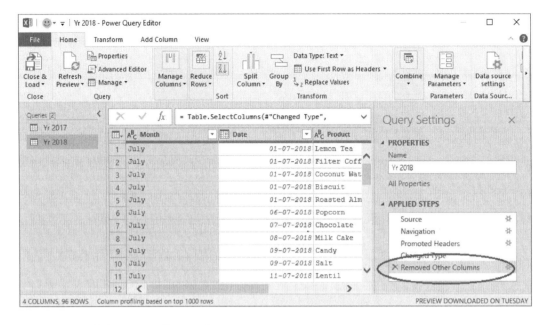

8.15.5.2 Merge Queries

We will now merge the queries by using the option 'Home -> Merge Queries'. In the Merge window the current query is shown, now we will select the other query in the dropdown list for merge. Also highlight the matching columns for merge, say 'Product' in this case and click OK with the default 'Join Kind' selected. There are different merging options or Join Kind, which are explained in chapter 8.15.6.

A new Column is added that contains the merged Sales data from the year 2017. This column has an expand icon and the rows say Table.

On clicking the expand icon on that column, we get a window in which we can again select the column we want to see. Select the check box of the desired columns and click OK.

The column is expanded to show Yr 2017's Product information and their corresponding Total Sale values.

Use 'File->Close & Load' to save the queries.

In order to view the columns that were removed earlier in the Query Editor, select 'Removed Other Columns' in the 'Applied Steps', right click and click 'Delete'.

Excel will ask for confirmation before deleting the step. Click 'Delete' on the 'Delete Step' dialog box. All the columns that were removed earlier get added in the Query Editor.

8.15.5.3 Add new Column by Examples

You can also add new columns of data in the Query Editor by simply providing one or more sample values for your new column. You can create a new column example from a current selection, or from providing input based on all (or selected) columns in a given table. In the Power Query Editor, go to 'Add Column-> Column From Examples-> From All Columns' as shown in screenshot below.

Power Query Editor adds a new column on the right-hand side of the data range. In the example given below, in row one type 'North, 66000' and press Ctrl + Enter. In the Merged column, data in all rows are filled automatically. Based on the value entered by the user, Power Query identifies the pattern, that is, 'Region, Total Sale' in the example below and fills data in other rows accordingly. Click 'OK' to confirm the changes.

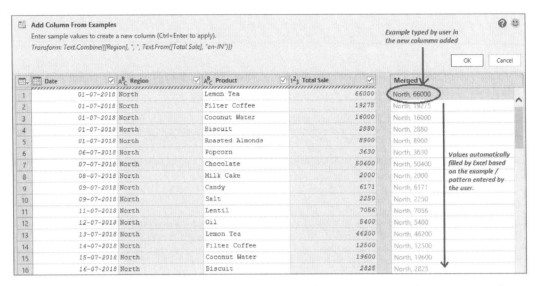

Note that in more complex data sets you may need to give Power Query two or three examples before it can correctly detect the pattern.

8.15.5.4 Insert a Custom Column

You can add an Index or Custom column to your current query in the Power Query Editor.

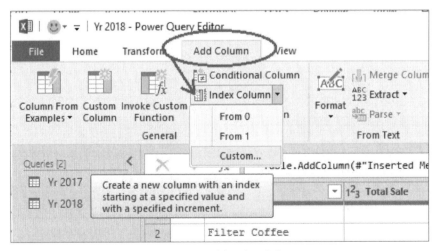

Figure 8-38: Add Index Column

To add an Index, go to 'Add column->Index Column' and select any one of the three options, that is, 'From 0' to create a new column with an Index starting at 0, 'From 1' to create a new column with an Index starting at 1 and 'Custom' in case you want to create a column with the Index starting at a specified value with specified increment.

In the 'Add Index custom' dialog box you can specify the 'Starting Index' and the 'Increment' as given in screenshot below.

Figure 8-39: Add Index Column (Custom)

You can also create a Custom Column, that is, you define the formula based on which the data will be populated in the column. To create a custom column, go to 'Add Column->Custom Column'.

Figure 8-40: Add Custom Column

In the Custom Column dialog box, you can specify the name of the new column to be added and the custom formula by using the available columns from the existing query. To create the custom formula, select the column from the 'Available Columns' list and click 'Insert'. You can use multiple reference columns as long as you separate them with some operator. In the example below, we are adding a new custom column named 'Net Sale' that will be calculated using the formula '[Total Sale] - ([Returned Units]*[Price per Unit])'.

Click OK to add the custom column in the existing query. To save the new column in the query, click 'File -> Close & Load'.

8.15.5.5 Split a Column

Query editor gives you options to split a column of text into multiple columns By Delimiter, By Number of Characters, By Positions, By Lowercase to Uppercase, By Uppercase to Lowercase, By Digit to Non-Digit and By Non-digit to Digit.

In the example below, we will split text in column 'Merged' by using a delimiter. Select the 'Merged' column and go to 'Home->Split Column->By Delimiter'.

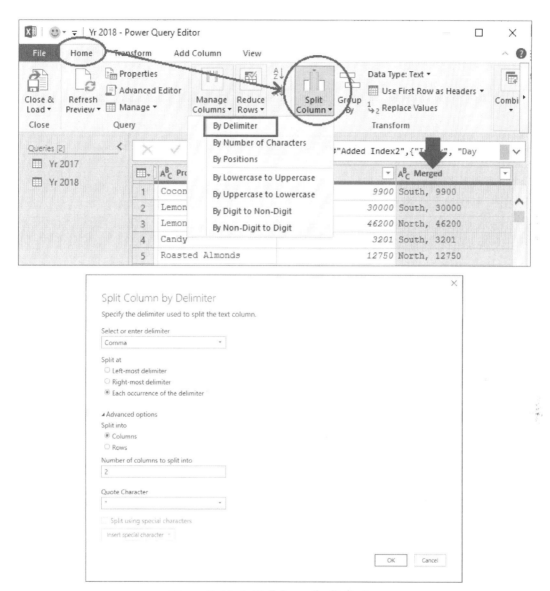

Figure 8-41: *Split Column By Delimiter*

In the 'Split Column by Delimiter' dialog box, you can select a delimiter from the existing list or create your own using the custom option. You can also specify the other parameters like the position to split at, whether it should be split into columns or rows etc. Click 'OK' to complete.

The text in the 'Merged' column is now split by the delimiter 'Comma' into two columns 'Merged.1' and 'Merged.2' as given in the preceding screenshot.

8.15.6 Different Merging options

Before we close this topic, we will quickly look at the different Join Kind (Merge Types), which is very important as we can get a totally different result set when choosing a different type of merge. There are six different kinds as seen in the following screenshot.

8.15.6.1 Left and Right tables/queries

Let's understand the concept of 'Left and Right' tables (or queries). When we merge two datasets with each other, the first query is considered as LEFT and the second as RIGHT. In the example below the Sales data of year 2018 is considered first and the data of year 2017 is second.

8.15.6.2 Join Kind / Merge types

Now we will look at the different Join Kind or Merge Type options available.

- Left Outer (All from first, matching from second) - This means the LEFT query is the important one. All records from this query (LEFT or FIRST) will be seen in the result set along with their matching rows in the right (or second table). In the LEFT Outer merge, only records from the Left table with matching rows from the right table will be selected.

- Right Outer (all rows from second, matching from first) - All rows from the RIGHT (or second) table will be seen with matching rows from the left (or first table).

- Full Outer (all rows from both) – As the name suggests, it will return all rows from both tables (matching and non-matching).

- Inner (only matching rows) - This method only selects matching rows. We will not have any record with null values (because these records are generated as a result of not matching)

- Left Anti (rows only in first) - This method only selects unmatched rows from the first table.

- Right Anti (rows only in second) - This method only selects unmatched rows from the second table.

8.15.7 Recent Sources and Existing Connections

You can connect and create query from the set of frequently used sources by clicking 'Data->Recent Sources'.

In the Recent Sources dialog box, you can then browse through your recently connected sources, select one, and then click 'Connect' to continue with the import flow.

You can view the existing connections in the workbook by clicking on 'Data->Existing Connections'.

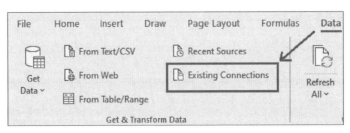

The Existing Connections dialog will appear, and you can then import from the available ODC (Office Database Connection) files, existing workbook connections or tables.

CHAPTER 9
Complex Data Analysis using ToolPak

Analysis ToolPak helps in developing complex statistical or engineering analyses. Users have to only provide the data to be analyzed and its required parameters for each analysis, and the tool uses the appropriate functions to calculate and display results. This reduces the challenge users face with no prior knowledge of statistics.

9.1 Enabling Analysis ToolPak in Excel

First, we need to make sure that we have the Analysis ToolPak enabled or added. Go to menu 'File-> Options-> Add-ins'. The Excel options window will display all the add-ins grouped as per their status. Confirm that Analysis ToolPak is under the active add-ins.

If not present, it can be added by selecting 'Excel Add-ins' under 'Options->Add-ins-> Manage' and click 'Go...' In the next window select the checkbox for Analysis ToolPak and click OK. Data Analysis option under Data should appear and on clicking it, a window is launched displaying the list of analysis tools. In this section we will discuss a few of these important tools.

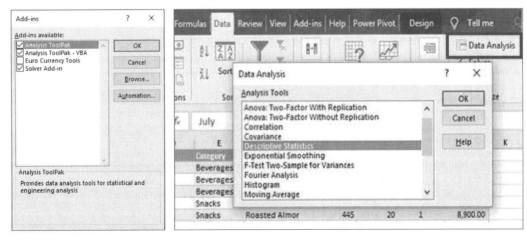

9.2 Descriptive Statistics in Excel

Descriptive statistics uses the data to provide a description of the population. Let us take a sample data of students age and use the Descriptive Statistics tool of Excel and see the details that it generates.

Age of Students: 3, 5, 7, 9, 4, 2, 2, 4, 6, 8, 15, 4, 20, 6, 10, 4, 5, 9, 11, 1, 6, 9, 4, 5, 13, 17, 7, 9, 6, 10

Put these figures in one column of Excel and select the option 'Data-> Data Analysis', and in the Data analysis window select 'Descriptive Statistics' and click OK. In the Descriptive Statistics dialog box, as shown in below screenshot, select the Input Range, set the Output Range and click the Summary Statistics check box and click OK.

The summary is added in two columns, starting with the cell specified in the output range. The first column is the descriptive statistic and the second is its corresponding value. The result of the Descriptive Statistics tool can be seen in below screenshot, in the cells ranging from D3 to E17; thirteen statistics are calculated by default. For better understanding, the meaning of each statistic has been shown in column G and in column H the corresponding Excel function that can be used independently for calculation.

	A	B	C	D	E	F	G	H
2		Age of Students						
3		3		*Age of Students*			Statistics Meaning	Excel function
4		5						
5		7		Mean	7.4		= average of the data values	=AVERAGE($B$3:$B$32)
6		9		Standard Error	0.8		= gives reliability of the mean	
7		4		Median	6.0		= middle value of the data set	=MEDIAN($B$3:$B$32)
8		2		Mode	4.0		= value that appears most often in the set	=MODE($B$3:$B$32)
9		2		Standard Deviation	4.5		= describes the spread of the data	=STDEV.P($B$3:$B$32)
10		4		Sample Variance	20.0		= deviation of a set of data from the mean value	=VAR.P($B$3:$B$32)
11		6		Kurtosis	1.3		= pointedness of a peak in the distribution	=KURT($B$3:$B$32)
12		8		Skewness	1.1		= measure of symmetry in distribution	=SKEW.P($B$3:$B$32)
13		15		Range	19.0		= difference between max and min value	
14		4		Minimum	1.0		= minimum value in the distribution	=MIN($B$3:$B$32)
15		20		Maximum	20.0		= maximum value in the distribution	=MAX($B$3:$B$32)
16		6		Sum	221.0		= total of the data values	=SUM($B$3:$B$32)
17		10		Count	30.0		= total number of values in the set	=Count($B$3:$B$32)
18		4						

For understanding the statistics in greater detail, please refer to the documentation or an expert related to the subject. This example is only intended to describe the capabilities of Excel and its usage for better data analysis.

9.3 ANOVA in Excel

Analysis of Variance (ANOVA) is a hypothesis testing technique; useful statistical function that lets you test different data sets to figure out the extent of difference among them. ANOVA analysis tools provide different types of variance analysis; Single Factor, Two Factor With/Without Replication.

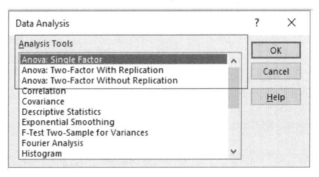

9.3.1 ANOVA: Single Factor

Single Factor or One-Way ANOVA is used to check whether there is any significant difference between the means of three or more unrelated groups.

First, we set up the hypothesis. ANOVA uses a Null hypothesis and an Alternate hypothesis.

$$H0: \mu1 = \mu2 = \mu3 = \ldots = \mu N \qquad \text{i.e., Null Hypothesis}$$

H1: μ1 ≠ μM; at least one of the means is different.   i.e., Alternate Hypothesis
where, μ1, μ2, μN are sample means and N is the number of samples.

The null hypothesis states that all the sample means are equal, or the factor did not have any significant effect on the results. Whereas, the alternate hypothesis states that at least one of the sample means is different from another. Let us understand this with the help of an example.

24 people were selected for testing weight loss methods. They were divided into 3 groups; 8 people who did only exercise, 8 people were put on a low-fat diet and 8 did exercise and followed the diet. Weight loss per kg by using different methods was recorded, as in table below.

	A	B	C	D	E	F	G	H	I	J
1										
2										
3					Weight Loss per kg					
4		Exercise	3	2	1	3	4	1	2	2
5		Low fat Diet	1	2	2	1	2	3	1	1
6		Exercise + Diet	3	5	4	2	3	5	2	2
7										

We can use ANOVA to compare these 3 weight loss methods and depict how different these samples are from one another. Here, weight is the only one factor. We will use the Excel ANOVA tools to generate the results. Go to 'Data -> Data Analysis' and select 'ANOVA Single Factor' and click OK. A window in launched, enter the Input Range, Output Range and click OK.

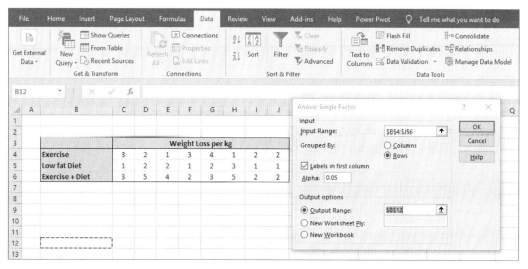

The result is displayed in the cells starting with the given Output Range.

◢	A	B	C	D	E	F	G	H
10								
11								
12		Anova: Single Factor						
13								
14		SUMMARY						
15		*Groups*	*Count*	*Sum*	*Average*	*Variance*		
16		Exercise	8	18	2.25	1.071428571		
17		Low fat Diet	8	13	1.625	0.553571429		
18		Exercise + Diet	8	26	3.25	1.642857143		
19								
20								
21		ANOVA						
22		*Source of Variation*	*SS*	*df*	*MS*	*F*	*P-value*	*F crit*
23		Between Groups	10.75	2	5.375	4.93442623	0.017512071	3.466800112
24		Within Groups	22.88	21	1.089285714			
25								
26		Total	33.63	23				
27								

where,

SS = Sum-of-Squares for between-group variability

df = degrees of freedom

MS = Measure of between-group variability i.e., SS / df

F = Between group variability / Within group variability

Between Group Variability' refers to the difference between the grand mean/ means of individual data samples. Within-Group Variability' is an indication of the variability factor inside individual data samples owing to the dissimilarity of various constituting sample values.

P-value = Calculated probability, is the probability of finding the observed, or more extreme, results when the null hypothesis (H 0) of a study question is true

F crit = F-critical value, determined by looking at the F distribution tables corresponding to alternative right-tail probabilities (α) / alpha level

Alpha Levels / Significance Levels = It is the probability of making the wrong decision when the null hypothesis is true. Most used alpha level is 0.05 that is 5%, that means the confidence level is 95%

Here we are concerned with 'F-value', which in this case is greater than the F-critical value for the alpha level selected (0.05). Therefore, we reject the null hypothesis and say that at least one of the three samples have significantly different means and thus belong to an entirely different population. Another measure is the 'p-value', which if it is less than the alpha level selected (0.05), we reject the null hypothesis.

ANOVA has a limitation that it does not tell us which groups are different. Hence, we need to drill down. A t-Test can be used here, to test each pair of mean to tell us exactly which groups have a difference in means.

9.3.2 t-Test following ANOVA

Two-Sample t-Test analysis tools test for equality of the population means that underlie each sample. In order to find which groups, have a difference in means in the above example, we will do the t-Test for the following group combinations; (i) Group 1 vs Group 2 (ii) Group 1 vs Group 3 (iii) Group 2 vs Group 3.

Go to 'Data-> Data Analysis' and select 't-Test': Two-Sample Assuming Equal Variances and click OK.

Enter the Cell Range for Group 1 and Group 2 in Variable 1 and Variable 2 Range respectively and specify the Output Range. The results are shown in three columns as seen in the following screenshot.

	A	B	C	D	E	F	G	H	I	J	K	L	M	N
1														
2														
3			Weight Loss per kg									t-Test: Two-Sample Assuming Equal Variances		
4	Group 1	Exercise	3	2	1	3	4	1	2	2				
5	Group 2	Low fat Diet	1	2	2	1	2	3	1	1			Group 1	Group 2
6	Group 3	Exercise + Diet	3	5	4	2	3	5	2	2		Mean	2.25	1.625
7												Variance	1.071428571	0.553571429
8												Observations	8	8
9												Pooled Variance	0.8125	
10												Hypothesized Mean Difference	0	
11												df	14	
12												t Stat	1.386750491	
13												P(T<=t) one-tail	0.093601746	
14												t Critical one-tail	1.761310136	
15												P(T<=t) two-tail	0.187203492	
16												t Critical two-tail	2.144786688	

We will repeat the same process for the other two group combinations and compare the results.

	K	L	M	N	O	P	Q	R	S	T	U	V
1												
2												
3		t-Test: Two-Sample Assuming Equal Variances				t-Test: Two-Sample Assuming Equal Variances				t-Test: Two-Sample Assuming Equal Variances		
4												
5			Group 1	Group 2			Group 1	Group 3			Group 2	Group 3
6		Mean	2.25	1.625		Mean	2.25	3.25		Mean	1.625	3.25
7		Variance	1.071428571	0.553571429		Variance	1.07142857	1.6428571		Variance	0.553571429	1.642857143
8		Observations	8	8		Observations	8	8		Observations	8	8
9		Pooled Variance	0.8125			Pooled Variance	1.35714286			Pooled Variance	1.098214286	
10		Hypothesized Mean Difference	0			Hypothesized Mean Difference	0			Hypothesized Mean Difference	0	
11		df	14			df	14			df	14	
12		t Stat	1.386750491			t Stat	-1.7167902			t Stat	-3.101271703	
13		P(T<=t) one-tail	0.093601746			P(T<=t) one-tail	0.05402459			P(T<=t) one-tail	0.003906316	
14		t Critical one-tail	1.761310136			t Critical one-tail	1.76131014			t Critical one-tail	1.761310136	
15		P(T<=t) two-tail	0.187203492			P(T<=t) two-tail	0.10804918			P(T<=t) two-tail	0.007812632	
16		t Critical two-tail	2.144786688			t Critical two-tail	2.14478669			t Critical two-tail	2.144786688	

We are interested in the p values, highlighted in yellow. P value for Group 2 and Group 3 is less than the alpha level selected (0.05), which means that Group 2 and Group 3 have less than 5% chance of belonging to the same population.

9.3.3 ANOVA: Two Factor with Replication

This analysis tool is useful when data can be classified along two different dimensions. Let us understand using the following example.

A children health drink company did a test on 16 students from two schools in 3 different age groups. Students of school A drank the health drink for over a year before the tests were conducted, while the students of school B did not. The following table shows the test scores.

	Age Group (yrs)		
Group	2 to 5 yrs	5 to 8 yrs	8 to 12 yrs
A (Health Drink)	6	4	8
	5	6	9
	2	9	7
	4	8	6
	5	5	9
	5	6	10
	2	9	7
	4	8	6
B (No Drink)	1	5	6
	3	4	4
	2	5	6
	1	3	6
	1	4	8
	2	5	5
	1	6	8
	3	3	7

Now since we have 2 factors; Age and Health drink and have 8 observations for each combination, we will use Two Factor with Replication. Go to 'Data-> Data Analysis' and select 'ANOVA: Two Factor with Replication' and click OK.

	Age Group (yrs)		
Group	2 to 5 yrs	5 to 8 yrs	8 to 12 yrs
A (Health Drink)	6	4	8
	5	6	9
	2	9	7
	4		
	5		
	5		
	2		
	4		
B (No Drink)	1		
	3		
	2		
	1		
	1	4	8
	2	5	5
	1	6	8
	3	3	7

Data Analysis

Analysis Tools

Anova: Single Factor
Anova: Two-Factor With Replication
Anova: Two-Factor Without Replication
Correlation
Covariance
Descriptive Statistics
Exponential Smoothing
F-Test Two-Sample for Variances
Fourier Analysis
Histogram

OK   Cancel   Help

Enter the Input Range which is, the complete data set. Rows per Sample is 8 in this case as we have 8 observations each and enter the Output Range to the desired cell where you want the results to be displayed.

First screenshot:

	A	B	C	D	E	F	G	H	I	J	K
2				**Age Group (yrs)**							
3		**Group**	2 to 5 yrs	5 to 8 yrs	8 to 12 yrs						
4		A (Health Drink)	6	4	8						
5			5	6	9						
6			2	9	7						
7			4	8	6						
8			5	5	9						
9			5	6	10						
10			2	9	7						
11			4	8	6						
12		B (No Drink)	1	5	6						
13			3	4	4						
14			2	5	6						
15			1	3	6						
16			1	4	8						
17			2	5	5						
18			1	6	8						
19			3	3	7						

Anova: Two-Factor With Replication ? ✕

Input
Input Range: $B$3:$E$19
Rows per sample: 8
Alpha: 0.05

Output options
● Output Range: $G$2
○ New Worksheet Ply:
○ New Workbook

OK
Cancel
Help

Second screenshot:

	A	B	C	D	E	F	G	H	I	J	K	L	M
2				Age Group (yrs)			Anova: Two-Factor With Replication						
3		Group	2 to 5 yrs	5 to 8 yrs	8 to 12 yrs								
4		A (Health Drink)	6	4	8		SUMMARY	2 to 5 yrs	5 to 8 yrs	8 to 12 yrs	Total		
5			5	6	9		*A (Health Drink)*						
6			2	9	7		Count	8	8	8	24		
7			4	8	6		Sum	33	55	62	150		
8			5	5	9		Average	4.125	6.875	7.75	6.25		
9			5	6	10		Variance	2.125	3.55357	2.21428571	4.8913		
10			2	9	7								
11			4	8	6		*B (No Drink)*						
12		B (No Drink)	1	5	6		Count	8	8	8	24		
13			3	4	4		Sum	14	35	50	99		
14			2	5	6		Average	1.75	4.375	6.25	4.125		
15			1	3	6		Variance	0.78571	1.125	1.92857143	4.72283		
16			1	4	8								
17			2	5	5		*Total*						
18			1	6	8		Count	16	16	16			
19			3	3	7		Sum	47	90	112			
20							Average	2.9375	5.625	7			
21							Variance	2.8625	3.85	2.53333333			
24							ANOVA						
25							*Source of Variation*	SS	df	MS	F	P-value	F crit
26							Sample (Rows)	54.1875	1	54.1875	27.7123	4.5E-06	4.07265
27							Columns	136.625	2	68.3125	34.9361	1.2E-09	3.21994
28							Interaction	2.375	2	1.1875	0.60731	0.54953	3.21994
29							Within	82.125	42	1.95535714			
31							Total	275.313	47				

Based on the results we will determine if either of two categorical factors; that is Age and Health Drink and/or the interaction between these two factors, has had a significant effect on the data set.

The P-value of the two factors individually is less than the alpha level (0.05), so we can say that the effect of Age and Health Drink is statistically significant. P-value for interaction is greater than alpha level, so the interaction effect between Age and Health Drink is not statistically significant.

Check the F value against the F-crit value. If the F value is greater than the F critical value it indicates that there is a significant difference between the test scores.

9.3.4 ANOVA: Two Factor without Replication

For this tool it is assumed that there is only a single observation for each pair.

		Age Group (yrs)		
Group		2 to 5 yrs	5 to 8 yrs	8 to 12 yrs
A (Health Drink)		6	4	8
B (No Drink)		1	5	6

Go to 'Data-> Data Analysis' and select 'ANOVA: Two Factor without Replication' and click OK.

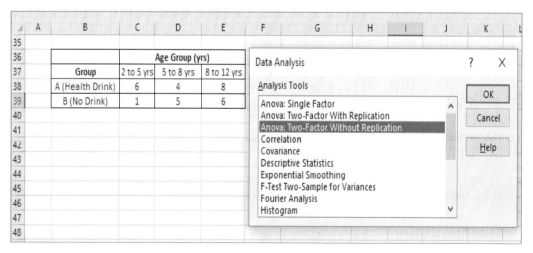

Specify the Input and Output Range and click OK.

Interpretation of the results is the same as before. We again look at the p-Value and the F value against the F-crit.

CHAPTER 10
Forecasting in Excel

Forecasting is the process of making predictions of the future based on historical time-based data (past and present data), commonly by analysis of trends. The ability to forecast helps in effective and efficient planning, for example predicting things like future sales, inventory requirements, or consumer trends. In Excel the one-click forecasting features, that is, the Forecast Sheet along with new forecasting sheet functions have been introduced for better and ease of forecasting. Excel also has analysis tools like 'What-if Analysis' tools to help predict the future. What-If Analysis in Excel allows you to try out different scenarios for formulas/data, even when the data is incomplete.

10.1 Forecast Sheet - One-click forecasting

'Forecast Sheet' option is available in Excel on the 'Data' tab, under the Forecast group. We will create a Forecast Sheet for our existing Sales data (including timelines and sales values) to predict future sales. It must be noted that in order to use this feature and get accurate results, the data set should have two data series that is, with date/time entries for timelines and corresponding values like sales and so on. And the timelines should have consistent intervals between its data points. For example, timelines can have monthly intervals (with values on the 1st of every month), yearly intervals, or numerical intervals. Forecasts will still be accurate if the timeline series is missing up to 30% of the data points or has several numbers with the same time stamp.

10.1.1 Create Forecast Worksheet

Open the Excel sheet with the time-based sales data for which forecast is to be created. To create a forecast, select any cell in the data series and go to the 'Data' tab, in the 'Forecast' group select 'Forecast sheet' option. Excel automatically selects the rest of the data and a 'Create Forecast Worksheet' dialog box is launched.

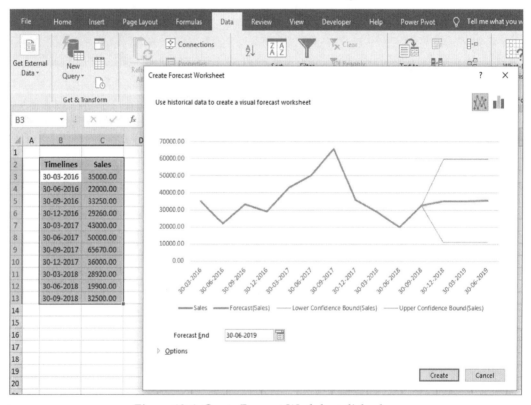

Figure 10-1: Create Forecast Worksheet dialog box

Click 'Create' on the 'Create Forecast Worksheet'. Excel creates a new worksheet that contains both a table of the historical and predicted values, and a chart that expresses this data.

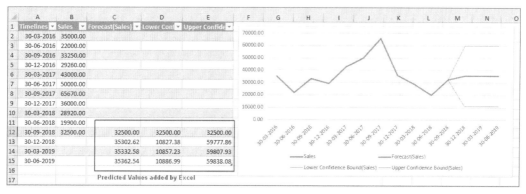

Figure 10-2: *New Forecast Sheet with table & graph*

10.1.2 Customize Forecast using Options

In the above section we created the forecast with default settings. Excel allows for various customizations, click Options to change the Chart type, Forecast End/Start dates, and so on.

Figure 10-3: *Forecast Options*

- Confidence Level - The confidence interval helps to figure out the accuracy of the prediction. It is the range surrounding each predicted value —in which 95% (default value) of future points are expected to fall—based on the forecast (with normal distribution). A smaller interval implies more confidence in predicting a specific point.

- Seasonality - It is a number for the length (number of points) of the seasonal pattern and is automatically detected. By choosing 'Set Manually' and picking a number, you can override the automatic detection. For example, in a yearly sales cycle, with each point representing a month, the seasonality is 12. For this to work properly it's better to have more repeating cycles in the historical data, at least 2–3 full seasonal cycles.

- Timeline Range – You can change the timeline range. Note that when changing the timeline range the corresponding values range also needs to be changed.

- Values Range – You can change the value range keeping in mind that both Timeline Range and Value Range need to be identical.

- Fill Missing Points Using – In case the data series have some missing points, Excel uses interpolation, meaning that a missing point will be completed as the weighted average of its neighboring points as long as fewer than 30% of the points are missing. To treat the missing points as zeros instead, click Zeros in the list.

- Aggregate Duplicates Using - In case the data contains multiple values with the same timestamp, Excel will average the values. You can use another calculation method from the list such as Median, Sum and so on.

- Include Forecast Statistics – If checked, additional statistical information on the forecast will be included in a new worksheet.

- Forecast Start: You can specify the date for the forecast to begin. To get an idea of the accuracy of the forecast, try changing the forecast start date to a date before the last historical point. This allows you to see how your prediction would have looked had it been calculated only over the earlier subset.

In our Sales example, we have changed the Forecast Start date to a date before the last historical data, seen in the following screenshot. Forecasted values or predictions are close to the actual values.

Figure 10-4: *Forecast Sheet with forecast statistics*

10.2 FORECAST Functions

Excel has new forecasting functions that are used for predicting future values. Even when we use the one-click forecasting feature for creating Forecast Sheets (see 10.1), Excel uses FORCAST functions for calculations.

Go to the Forecast Sheet created, as in example shown in Figure 10-4. Go to the 'Formulas' tab and select 'Show Formulas' from the 'Formula Auditing' group. All the formulas used by Excel to predict the future values and the formulas used for showing forecast statistics are shown instead of values in the Excel worksheet.

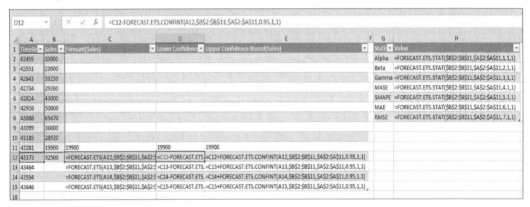

Figure 10-5: Forecast sheet with Formulas

10.2.1 FORECAST.ETS

Calculates or predicts a future value based on existing (historical) values by using the AAA version of the Exponential Smoothing (ETS) algorithm. The predicted value is a continuation of the historical values in the specified target date, which should be a continuation of the timeline.

Syntax is

"=FORECAST.ETS(target date, values, timeline, [seasonality], [data completion], [aggregation])"

For predicting the value of A12 in example given in Figure 95, the formula used is

"=FORECAST.ETS(A12, $B$2:$B$11, $A$2:$A$11, 1, 1)" where,

Argument	Value	Description
target date	A12	***30-09-2018*** – The data point for which you want to predict a value

Contd...

Values	$B$2:$B$11	**Sales values** – The historical values, for which you want to forecast the next points
timeline	$A$2:$A$11	**Dates** – The timelines corresponding to the values
seasonality	1	**Detect Automatically** was selected in Options, in the Forecast Sheet example (which Excel automatically calculates).
		Optional parameter, Default is 1.
		0 indicates no seasonality, meaning the prediction will be linear. Positive whole numbers will indicate to the algorithm to use patterns of this length as the seasonality.
data completion	1	**Filling Missing Points Using** – **Interpolation** was selected in Options, in the Forecast Sheet example.
		Optional parameter, Default is 1.
		0 will indicate the algorithm to account for missing points as zeros.
aggregation	omitted	**Aggregate Duplicates Using** – **Average** was selected in Options, in the Forecast Sheet example.
		Optional parameter, Default is 1.
		The default value of 1 will use AVERAGE, while other options are 2-COUNT, 3-COUNTA, 4-MAX, 5-MEDIAN, 6-MIN, 7-SUM

10.2.2 FORECAST.ETS.CONFINT

Returns a confidence interval for the forecast value at the specified target date. A confidence interval of 95% means that 95% of future points are expected to fall within this radius from the result FORECAST.ETS forecasted (with normal distribution). Using a confidence interval can help grasp the accuracy of the predicted model. A smaller interval would imply more confidence in the prediction for this specific point.

Syntax is

"=FORECAST.ETS.CONFINT(target date, values, timeline, [confidence level], [seasonality], [data completion], [aggregation])"

For calculating the Upper and Lower Confidence bounds of A12 in example given in Figure 95, the formulas used are

"=C12+FORECAST.ETS.CONFINT(A12, $B$2:$B$11, $A$2:$A$11, 0.95, 1, 1)" and

"=C12-FORECAST.ETS.CONFINT(A12, $B$2:$B$11, $A$2:$A$11, 0.95, 1, 1)"

Note that to calculate the Upper bound, the C12 value is added to the result of the FORECAST.ETS.CONFINT function, while it is subtracted in case of Lower bound calculation. FORECAST.ETS.CONFINT function is the same that is,

"=FORECAST.ETS.CONFINT(A12, $B$2:$B$11, $A$2:$A$11, 0.95, 1, 1)" where,

Argument	Value	Description
target date	A12	***30-09-2018*** – The data point for which you want to predict a value
Values	$B$2:$B$11	***Sales values*** – The historical values, for which you want to forecast the next points
timeline	$A$2:$A$11	***Dates*** – The timelines corresponding to the values
confidence level	0.95	***Confidence Interval - 95%*** was selected in Options, in the Forecast Sheet example. Optional parameter. A numerical value between 0 and 1 (exclusive), indicating a confidence level for the calculated confidence interval
seasonality	1	***Detect Automatically*** was selected in Options, in Forecast Sheet example (which Excel automatically calculates). Optional parameter, Default is 1. 0 indicates no seasonality, meaning the prediction will be linear. Positive whole numbers will indicate to the algorithm to use patterns of this length as the seasonality.
data completion	1	***Filling Missing Points Using – Interpolation*** was selected in Options, in Forecast Sheet example. Optional parameter, Default is 1. 0 will indicate the algorithm to account for missing points as zeros.
aggregation	omitted	***Aggregate Duplicates Using – Average*** was selected in Options, in Forecast Sheet example. Optional parameter, Default is 1. The default value of 1 will use AVERAGE, while other options are 2-COUNT, 3-COUNTA, 4-MAX, 5-MEDIAN, 6-MIN, 7-SUM

10.2.3 FORECAST.ETS.STAT

The Excel FORECAST.ETS.STAT function calculates a specified statistical value, relating to a time series forecasting.

Syntax is

"=FORECAST.ETS.STAT(values, timeline, statistic type, [seasonality], [data completion], [aggregation])"

For displaying the Forecast Statistics in the example given in Figure 95, the formula used is "=FORECAST.ETS.STAT($B$2:$B$11, $A$2:$A$11, **1**, 1, 1)" where the third parameter changes from 1 to 8 for different statistics.

Argument	Value	Description
Values	$B$2:$B$11	*Sales values* – The historical values, for which you want to forecast the next points
timeline	$A$2:$A$11	*Dates* – The timelines corresponding to the values
statistic type	1-8	See the following table
seasonality	1	*Detect Automatically* was selected in Options, in the Forecast Sheet example (which Excel automatically calculates). Optional parameter, Default is 1. 0 indicates no seasonality, meaning the prediction will be linear. Positive whole numbers will indicate to the algorithm to use patterns of this length as the seasonality.
data completion	1	*Filling Missing Points Using – Interpolation* was selected in Options, in the Forecast Sheet example. Optional parameter, Default is 1. 0 will indicate the algorithm to account for missing points as zeros.
aggregation	omitted	*Aggregate Duplicates Using – Average* was selected in Options, in the Forecast Sheet example. Optional parameter, Default is 1. The default value of 1 will use AVERAGE, while other options are 2-COUNT, 3-COUNTA, 4-MAX, 5-MEDIAN, 6-MIN, 7-SUM

Statistic Type

Alpha	Alpha parameters of ETS algorithm. Returns the **base value parameter**—a higher value gives more weight to recent data points.
Beta	Beta parameter of ETS algorithm. Returns the **trend value parameter**—a higher value gives more weight to the recent trend.

Contd…

Gamma	Gamma parameter of ETS algorithm. Returns the **seasonality value parameter**—a higher value gives more weight to the recent seasonal period.
MASE metric	Returns the **mean absolute scaled error metric**—a measure of the accuracy of forecasts.
SMAPE metric	Returns the **symmetric mean absolute percentage error** metric—an accuracy measure based on percentage errors
MAE metric	Returns the **mean absolute percentage error** metric—an accuracy measure based on percentage errors
RMSE metric	Returns the **root mean squared error metric**—a measure of the differences between predicted and observed values.
Step size detected	Returns the **step size** detected in the historical timeline.

10.3 What-if Analysis Tools

What-If Analysis in Excel allows you to try out different values or scenarios for formulas. We will use an example to understand the different What-if analysis tools; Scenario Manager, Goal Seek, Data Table, and Solver. These tools are available on the 'Data' tab, in 'Forecast' and 'Analyze' groups.

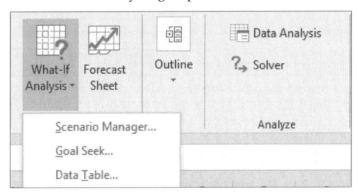

Figure 10-6: What-if Analysis tools

10.3.1 Scenario Manager

Using the 'What-if Analysis' tool 'Scenario Manager', you can create and save different scenarios that is, different input values that create different results. For example, a vendor wants to know the profit that he could make from his sale of Mangos at different price units.

Currently the vendor is selling 50% of the total number at the highest price and 50% at the lowest price, as seen in the following screenshot.

◢	A	B	C	D	E
1					
2		**Vendor Item : Mango**			
3		**Total Number**	150		
4					
5			**%age**	**Unit Price**	**Num**
6		Highest Price	50%	60	75
7		Lowest Price	50%	35	75
8					
9			**Total Profit**	**7125.00**	

Now he wants to know the profit if he sells different percentages (60%, 70%, 80%, 90%, and 100%) of Mangos at the highest price. One way is to create a table manually with different percentages like the one above and then calculate the total profits. Another easier way is to use the 'Scenario Manager' wherein each different percentage is a different scenario.

Go to the 'Data' tab, in the 'Forecast' group, click on 'What-if Analysis' and select 'Scenario Manager' (see Figure 10-6). A Scenario Manager dialog box is launched.

Figure 10-7: *What-if Analysis: Scenario Manager*

Following are the steps to be followed to create Scenarios.

Step 1: Click on 'Add…' in the 'Scenario Manager' dialog box (Figure 10-7) and the 'Edit Scenario' dialog box is launched. Type the name of the scenario, enter the cell C6 in the 'Changing Cells' field that is, the highest percentage value. Add any comments you want and click OK.

Figure 10-8: *Scenario manager – Step 1*

Step 2: Enter the corresponding value 0.5 (that is, for 50%) in the Scenario Values, and click 'Add'.

Step 3: Create/Add new scenarios for the percentages 60%, 70%, 80%, 90%, and 100%. Go to 'Scenario Manager', click 'Add' and follow Step 1 & 2 to add the scenarios. The Scenario Manager dialog box will show all the scenarios as given below.

Figure 10-9: *Multiple Scenarios*

<u>*Step 4*</u>: To see the result, select the scenario you want to view and click 'Show'. The value in C6 cell will change that is, if you select scenario named '80% at Highest Price' the value of C6 will be 80% and the total profit gets calculated accordingly.

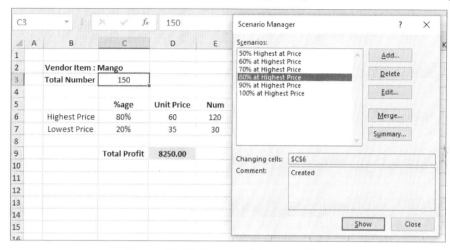

Figure 10-10: *Scenario Manager: Show*

In this case, you see the result of one scenario at a time. To see results for all the different scenarios, click on 'Summary...'. In the 'Scenario Summary' dialog box, select the report type and enter D9 in the result cells that is, the 'Total Profit' value cell in the sheet and click OK.

Figure 10-11: *Scenario summary*

A new worksheet named 'Scenario Summary' is created by Excel with the consolidated results of all the scenarios created.

	Current Values:	50% Highest at Price	60% at Highest Price	70% at Highest Price	80% at Highest Price	90% at Highest Price	100% at Highest Price
Scenario Summary							
Changing Cells:							
$C$6	80%	50%	60%	70%	80%	90%	100%
Result Cells:							
$D$9	8250.00	7125.00	7500.00	7875.00	8250.00	8625.00	9000.00

Notes: Current Values column represents values of changing cells at
time Scenario Summary Report was created. Changing cells for each
scenario are highlighted in gray.

Figure 10-12: *Scenario Summary sheet*

If the 'Report Type' was selected as 'Scenario PivotTable Report' then a new worksheet named 'Scenario PivotTable' is created by Excel.

	A	B	C
1	$C$6 by	(All) ▼	
2			
3	Row Labels ▼	$D$9	
4	100% at Highest Price	9000	
5	50% Highest at Price	7125	
6	60% at Highest Price	7500	
7	70% at Highest Price	7875	
8	80% at Highest Price	8250	
9	90% at Highest Price	8625	
10			

Figure 10-13: Scenario PivotTable Report

10.3.2 Goal Seek

Scenario manager is good for known variables, however, sometimes it is desirable to work backwards. Goal Seek is in a way opposite to the Scenario Manager that is, you start with the desired result, and it calculates the input value that will give you that result.

Using the same example of selling Mangos, now the vendor wants to know how many will have to be sold at the highest price to make a profit of say 8500. Go to the 'Data' tab, in the 'Forecast' group select 'What-if Analysis' and click on 'Goal Seek' (see Figure 10-6).

Figure 10-14: Goal Seek

In the 'Goal Seek' dialog box, select D9 in 'Set Cell' field (the Total Profit cell), in the 'To value' enter 8500 (the goal to achieve) and select C6 in the 'By changing cell' and click OK. The 'Goal Seek Status' dialog is opened, and the worksheet is updated to show that the vendor will have to sell 87% Mangos at the Highest price to make a profit of 8500. Click OK to close the Goal Seek Status dialog box.

Figure 10-15: *Goal Seek Status*

10.3.3 Data Table

Data Table lets you see how changing one or two values will affect the bottom line, by creating one variable data table or a two variable data table respectively.

10.3.3.1 One Variable Data Table

In previous section we created different scenarios using 'Scenario Manager', to know the total profits that vendor will make on selling different numbers (%) of Mangos at the highest price (see 10.3.1) and also created the Scenario Summary (see Figure 10-12). Instead of creating scenarios, we can also use Data Table to do the same thing.

In cell C12 type the formula '=D9' to get the 'Total Profit' value and in the column B that is, cell range B13-B17, enter the different percentages (Mangos to be sold at highest price) for which we want to find the 'Total Profits'. Select the cell range B12 to C17 and go to the 'Data' tab, in the 'Forecast' group select 'What-if Analysis' and click on 'Data Table'.

Figure 10-16: *Data Table dialog box – one variable*

Click on the 'Column input cell' box (as the percentages are in a column) and select cell C6 because the percentages refer to cell C6 (% sold for the highest price). With the formula in cell C12, Excel knows that it should replace cell C6 with 60% to calculate the total profit, replace cell C6 with 70% to calculate the total profit, and so on. Click Ok and the corresponding total profit values are inserted against the percentages.

	A	B	C	D	E
4					
5			%age	Unit Price	Num
6		Highest Price	50%	60	75
7		Lowest Price	50%	35	75
8					
9			Total Profit	7125.00	
10					
11					
12			7125.00		
13		60%	7500		
14		70%	7875		
15		80%	8250		
16		90%	8625		
17		100%	9000		
18					

Figure 10-17: One Variable Data Table Result

10.3.3.2 Two Variable Data Table

Now if we want to also see what the profits will be if the unit price is also changed along with the percentage, we can make use of the two variable data table.

In cell B12 type the formula '=D9', type the different percentages in column B in cells B13 to B17 and type the different unit price in row 12 in cells C12 to E12. Select the cell range B12 to E17, go to the 'Data' tab, in the 'Forecast' group select 'What-if Analysis', and then click on 'Data Table…'.

	A	B	C	D	E	F	G	H	I
4									
5			%age	Unit Price	Num				
6		Highest Price	50%	60	75				
7		Lowest Price	50%	35	75				
8									
9			Total Profit	7125.00					
10									
11									
12		7125.00	60	75	85	Data Table		?	✕
13		60%							
14		70%				Row input cell:		$D$6	⬆
15		80%				Column input cell:		$C$6	⬆
16		90%							
17		100%				OK		Cancel	
18									

Figure 10-18: Data Table dialog box – two variables

Click on the 'Row input cell' box (the unit prices are in a row) and select cell D6. And in the 'Column input cell' box (the percentages are in a column) select cell C6. Together with the formula in cell B12, Excel knows that it should replace cell D6 with 60 and cell C6 with 60% to calculate the total profit, replace cell D6 with 60 and cell C4 with 70% to calculate the total profit, and so on. Click Ok and the corresponding total profit values are inserted in the two-dimensional table.

	A	B	C	D	E	F
4						
5			%age	Unit Price	Num	
6		Highest Price	50%	60	75	
7		Lowest Price	50%	35	75	
8						
9			Total Profit	7125.00		
10						
11						
12		7125.00	60	75	85	
13		60%	7500	8850	9750	
14		70%	7875	9450	10500	
15		80%	8250	10050	11250	
16		90%	8625	10650	12000	
17		100%	9000	11250	12750	
18						

Figure 10-19: *Two Variable Data Table Result*

Results show that if 60% of the Mangos are sold at the highest price of 60, the total profit is 7500 and if they are sold at the highest price of 85, the total profit is 9750, and so on.

10.3.4 Solver Add-In

Solver is a Microsoft Excel add-in program you can use for what-if analysis. Solver can be used to find an optimal (maximum or minimum) value for a formula in one cell (called the objective cell) subject to constraints, or limits, on the values of other formula cells on a worksheet.

Make sure that Solver Add-in is active. Go to the 'File' menu and select 'Options'. In the 'Excel Options' dialog box, go to Add-Ins and ensure that Solver Add-in is active.

If not active, then for 'Manage' select 'Excel Add-Ins' and click 'Go…'.

Select the checkbox for 'Solver Add-In' and click Ok. Solver Add-In will now be shown under the Active Application Add-Ins and also in the 'Data' tab under the 'Analysis' group (see Figure 10-6).

To see how Solver helps in solving a problem, we will use the following example.

A vendor sells three types of fruits; Mangos, Apples, and Strawberries; and makes a unit profit of 300,150 and 80 respectively. The total capital available to him is 50000 and the total space is 250. Also known is the amount of space and capital that each unit of fruit requires. All the information has been put in a worksheet as given below. In order to maximize his profits, the vendor wants to know the optimal order (that is, how many to order of each fruit type), taking into consideration the space and capital constraints he has.

	A	B	C	D	E	F	G
1							
2			Unit Profit	Space Req per unit	Capital Req per unit	Order	
3		Mangos	300	3	85	0	
4		Apples	150	2	120	0	
5		Strawberries	80	5	74	0	
6							
7		Space Available	250		Space Utilized	0	
8		Capital Available	50000		Capital Utilized	0	
9							
10					Total Profit	0	

Now let us understand the problem we want to solve and the information we know which will help us in using the Solver tool.

Objective: Vendor needs to know optimal number of fruits to order of each type (Mangos, Apples and Strawberries) to maximize the Total Profit.

Constraints: Vendor has a limited amount of space (250) and capital (50000). So, order should be such that it is within these limits, knowing that each Mango uses 3 units of space and 85 units of capital, Apples uses 2 and 120, and Strawberries uses 5 and 74 units respectively.

To ease our calculations, we defined names for cell ranges and added formulas in the sheet. Defined names are as shown in the Names Manager dialog box. Go to 'Formulas' tab, select 'Name Manager', where you will see the existing or defined names in the dialog box. You can create new defined names or named ranges by clicking on 'New' (see 3.3).

These defined names are used in the formulas using the SUMPRODUCT function (see function details in section 3.10.5) to calculate the utilization and total profits, as given in the following screenshot.

| Profits | ▾ | ⋮ | × | ✓ | *fx* | =SUMPRODUCT(UnitProfit,order) |

	A	B	C	D	E	F	G
1							
2			Unit Profit	Space Req per unit	Capital Req per unit	Order	
3		Mangos	300	3	85	0	
4		Apples	150	2	120	0	
5		Strawberries	80	5	74	0	
6							
7		Space Available	250		Space Utilized	0	=SUMPRODUCT(SpaceReqd,order)
8		Capital Available	50000		Capital Utilized	0	=SUMPRODUCT(CapitalReqd,order)
9							
10					Total Profit	0	=SUMPRODUCT(UnitProfit,order)
11							

Now using this sheet, we can manually put values in Order and try out some permutations and combinations to find the optimal values. Below are two such combinations, wherein first the storage used is 241 that is, within the limit 250 and total profit is 10360, while in the second the storage utilization is maximum 250 but the total profit is less 7850 than first one.

	A	B	C	D	E	F
1						⬇
2			Unit Profit	Space Req per unit	Capital Req per unit	Order
3		Mangos	300	3	85	23
4		Apples	150	2	120	6
5		Strawberries	80	5	74	32
6						⬇
7		Space Available	250		Space Utilized	241
8		Capital Available	50000		Capital Utilized	5043
9						
10					Total Profit	10360

	A	B	C	D	E	F
1						⬇
2			Unit Profit	Space Req per unit	Capital Req per unit	Order
3		Mangos	300	3	85	12
4		Apples	150	2	120	7
5		Strawberries	80	5	74	40
6						⬇
7		Space Available	250		Space Utilized	250
8		Capital Available	50000		Capital Utilized	4820
9						
10					Total Profit	7850

Here is where Solver helps us in getting an optimal solution without manually trying out different combinations. Go to the 'Data' tab, in the 'Analysis' group click on 'Solver' and the Solver Parameters window gets launched. Enter 'Profits' that is, the defined name for cell F10, for Objective, click on Max, enter 'order' that is, F3:F5 for Changing Variable cells, and select the 'Simplex LP' solving method. For adding a constraint, click on 'Add' and enter the values in the dialog box which are, F7:F8 (Used) <= C7:C8 (Available). Click on OK to go back to the Solver Parameters window.

Figure 10-20: Solver: Add Constraints dialog box

Figure 10-21: Solver Parameters

Click on 'Solve' and it launches a 'Solver Results' dialog box.

Figure 10-22: Solver Results

Click Ok to see the results in the sheet.

	B	Unit Profit	Space Req per unit	Capital Req per unit	Order
3	Mangos	300	3	85	83.33333
4	Apples	150	2	90	0
5	Strawberries	80	5	74	0
6					
7	Space Available	250		Space Utilized	250
8	Capital Available	50000		Capital Utilized	7083.333
9					
10				Total Profit	25000

So, the optimal solution is to order only 84 units of Mangos to get the maximum profit that is, 25000. Now add another constraint such that not more than 55 Mangos and 30 Apples can be ordered.

Click on Solve and in the Solver Results dialog box click on OK.

⊿	A	B	C	D	E	F
1						⇩
2			Unit Profit	Space Req per unit	Capital Req per unit	Order
3		Mangos	300	3	85	55
4		Apples	150	2	90	30
5		Strawberries	80	5	74	5
6						⇩
7		Space Available	250		Space Utilized	250
8		Capital Available	50000		Capital Utilized	7745
9						
10					Total Profit	21400

With new constraints on the maximum number of Mangos and Apples that can be ordered, the maximum profit of 21400 can be reached by ordering 55 Mangos, 30 Apples, and 5 Strawberries units. Space utilization in this case is 250, that is complete utilization.

You can also save this as a scenario, click on 'Save Scenario' in the Solver Results window (see Figure 10-22). It opens a Save Scenario dialog box where you enter the name and then click OK.

This scenario is saved by the given name and can be viewed in the Scenario Manager (see Figure 10-7)

CHAPTER 11

Mail Merge
using Excel

Mail Merge is a feature that helps in creating multiple documents at once, which are identical with respect to layout, text, formatting, graphics and so on, except for some sections that vary and are personalized.

Mail Merge is a supported feature in the Microsoft Office suite, and you can utilize it to create bulk labels, letters, envelopes, or send out multiple emails from Microsoft Word using an Excel workbook. Excel in this case becomes the data source or database from where the specific information is picked for customizing or personalizing the document. We can also perform Mail Merge from Excel itself without using Word. This would require writing some formulas and a Macro (VBA) in the Excel.

In this chapter we will explain both the methods of Mail Merge with the help of examples.

11.1 Mail Merge from Word using Excel

This is the most used method of using Mail Merge feature. We will take an example for generating pay slips and sending emails to employees. Companies generally have a single payslip template that is used for each employee. Hence in the payslip layout, the formatting remains the same but for each employee the contents or data values differ. Mail Merge involves three documents; the data source or database, document template, and the resultant Mail Merged document. We will create each of them one by one for our example.

11.1.1 Preparing the database

Excel is our data source or the database from where the employee specific information will be picked to generate individual pay slips. Add all the information in the Excel database that you want to use in the generated document. The first row is the header row, with descriptive and unique labels to identify the data in the columns or cells beneath. These labels will be used as tags in the template to correlate the Excel database and the template while generating payslips using Mail Merge. We have created our sample database in a new Excel file, in a worksheet named "Sheet 1". The following screenshot shows the example that we will use.

	A	B	C	D	E	F	G	H	I	J	K
1	Name	Employee ID	Email	Designation	Basic	Allowance	Others	Tax	Net Payable	Salary Month	Salary Year
2	Karthik G S	10011	kgs@abs.com	Strategy Lead	47000.00	9400.00	4700.00	3915.10	57184.90	June	2018
3	Neelakshi S	10012	ns@abc.com	Architecture Lead	56000.00	11200.00	6720.00	4664.80	69255.20	June	2018
4	Puja N	10013	pn@abc.com	Quality Lead	46200.00	9240.00	3696.00	3848.46	55287.54	June	2018
5	Avinash P	10015	ap@abc.com	Analytics Lead	46200.00	9240.00	4158.00	3848.46	55749.54	June	2018
6	Karthik G S	10011	kgs@abs.com	Strategy Lead	43000.00	8600.00	4300.00	3581.90	52318.10	April	2018
7											

Figure 11-1: Mail Merge: Excel database example

In above database, first row is the header row that has descriptive labels such as Name, Employee ID, Email and so on, and subsequent rows have information. For each of the four employees we have given their unique employee id, email, designation, salary break up that is, earnings: basic, allowance, others and deductions: tax and then the total net payable. The last two columns specify the month and year for which the payslip is to be generated. After completing the data entry in the Excel file, save it for later use.

Using this information, we will generate the payslip of all four employees for June 2018 and the payslip of one employee for the month of April 2018, just to show how data changes based on row information. Each row corresponds to one payslip (one record) and each column corresponds to a field that will be inserted in the document generated.

11.1.2 Creating the template

Next step is to create the payslip template in Microsoft Word. This template will have some common text and some text will vary that is, enclosed within "<<>>", denoting them as tags to be mapped with the data source. Open a new Word document and insert the text, like our example as seen in the following screenshot and save the document.

COMPANY – ABC LTD			
PAYSLIP FOR << Salary Month>> << Salary Year>>			
Employee Name: <<Name>> Designation: <<Designation>>		Employee Id: << Employee ID>>	
Earnings		Deductions	
Basic Salary	<<Basic>>	Taxes	<<Tax>>
Spl. Allowance	<<Allowance>>		
Others	<<Others>>		
		Net Payable: <<Net Payable>>	

Figure 11-2: Mail Merge: Word template

Note that the text within "<<>>" have the same name as the column labels in the header row for the Excel database, which makes it easier to correlate or map the template and database.

11.1.3 Generating the Merged document

Open the Word template created for payslip generation and go to menu 'Mailings'. Select the option 'Start Mail Merge-> Step-by-Step Mail Merge Wizard…'.

Figure 11-3: Mail Merge: step by step wizard

We will use the Step-by-Step Mail Merge Wizard to create the Mail Merge document and explain each step as we go.

On clicking the 'Step-by-Step Mail Merge Wizard' option, you can see the Mail Merge option on the right-hand side pane. You can move, size, or close this pane as per your convenience, using the options that are given. We will keep it as is for our example.

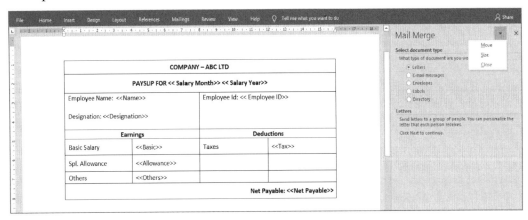

In Step 1, we will select the document type as 'Letters, and click on the 'Next: Starting document'. In Step 2, select 'Use the current document', as this is our payslip template that we want to use for Mail Merge and click on 'Next->Select recipients'.

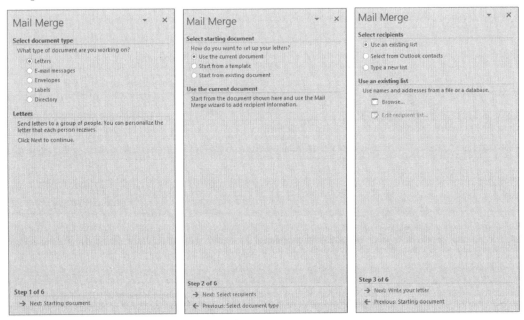

Figure 11-4: Mail Merge: Steps 1-3

In Step 3, we will connect the Word with the Excel database to get the recipients. Click on 'Browse...' and select the Excel file in which we created the employee info database for payslips and click OK. Another window is launched showing all the sheets of the workbook; select Sheet1 as we have the data in there. Click the checkbox indicating that the first row of data contains column headers, this way Excel will know the names to pick for merge.

Click OK and it launches another window displaying the records from the Excel database that is, information from the selected 'Sheet 1'. You can select/deselect the rows that you want to use for Mail Merge. We will select all and click OK to go to the next step.

Figure 11-5: Mail Merge: Select recipients window

On clicking OK it moves back to the Mail Merge pane and displays our selection.

Again, click on 'Next: Write your letter' and select 'More Items...' to launch a dialog box to insert merged fields.

Figure 11-6: Mail Merge: Insert Merge Field dialog

Now, in the word document select the text to be replaced for example, <<Name>>, choose the field from the Insert Merge field dialog 'Name' and click Insert. Similarly do this for all the other texts that we had inserted with '<<>>' in our template. The

Insert Merge Field option also comes from 'Mailings->Insert Merge Field' as given below.

Figure 11-7: Mail Merge: Insert Merge Field

After you replace all the text with fields from the database, click on 'Next->Preview your letters' and see how it replaces the tags with actual values.

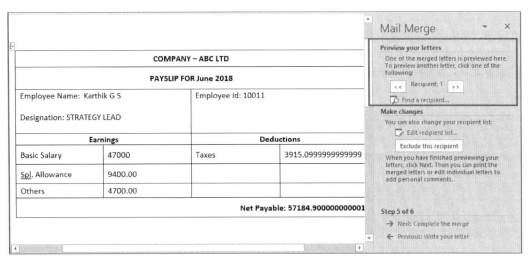

Figure 11-8: Mail Merge: Preview letters

It displays the first record and you can traverse through all the records and see the preview that is, preview all the payslips using the Next and Previous arrows.

If you perform a Mail Merge in Microsoft Word and use a Microsoft Excel worksheet as the data source for the recipient list, some of the numeric data may not retain its formatting when it is merged. For example, in the above preview the 'Base Salary' does not have any decimals while 'Taxes' shows multiple decimal places. We can format the merged field codes in Word to display a specific consistent format.

Select the merged field for 'Taxes', right-click and select 'Toggle Field Codes' or press the SHIFT+F9 shortcut key.

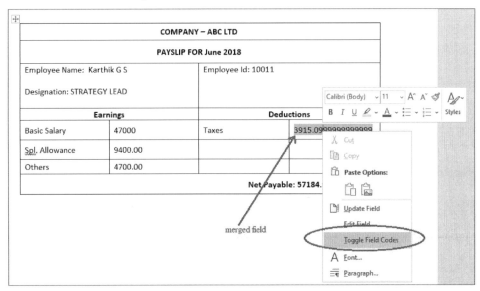

It will display the merged field code as {MERGEFIELD Tax} instead of the value 3915.099999999999. Modify the merged field code to {MERGEFIELD Tax \# 0.00} and again click Toggle Field Codes. You will see that now it displays the value as 3915.10 for Taxes. You can also use the option 'Update Field' in the right-click menu to reflect the changes. The Merged field codes are explained in more detail with examples later in this chapter.

After you have corrected the formatting and other aspects, and previewed all payslips, it's time to click 'Complete the merge' option as given in Figure 11-9.

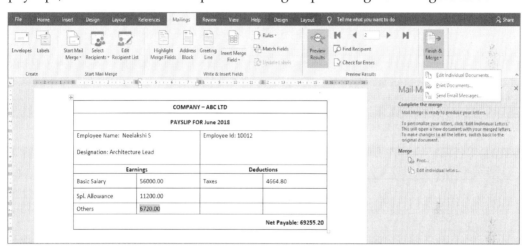

Figure 11-9: Mail merge: Complete the merge

In the next step you get the option to either Print the documents, send email messages, or edit the individual documents.

11.1.3.1 Print Documents

Figure 11-10: Merge to Printer

In the 'Merge to Printer' dialog box you can choose to either print 'All' the records that get generated, only 'Current record', or some specific records by giving the record numbers in 'From' and 'To' fields. On clicking OK the print dialog is launched for printing.

11.1.3.2 Send Email Messages

Figure 11-11: Merge to E-mail

In the 'Merge to E-mail' dialog box, the 'To' message options field shows the list of database fields to select, which is, Email in our case. You can also specify the Subject line, Mail format (attachment, text or html), and the records to send. Click OK to send email to recipients. By default, it tries to connect with Microsoft Outlook.

11.1.3.3 Edit Individual Documents

Figure 11-12: Merge to Edit

'Edit Individual Documents' option allows you to edit the generated documents and save them. It opens a new merged document for editing, with the selected records. Preferably, personalization's like special notes should be handled in the data source itself by adding a notes column to enter comments and so on; that is a better and easier way to handle.

11.1.4 Merged Field Codes

Field codes can be formatted in Word. In this section we will see how to format numbers, date and time with help of some examples.

To format a numeric merge field, use the \# switches mentioned in the following table.

Switch	Description	Example
\# 0	For rounded whole numbers	NUM = 4.5 {NUM \# 0} displayed as 5 (roundup) NUM = 3.1 {NUM \# 0} displayed as 3
\# ,0	For rounded whole numbers with a thousand separator	NUM = 3500 {NUM \# ,0} displayed as 3,500
# ,0.00	For numbers accurate to two decimal places, with a thousand separator	NUM = 3500 {NUM \# ,0.00} displayed as 3,500.00
\# $,0	For rounded whole dollar with a thousand separator	NUM = 3500 {NUM \# $,0} displayed as $3,500
\# 0%	For percentage	NUM = 8 {NUM \# 0%} displayed as 8%

To format a date and time merge field, use the \@ switches mentioned in the following table

Switch	Example
\@ dd-MMM-yy	Formats as: 13-Mar-18
\@ dd/MM/yyyy	Formats as: 13/03/2018
\@ dd MMMM yyyy	Formats as: 13 March 2018
\@ dddd, dd MMMM yyyy	Formats as: Tuesday, 13 March 2018
\@ HH:mm	Formats as: 14:45
\@ HH:mm:ss	Formats as: 14:45:30
\@ h:mm:ss AM\PM	Formats as: 2:45:30 PM

Mailings Ribbon

On the Mailings tab of a Word document, we have some useful options that can also be used directly from the Ribbon apart from been accessed via the wizard pane like:

- 'Preview Results', which helps to toggle between actual values and Mail Merge template, using the Navigation arrows to traverse and preview the records.

- 'Find Recipient' to find records based on the different fields like Employee Id, Name and so on.

- 'Check for Errors' that gives multiple options for example simulate merge and report errors, complete merge and report errors as encountered, or report at the end in a new document,

- 'Highlight Merge Fields' under the Write & Insert Fields group, is a toggle button to select/deselect all the merged fields in the document. You can also use the ALT+F9 shortcut key.

- 'Select Recipients' and 'Edit Recipients List' under the 'Start Mail Merge' groups help to select new recipients / data source and modify the existing recipients list respectively.

11.2 Mail Merge from Excel (without Word)

We will use the same payslip generation example to show how to do Mail Merge from within the Excel without using Word. In case of a small letter, email, and so on, this method might be easier but as you will see, generating a payslip via this method is tedious and not that easy as compared to using Word Mail Merge. This method involves preparing a Mail Merge template in Excel, using Excel as the data source or the database and then generating the merged document.

In our example we will make use of the function INDIRECT, Named Ranges, and one simple Macro. Macros are discussed in more details in Chapter 13 and for our example here you can just go and copy paste the code as described.

Note that the Excel file should have Macros enabled. If not then save the existing Excel as Macro enabled Excel that is, it will get saved with file extension '.xlsm'.

11.2.1 Prepare database in Excel

We will use the same Excel database for the payslip generation that we created for Mail Merge with Word, (see section 11.1.1). Open the Excel file and rename the sheet in which we have the employee information as "Data".

	A	B	C	D	E	F	G	H	I	J	K
1	Name	Employee ID	Email	Designation	Basic	Allowance	Others	Tax	Net Payable	Salary Month	Salary Year
2	Karthik G S	10011	kgs@abs.com	Strategy Lead	47000.00	9400.00	4700.00	3915.10	57184.90	June	2018
3	Neelakshi S	10012	ns@abc.com	Architecture Lead	56000.00	11200.00	6720.00	4664.80	69255.20	June	2018
4	Puja N	10013	pn@abc.com	Quality Lead	46200.00	9240.00	3696.00	3848.46	55287.54	June	2018
5	Avinash P	10015	ap@abc.com	Analytics Lead	46200.00	9240.00	4158.00	3848.46	55749.54	June	2018
6	Karthik G S	10011	kgs@abs.com	Strategy Lead	43000.00	8600.00	4300.00	3581.90	52318.10	April	2018
7											

11.2.2 Prepare Mail Merge template in Excel

We will create the Mail Merge template in the same Excel workbook or file that has the Excel database. Create a new sheet in the workbook and name it as "Form". Now add the payslip entries (see section 11.1.2) in the sheet as given in the following screenshot. In addition, we will add three more entries; 'Current Record' – for displaying the corresponding values in the payslip fields, 'From & To' – for specifying the records for Print Preview.

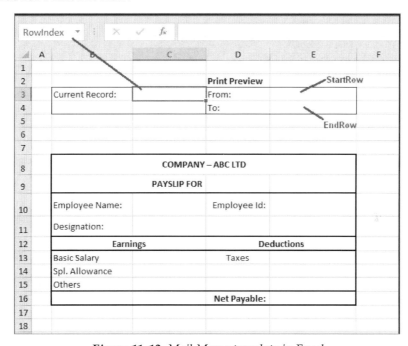

Figure 11-13: *Mail Merge template in Excel*

We will also use Named Ranges (see section 3.3) and name the cells; C3 as 'RowIndex', E3 as 'StartRow' and E4 as 'EndRow'. These will be used later in the Macro that will be used in this example.

In the Print Preview, we only want the payslip entries to be shown. To do that we will set the Print Area by selecting the cell range A6 to F18 and go to menu 'Page Layout->Print Area->Set Print Area'.

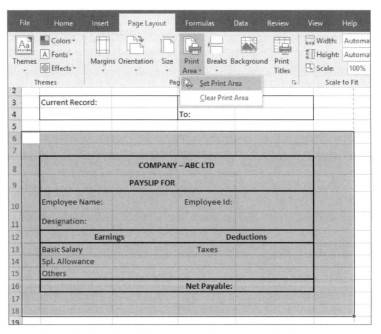

Figure 11-14: *Mail Merge template in Excel: Set Print Area*

Again, select the cell range A6 to F18 and go to menu option 'Home->Font->Fill Color'. Select the fill color as white, so that the print area background is all white and we do not see the row and column lines. It will look like text on a plain white sheet.

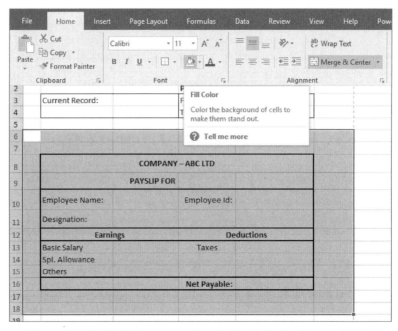

Figure 11-15: *Mail Merge template in Excel: Set background color*

Next step is to add some formulas and new named ranges that will be used in displaying the employee information in the template created.

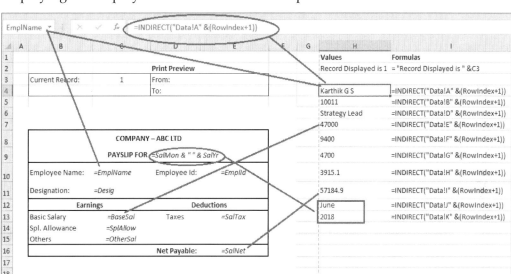

We have linked the employee information in column H, with help of the INDIRECT function (see formula in column I, for function help see section 3.12.4), which is in the same workbook or file but in a different sheet named 'Data' (see 11.2.1 & 11.1.1). Each cell in column H, from H4 to H13 has been given a name. And these defined names are used in the formulas in the payslip template area to fill the values.

Note that in formulas for example, '=INDIRECT("Data!A" &(RowIndex+1))' we are adding 1 to the RowIndex (defined name for cell C3). The reason being that the first row in the employee database sheet 'Data' is the header row, so we want to skip that. Hence, when we specify 1 for the Current Record field, in the formulas the first actual record in row 2 is picked and so on.

For example, cell H4 is named 'EmplName' that is used in cell C10 formula (=EmplName) to specify the value of the current record (which is 1), against the 'Employee Name:' field. Similarly, cell I17 is named 'BaseSal' indicating the Base Salary value in cell C13. And cells H12 & H13 are named 'SalMon' & 'SalYr' to print the Salary Month and Year of the Payslip that is, used in formula in cell D9 (=SalMon & " " & SalYr).

Now that all the formulas are set, we can view the different payslips of employees by changing the number in the 'Current Record' field (cell C3).

First Record - Current Record =1

	A	B	C	D	E	F	G	H
1								
2				Print Preview				Record Displayed is 1
3		Current Record:	1	From:				
4				To:				Karthik G S
5								10011
6								Strategy Lead
7								47000
8			COMPANY – ABC LTD					9400
9			PAYSLIP FOR June 2018					4700
10		Employee Name:	Karthik G S	Employee Id:	10011			3915.1
11		Designation:	Strategy Lead					57184.9
12		Earnings		Deductions				June
13		Basic Salary	47000	Taxes	3915.1			2018
14		Spl. Allowance	9400					
15		Others	4700					
16				Net Payable:	57184.9			
17								

Third Record - Current Record =3

	A	B	C	D	E	F	G	H
1								
2				Print Preview				Record Displayed is 3
3		Current Record:	3	From:				
4				To:				Puja N
5								10013
6								Quality Lead
7								46200
8			COMPANY – ABC LTD					9240
9			PAYSLIP FOR June 2018					3696
10		Employee Name:	Puja N	Employee Id:	10013			3848.46
11		Designation:	Quality Lead					55287.54
12		Earnings		Deductions				June
13		Basic Salary	46200	Taxes	3848.46			2018
14		Spl. Allowance	9240					
15		Others	3696					
16				Net Payable:	55287.54			
17								

11.2.3 Print Preview the merged documents

In order to see the Print Preview of each record, we will write a small Macro and attach it to a control. To add a control in the sheet, insert a rectangular shape via the menu option 'Insert->Illustrations->Shapes', with the text 'Print Preview' in cell E2 of the sheet 'Form' as seen in the following screenshot. Select the inserted shape and format it as you like by using the 'Drawing Tools->Format' option.

Select the inserted rectangular shape and select the 'Assign Macro' option in the right-click menu. 'Assign a Macro' dialog box will be launched, click on 'New' to add the Macro code.

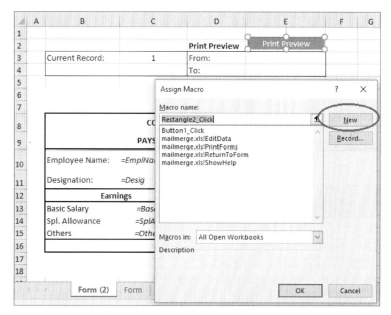

Figure 11-16: Add new macro for control

This will open the Microsoft Visual Basic Application (VBA) editor. Copy the code in the editor and save the file.

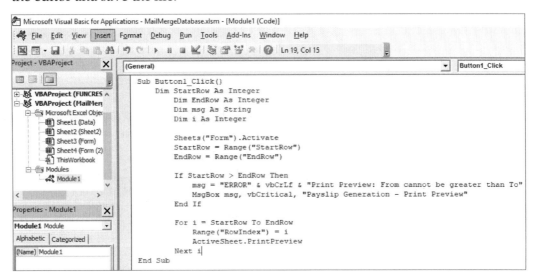

Code sample:

```
Sub Button1_Click()

    Dim StartRow As Integer

        Dim EndRow As Integer

        Dim msg As String

        Dim i As Integer

        Sheets("Form").Activate

        StartRow = Range("StartRow")

        EndRow = Range("EndRow")

        If StartRow > EndRow Then

            msg = "ERROR" & vbCrLf & "Print Preview: From cannot be greater than To"

            MsgBox msg, vbCritical, "Payslip Generation - Print Preview"

            End If

        For i = StartRow To EndRow

            Range("RowIndex") = i

            ActiveSheet.PrintPreview

            Next i

    End Sub
```

Now everything is set for Print Preview. To see the Print Preview of records 1 to 3, enter the numbers 1 and 3 in the sheet in cells E3 and E4 respectively and then click on the 'Print Preview' control (which we just added a Macro to). Excel will launch 3 print preview windows like below.

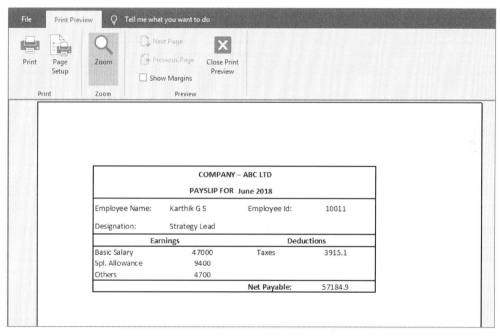

Figure 11-17: *Print Preview of Merged document*

CHAPTER 12
Create Custom Excel Template

Microsoft Excel gives you the option to create a New Excel file from scratch using the 'Blank Workbook' option or use any of the predefined templates in the Microsoft Office Online.

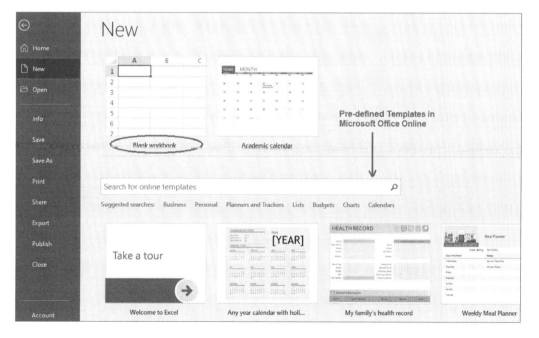

Many times, it so happens that you either create the same types of Excel spreadsheets repeatedly or instead you open an existing file, clear the old data before use and save it as a different file. Creating a custom template, that is a predesigned workbook or a worksheet where the main work has already been done for you, can help make that process a lot smoother.

You can create a custom template from scratch or a blank workbook or from an existing file. To save the file as a template, go to 'File->Save As' and select the file type as 'Excel Template (*.xltx)' or 'Excel 97-2003 Template (*.xlt)' or 'Excel Macro-Enabled Template (*.xltm)'. By default, the location where custom templates are saved is 'C:\Users\<*User Name*>\Documents\Custom Office Templates'. To change the default location, go to 'File->Options', select 'Save' and type the new location in the 'Default personal templates location' field.

You can save the following settings in the Excel Template

- Number and type of sheets
- Cell styles and formats
- Page layout and print areas for each sheet
- Hidden areas to make certain sheets, rows, columns or cells invisible
- Protected areas to prevent changes in certain cells
- Text that you want to appear in all workbooks created based on a given template, such as column labels or page headers
- Formulas, hyperlinks, charts, images and other graphics
- Excel Data validation options such as drop-down lists, validation messages or alerts, etc.
- Calculation options and window view options, e.g. freezing the header row
- Macros and ActiveX controls on custom forms

We will use the example of chapter 11.2.2 Prepare Mail Merge template in Excel for illustrating how to create a custom template from an existing file. The workbook created in this example has two worksheets. Worksheet named 'Data' has the employee salary details, where each row corresponds to a single employee.

	A	B	C	D	E	F	G	H	I	J	K
1	Name	Employee ID	Email	Designation	Basic	Allowance	Others	Tax	Net Payable	Salary Month	Salary Year
2	Karthik G S	10011	kgs@abs.com	Strategy Lead	47000.00	9400.00	4700.00	3915.10	57184.90	June	2018
3	Neelakshi S	10012	ns@abc.com	Architecture Lead	56000.00	11200.00	6720.00	4664.80	69255.20	June	2018
4	Puja N	10013	pn@abc.com	Quality Lead	46200.00	9240.00	3696.00	3848.46	55287.54	June	2018
5	Avinash P	10015	ap@abc.com	Analytics Lead	46200.00	9240.00	4158.00	3848.46	55749.54	June	2018
6	Karthik G S	10011	kgs@abs.com	Strategy Lead	43000.00	8600.00	4300.00	3581.90	52318.10	April	2018
7											

Form | **Data** | ⊕

Clear only the contents, retaining the formulas, from the 'Data' sheet. You can do it manually or use the 'Go to Special' command that is a quicker method. 'Go to Special' command is under 'Home->Find & Select' menu. In the Go to Special dialog box select 'Constants' and uncheck everything except 'Numbers', 'Text' and click OK.

All numbers and texts are highlighted in the sheet. Deselect the first row, that is the table header row, so that it does not get removed. Press 'Delete' to clear the contents. Now the 'Data' sheet is clean, with only the header row and formulas, to be used as part of the template.

The other worksheet named 'Form' has the payslip format with formulas, references to display data from the 'Data' sheet based on values entered in the input fields and the button control with macro attached for printing the document.

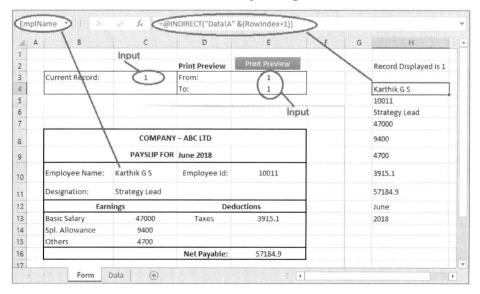

This sheet is already clean and ready for use. Now save this workbook as a template by saving this as a 'Excel Macro-Enabled Template (*.xltm)', that is, a file named 'MailMergeDatabase.xltm'.

Next time when you want to use this template to create a new Excel file, go to 'File->New' and select your custom template under Personal tab. All your custom templates are listed under the Personal tab section.

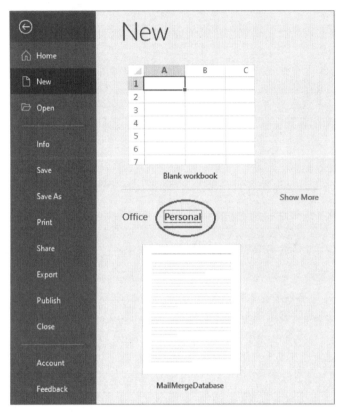

CHAPTER 13
Macros in Excel

A Macro is a piece of programming code in VBA that runs in Excel and helps in automating routine tasks. It is an action or a set of actions that you can run as many times as you want. VBA is an acronym for Visual Basic for Applications, a programming language that is used to create or record Macros in Excel. In this chapter we will give an overview of VBA language, Recording & Writing Macros, and their usage with the help of examples.

Note that in order to use the Macros, the Excel workbook or file should be Macro enabled that is, saved as a Macro enabled file with extension '.xlsm'. Open Microsoft Excel and create a new file using the 'Blank Workbook' template. Go to 'File->Save As' and select the destination folder by double-clicking on the folder name. In the 'Save As' dialog box, specify the file name in the 'File Name' field and select the 'Save as type' as 'Excel Macro-Enabled Workbook (*.xlsm)'.

13.1 VBA Quick overview

Visual Basic for Applications (VBA) is a subset of the powerful Visual Basic programming language and is included with most MS Office applications. Although VBA gives you the ability to automate processes within and between MS Office applications, it is not necessary to know VBA code or computer programming if the Macro Recorder does what you want.

VBA uses English like statements to write instructions and has a short learning curve. The user interface (UI) is like the paint program, where you can drag, drop, and align controls.

13.1.1 Basic language constructs

In this section we will discuss the basic constructs of the language that will help in writing simple Macros.

- Variables: Are descriptive names for an integer, string, date, and so on, that are stored in a computer memory or storage system. They can be assigned a value to be used later in the code to execute.

- Constant: Is like a variable that once assigned cannot be modified by code. Keyword 'Const' is used to declare constant variables. The scope can be private or public, by default it is private.

- Operators: Like operators used in Excel formulas, arithmetic operators like '+' (addition), '- '(subtraction), '*' (multiplication) and '/' (division) can be used here as well.

- Logical operators: OR, AND, NOT can be used in conditional IF statements.

13.2 Enabling Developer tab

Macros are one of the developer features, available on the Developer tab. By default, the Developer tab is hidden in Excel, but we can enable it from the File menu by going to 'File->Options->Customize Ribbon.' Click on the checkbox for 'Developer' under 'Main Tabs' and then click OK.

Figure 13-1: Enable Developer Tab

The Developer tab is added in Excel as a main tab with the following options for recording Macros, writing Macro code in VBA, and so on.

Figure 13-2: *Developer tab Ribbon*

13.3 Create Macro

We will create a simple Macro that will display "Hello *Name*" on clicking a button, where *Name* will be picked from a cell in the Excel sheet. First, we will add a button control in the Excel and then assign a new Macro to it. Open a Macro enabled Excel file, go to the Developer tab and click 'Insert' to select 'Command button' under ActiveX Controls. Click anywhere in the Excel sheet to insert the Command button.

Right-click on the Command Button and click 'View Code' to go to VBA editor. We will write our code in the editor.

On clicking 'View Code', the VBA editor displays the default method or function for the command button. It is an empty method, where we will write the code.

We will insert the code in the 'CommandButton1_Click' method, code and the explanation of the code (in red) is given below.

```
CommandButton1

    Private Sub CommandButton1_Click()

        Dim name As String ──────────────── Variable "name" declared as String

        name = Range("B5").Value ────────── "name" assigned value in cell B5

        Range("D2").Value = "Hello " & name ──── "Hello" and "name" variable value are concatenated
                                                  and assigned to cell D2
    End Sub
```

Figure 13-3: Macro code

Save and close the VBA editor to go back to the Excel sheet. In the cell B5 enter any text, say "World" and then click on the command button. "Hello World" will be inserted in cell D2, as per the Macro code. Now change the text in cell B5 to "Children" and again click on the command button. "Hello Children" is inserted in D2, without changing anything in the Macro code and by just entering a new text in B5.

Figure 13-4: Macro assigned to command button

Another example of Macro code has been given in the mail merge payslip generation example in Chapter 11.2.3

13.4 Record Macro

In Excel we can also record a Macro, where it basically records and saves every mouse click and keystroke, we make. After recording when the Macro is run it performs the same steps. We will now record a Macro to export a '.csv' file into Excel and run the Macro to see the results. Identify a '.csv' file to import, in our case we have a file name "capitals.csv".

Open a Macro enabled Excel file, go to the Developer tab and click on the 'Record Macro' option. It opens a Record Macro dialog box. Enter the Macro name, shortcut key you want to assign with this Macro, scope of the Macro—this workbook, new workbooks, all open workbooks, and so on—and a description of what the Macro is intended to do.

Click on OK to start recoding the Macro. We will do the following steps,

- Select cell A1
- Go to the 'Data' tab and select 'Get External Data->From text'
- In the 'Import Text File' dialog, browse and select the file 'capitals.csv'
- Click 'Import' in the dialog box
- Follow the 'Import from Text' process as described in Chapter 1.10.1 so that the CSV file data will be imported in the Excel file

- Go to the 'Developer' tab and select 'Stop Recording'

- Delete the imported data and save the file as a macro enabled Excel file.

When we record a Macro, Excel generates the code automatically based on the recorded actions that is, mouse clicks and keystrokes. We can go and see the code by going to the 'Developer' tab. Go to the option 'Macros' and select the recorded Macro name from the list and click 'Edit'. VBA editor will be opened with the code generated for the Macro.

Figure 13-5: *Recorded Macro code*

Now we will check if the recorded Macro works.

- Open the saved Macro enabled Excel file, which has the recorded Macro
- Go to the 'Developer' tab and click on 'Macros' to view the existing Macros in the file.

- Select the Macro 'import_csv_file' that we had recorded earlier and click 'Run'
- Once the Macro executes, it follows the same steps and import the data from csv to Excel

CHAPTER 14

Get help for your problem

In earlier chapters of this book, we discussed Excel features and functionalities in details. We hope that the examples used in those chapters clarified their usage and made your work easier. In this chapter we will try to help you further by mapping generic problem statements to Excel features and functionalities. These examples might trigger new ideas or thoughts for finding solution to your problems. A word of caution though, this is just a reference or guide and not an exhaustive list. We will highly advice you to go through all the chapters in order to make an informed decision.

Qs 1. Saju has a worksheet with formulas for calculating results based on data entered in specific cells. This sheet needs to be shared with other people for inputs with a condition that the sheet is protected, formulas are hidden, and users are only allowed to edit specific cells.

Below is the screenshot of the worksheet, where

a) columns 'Task List', 'Engineer Name', Planned End Date' and 'Delay (in days)' should be made non-editable

b) formula '=NETWORKDAYS(D2,E2)' in cell F2 and in subsequent cells of the column 'Delay (in days)' should be hidden

c) user should be able to input data only in the cells C2 to C8 in column named 'Status' and E2 to E8 in column named 'Actual Completion date'.

Editable Cell Range

Reference: Chapter - Protect Sheet 1.9.2

Ans:
- Select the complete sheet, go to 'Home->Format->Format Cells' or right click and under 'Format Cells -> Protection', uncheck "Lock" and "Hidden".
  - Note, by default all cells in a sheet are locked, so first we need to unlock all cells. You can also use the keyboard shortcut 'CTRL + 1' to launch the 'Format Cells' dialog box.
- Go to 'Review->Allow Edit Ranges' and click 'New' in the 'New Range' dialog box enter the range title, select the cell ranges as '=$C$2:$C$8,$E$2:$E$8' and click OK. Click OK in Allow Edit Ranges to go back to the sheet.
- To select all formulas entered in the sheet, go to 'Home -> Editing -> Find & Select -> Go To Special' and select "Formulas". This will select all formulas in the sheet, they will get highlighted in the sheet.
  - You can also use the keyboard shortcut 'CTRL + `' (that's known as the "grave accent," and you'll find it to the left of the 1 key on your keyboard, above the Tab button) to show formulas in all cells of the sheet.
- Right click and under 'Format Cells -> Protection', check "Lock" and "Hidden". This will mark the cells that have a formula for locking.
- Go to 'Review' tab and select 'Protect Sheet'. Add a password and if required uncheck "Select locked cells" in case you do not want to allow people to even select that cell. If you traverse with arrow keys, that cell will be skipped.
- Now all the cells with formula are locked, formula is not visible in the formula bar and only the selected range of cells are open for editing.

Qs 2. Archana keeps a note of her shopping items with dates. She wants to know the number of days she went out and bought something. There is a list of dates as shown below, with some duplicates and now we need to count the days.

	List of Dates
1	
2	05-Dec-2019
3	05-Dec-2019
4	05-Dec-2019
5	06-Dec-2019
6	12-Dec-2019
7	15-Dec-2019
8	02-Jan-2020
9	02-Jan-2020
10	02-Jan-2020
11	15-Jan-2020
12	21-Jan-2020

Reference: Chapters - FREQUENCY 3.15.4, Double Minus / Unary Operator 3.2.5

Ans:
- To calculate the number of days, use the formula
  '=SUM(--(FREQUENCY(I2:I12,I2:I12)>0))'

- In the function 'FREQUENCY(I2:I12,I2:I12)', we have specified the data array and bin array as I2:I12 and the return array will look like {3;0;0;1;1;1;3;0;0;1;1;0}

  You can see the function result by selecting the function in the formula bar and clicking insert function '*fx*'

- Expression inside SUM function '--(FREQUENCY(I2:I12,I2:I12)>0)' will return {1;0;0;1;1;1;1;0;0;1;1;0} and SUM returns 7.

Qs 3. A company has their sales data for the year and now they want to categorize the sales into four timeframes, each with specific start and end date. In the example below, the Quarters have been defined in cell range A2:C6. Based on the date of each item, as given in 'Dates' column, we need to calculate the quarter it falls and input the quarter name in the 'Quarter' column.

	A	B	C	D	E	F
1						
2	**Quarters**	**Start Date**	**End Date**			
3	QTR 1	01-02-2019	03-05-2019			
4	QTR 2	04-05-2019	02-08-2019			
5	QTR 3	03-08-2019	01-11-2019			
6	QTR 4	02-11-2019	31-01-2020			
7						
8						
9	**Dates**	**Item**	**Price per Unit**	**Qty**	**Total Sale**	**Quarter**
10	02-03-2019	Lemon Tea	330	200	66,000.00	
11	06-05-2019	Filter Coffee	257	75	19,275.00	
12	10-10-2019	Coconut Water	160	100	16,000.00	
13	05-12-2019	Biscuit	24	120	2,880.00	
14	01-02-2020	Almonds	445	20	8,900.00	
15	10-04-2019	Popcorn	22	165	3,630.00	
16	04-05-2019	Chocolate	420	120	50,400.00	
17	10-07-2019	Milk Cake	20	100	2,000.00	

Reference: Chapters - Logical Functions 3.9, Error Handling Functions 3.17.2

Ans:
- To find the quarter in which the specific date falls can be done in multiple ways. We will discuss two; one using nested IF and other using IFS function.
- Nested IF formula will look like:

   =IF(AND(A10<=$C$3,A10>=$B$3),$A$3,   *..... checks if QTR 1*

IF(AND(A10>=$B$4,A10<=$C$4),$A$4,   *..... checks if QTR 2*

IF(AND(A10>=$B$5,A10<=$C$5),$A$5,   *..... checks if QTR 3*

IF(AND(A10>=$B$6,A10<=$C$6),$A$6,   *..... checks if QTR 4*

"ERROR"))))   *.... otherwise Error*

- Nested IFs are difficult to manage if there are multiple levels. We can instead use function IFS. The formula then will look like:

=IFS(AND(A10>=$B$3,A10<=$C$3),$A$3,   *... logical test and value if true*

AND(A10>=$B$4,A10<=$C$4),$A$4,

AND(A10>=$B$5,A10<=$C$5),$A$5,

AND(A10>=$B$6,A10<=$C$6),$A$6)

- Note that in the preceding IFS function there is no error handling. In case the date does not lie in any of the quarters the function will return error '#N/A'. We can do error handling by incapsulating the IFS function with error function IFNA, and returning text "ERROR" in case IFS function returns '#N/A', as shown below:

=IFNA(IFS(.....), "ERROR")

- In both cases the result in the same, as shown below

9	Dates	Item	Price per Unit	Qty	Total Sale	Quarter
10	02-03-2019	Lemon Tea	330	200	66,000.00	QTR 1
11	06-05-2019	Filter Coffee	257	75	19,275.00	QTR 2
12	10-10-2019	Coconut Water	160	100	16,000.00	QTR 3
13	05-12-2019	Biscuit	24	120	2,880.00	QTR 4
14	01-02-2020	Almonds	445	20	8,900.00	ERROR
15	10-04-2019	Popcorn	22	165	3,630.00	QTR 1
16	04-05-2019	Chocolate	420	120	50,400.00	QTR 2
17	10-07-2019	Milk Cake	20	100	2,000.00	QTR 2

Qs 4. An employee's attendance data is provided to the Manager with the months listed in one row (#2), the week numbers in a column (column J) as shown in screenshot below. But the Manager wants to view the data such that the week numbers are listed in one row and the months are in a column.

	I	J	K	L	M
1					
2		Attendence	Jan	Feb	Mar
3		Wk 1	P	P	A
4		Wk2	P	P	P
5		Wk3	A	P	P
6		Wk4	A	P	A
7					

Ans: • You can use the Transpose feature of Excel, that is copy the cell range and use paste special with Transpose option ticked. But doing that creates duplicated data. If you don't want that, you can type a formula instead using the TRANSPOSE function.

- To use TRANSPOSE function, first select some blank cells such that you select the same number of cells as the original set of cells, but in the other direction. In the example below the original set of cells are in 5 rows and 4 columns and we should select blank cells in 4 rows and 5 columns.

J2			×	✓	f_x	=TRANSPOSE(J2:M6)	
	I	J	K	L	M	N	O
1							
2		Attendence	Jan	Feb	Mar		
3		Wk 1	P	P	A		→ 5 Rows & 4 Columns
4		Wk2	P	P	P		
5		Wk3	A	P	P		
6		Wk4	A	P	A		
7							
8		E(J2:M6)					→ 4 Rows & 5 Columns
9							
10							
11							
12							

- As in preceding example, with those blank cells still selected, type: =TRANSPOSE(J2:M6), where J2:M6 is the range of the cells you want to transpose.

- Press Enter to transpose the cell range

	I	J	K	L	M	N
1						
2		Attendence	Jan	Feb	Mar	
3		Wk 1	P	P	A	
4		Wk2	P	P	P	
5		Wk3	A	P	P	
6		Wk4	A	P	A	
7						
8		Attendence	Wk 1	Wk2	Wk3	Wk4
9		Jan	P	P	A	A
10		Feb	P	P	P	P
11		Mar	A	P	P	A
12						

- Note that by using TRANSPOSE function, we avoided making a copy of the original data, instead made a reference. Any modification of values in the original data will also reflect in the transposed cell range.

Qs 5. There is a list of students along with the courses they are enrolled in. A student can have multiple rows of data when they are enrolled in multiple courses. A report is to be generated where each student name is displayed once with a comma separated list of their courses.

	A	B
1	**Student Name**	**Subjects**
2	Shaun	English
3	Shaun	History
4	Shaun	Physics
5	Aarav	Maths
6	Aarav	Science
7	Aarav	Computers
8	Shannette	Science
9	Shannette	Computers
10	Shannette	History
11	Eshita	English
12	Eshita	Maths
13	Abhiraj	English
14	Shanaya	English
15		

Reference: Chapter 8 Putting Data in perspective with Pivots , 8.14.7 Adding Measures / Calculated Fields

Ans:
- This is classical example of having PivotTable with Text in Values area using DAX.

- Traditionally you can only summarize fields in Values area of a PivotTable using the different aggregation methods like taking the sum, average, minimum, maximum or standard deviation.

- First create a PivotTable. Select the Students data Table, go to 'Insert->PivotTable' and select the checkbox 'Add this data to the Data Model', as shown below

- Now 'Add a Measure'. Select the PivotTable, right click on the table of data found in the PivotTable Fields window and select 'Add Measure' from the menu.

- In the Measure dialog box, the Table Name is automatically filled, that is, 'StudentsData'. Enter the measure name, description and the formula. We will use the Data Analysis Expressions (DAX) to define custom calculations for Measure (or calculated field) in the DAX formula editor.

- Type the formula in DAX editor as =CONCATENATEX(StudentsData, [Subjects],",",""). You can check the formula for errors by clicking 'Check DAX Formula'
- Click OK to create the measure. The newly created measure will appear listed in the PivotTable Fields window with all the other fields and we can use this new measure just like any of the other fields.

- In the PivotTable Fields, select the 'Student Name' in Rows and 'Subject List' in the Values.

Qs 6. Can we share the PivotTable Report, as shown in screenshot below, that got generated in preceding problem Qs 5 via email?

Ans:
- You can share the PivotTable report over Outlook mail using 'Send to Mail Recipient' option in Excel. Note that you should have Outlook installed as part of Microsoft Office and it should be set as your default email app.

- By default, Excel doesn't have the 'Send to Mail Recipient' option available on the toolbar but you can add it easily in the Quick Access Toolbar (QAT). Select the small down arrow on the right-hand side of the Quick Access Toolbar and select 'More Commands'.

- In the 'Choose commands from' list, select 'All Commands', highlight 'Send to Mail Recipient' and click 'Add>>' and then OK button to add it in the QAT.

- Click on the 'Send to Mail Recipient' icon in the QAT, that is, 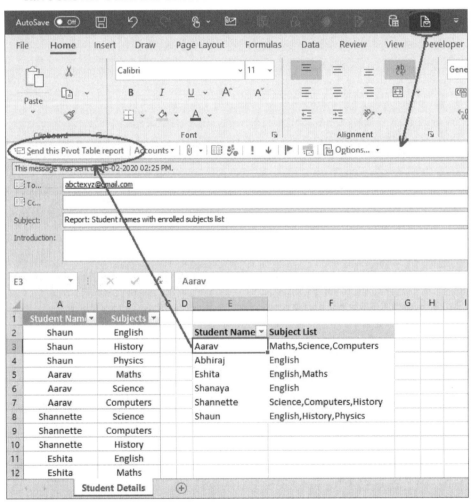 . The Mail dialog box is visible within the Excel.

- You can type in the recipient's email ids, subject of the email and specify if you want to send the complete sheet or the selected report. In the example given below, since we selected a cell inside the PivotTable Report, it is showing the option of 'Send this PivotTable Report'. Otherwise it would have shown 'Send this Sheet'.

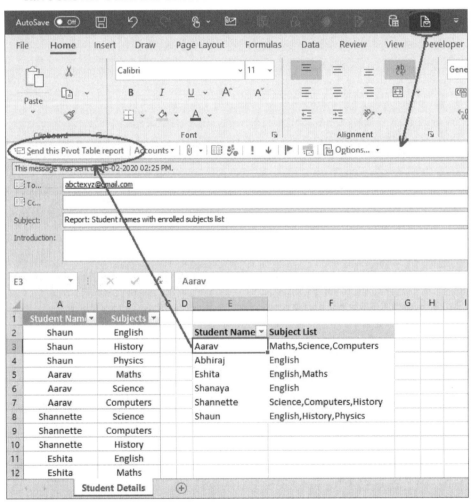

- Click on 'Send this PivotTable Report' to send the email from Outlook. The email received will be as shown in screenshot below.

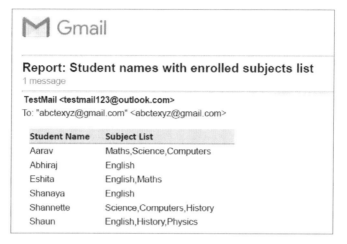

Qs 7. Avi wants to send personalized new year greetings to multiple people in one go. The graphics or image of the greeting is same for all and in order to personalize it, he wants to add individual names in the greetings text.

Reference: Chapter 11_Mail Merge using Excel_

Ans: Mail merge option can be used for sending the greetings, like the payslip example given in the above-mentioned chapter in reference.

Qs 8. Karthik has month wise sales data of his company's cloud subscription for the current year. For next year's strategy planning he is looking for a method to predict future sales and trends.

Reference: Chapter 10 Forecasting in Excel

Ans: Excel has an in-built forecasting feature than can help you in making future predictions and show trends based on time-based historical data. See example in the above-mentioned chapter.

Qs 9. In a project, Puja has created different graphs, charts etc. for showing the project status. For the project review with her manager, she wants a mechanism such that she can show different views on the fly, by just selecting or deselecting certain parameters.

Reference: Chapters - 8.6 Adding Slicers & Timelines, 8.12 Interactive Dashboard with PivotTables, Charts and Slicers

Ans: Excel has features like Slicers, Timelines that help users in creating different perspectives based on selection. See example in the above-mentioned chapter.

Qs 10. A builder is constructing a residential cum commercial complex with multiple condominiums and shopping towers, work for each will get completed at a certain date. Builder needs a single page graphical view for buyers to show them what will get constructed when.

Reference: Chapter 5.2 Creating a Milestone Chart in Excel

Ans: Milestone Chart is a very helpful visual or graphical tool and good indicator for reporting progress. See example in above-mentioned chapter.

Qs 11. Neelakshi wants to create a graphical representation of the reporting structure in her company. She is not good in graphics and is looking for a quick and easy solution.

Reference: Chapter 6.2 Organization Chart

Ans: Excel has the SmartArt feature using which the organization structure can be easily created. See example in above-mentioned chapter.

Qs 12. Sonam had recorded his last years data in an Excel file. Since that Excel file structure and format has been very helpful, he wants to record the current year and subsequent years data in similar file. Problem is that every time he wants to record new data, he must first clear the old data and then enter new data.

Reference: Chapter 12 Create Custom Excel Template

Ans: Creating a custom template, that is a predesigned workbook or a worksheet where the main work has already been done for you, can help make that process a lot smoother. See example in above-mentioned chapter.

Qs 13. A tours and travels company's executive is creating a tour package covering multiple countries. The executive received the flight and hotel charges in different currencies as shown in table below. He wants to publish the total cost of the tour package in a single currency, that is, in USD (US Dollar) and for that, he is looking for a quick solution. The solution should be generic such that it can be used for creating other tour packages and the formulas remain intact even if the conversion rates change.

Country	Symbol	Hotel Charges	Flight Charges
Netherlands	EUR	123.00	450.00
France	EUR	230.00	668.00
Switzerland	CHF Fr.	550.00	1500.00
United Kingdom	GBP	780.00	4352.00

Reference: Chapter 3.12 : Lookup and Reference functions, Chapter 3.3: Defined Names, Chapter 1.10: Importing data into Excel

Ans: • To convert the hotel and flight charges from different currencies to USD, firstly the conversion rates need to be determined. There are multiple web sites, banking organizations that publish the foreign currency conversion rates. For this example, consider the following conversion rate

Symbol	Rate
USD	1
EUR	0.92
CHF Fr.	0.97
GBP	0.81

Preceding table gives conversion rates of EUR, CHF Fr. and GBP for 1 USD. That is, 1 USD = 0.92 EUR / 0.97 CHF Fr. / 0.81 GBP.

- For ease of calculations, copy the above table in Excel sheet and define it as a named range "xtable". Benefit in using named range is that they do not change when the formula is copied to another location, so there is no chance of messing your formulas. Also, you can add or edit or delete items within the named range. Refer to "Defined Names" chapter for details.

Using VLOOKUP

- To find the charges in USD, we will divide the hotel / flight charges by the corresponding conversion rate. And to find the correct conversion rate, we will use the VLOOKUP function in the formula, as given in the screenshot below.

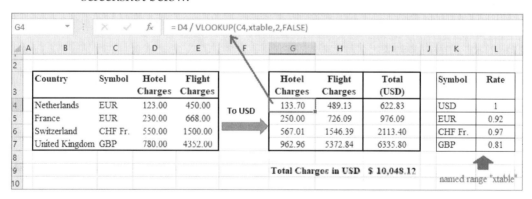

For example, the formula in cell G4 entered is "=D4 / VLOOKUP(C4,xtable,2,FALSE)". D4 is the hotel charges in EUR that needs to be converted to USD. Now from the named range "xtable', that is, cell range K3:L7 we will find the correct exchange rate using the VLOOKUP function, that is, EUR = 0.92.

- After converting each hotel and flight charges to USD, we will sum the individual charges to get the total charges in USD. Formula used in cell I9 is "=SUM(I4:I7)"

Using INDEX & MATCH

- We can also use the combination of INDEX and MATCH functions to find the correct conversion rate.

- That is, "VLOOKUP(C4,xtable,2,FALSE)" function used in formula above can be replaced by "=INDEX($L$4:$L$7,MATCH(C4,$K$4:$K$7,0))". Both return the same value as "0.92" corresponding to EUR.

- Function "MATCH(C4,$K$4:$K$7,0)" returns the position of the currency EUR in the exchange rate currency table, that is, 2 as shown in screenshot below.

- Function "=INDEX($L$4:$L$7,2)" then uses the return value of function MATCH to determine the exchange rate corresponding to EUR, that is, 0.92 as shown in screenshot below.

Using Live Currency Exchange Rates

- So far we did currency conversion using a defined exchange rate that we had fixed at the start. But as we know, the exchange rates change with time and so it should reflect in our solution too.

- Now we will see how to create a live list of currency rates; using the Excel feature of importing data from web. Go to "Data" tab, under "Get & Transform Data" group, select "From Web".

- In the URL field, add web link of your choice that gives exchange rates. We are using the URL: https://x-rates.com/table/?from=USD&amount=1 for this example. Click OK to confirm.

- Excel connects to the link and a list of all the tables on the page is shown in the Navigator dialog. Select the US Dollar Exchange Rates Table Converter and click "Load".

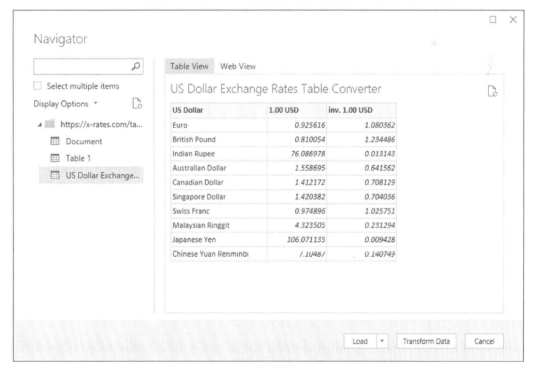

- On clicking "Load", the table is uploaded in the Excel worksheet as shown below

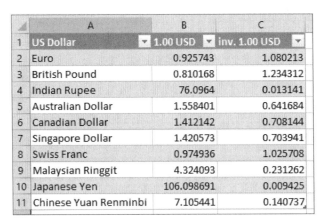

	A	B	C
1	US Dollar	1.00 USD	inv. 1.00 USD
2	Euro	0.925743	1.080213
3	British Pound	0.810168	1.234312
4	Indian Rupee	76.0964	0.013141
5	Australian Dollar	1.558401	0.641684
6	Canadian Dollar	1.412142	0.708144
7	Singapore Dollar	1.420573	0.703941
8	Swiss Franc	0.974936	1.025708
9	Malaysian Ringgit	4.324093	0.231262
10	Japanese Yen	106.098691	0.009425
11	Chinese Yuan Renminbi	7.105441	0.140737

- The table uploaded can now be used in currency conversion formulas. That is, in the VLOOKUP function used above, the "xtable" can be replaced with this table reference. Similarly, the INDEX and MATCH functions can use the cell range A1:C11.

- The exchange rates data in the preceding table is live, as it is a connection to a web link. It can be refreshed automatically, by specifying the refresh frequency in the 'Query Properties' dialog or manually by using the 'Refresh' option under 'Queries & Connections' group under the 'Data' tab.

Qs 14. A salary survey was conducted for IT companies across the world. We want to find the average salaries country wise and across different job types. Sample data is given below

	A	B	C	D	E
1	Country	Job type	Currency	Salary	Salary in USD
2	USA	CXO	USD	22000	
3	USA	Manager	USD	16000	
4	USA	Anaylst	USD	12000	
5	India	CXO	Indian Rupee	250000	
6	India	Manager	Indian Rupee	144000	
7	India	Anaylst	Indian Rupee	120000	
8	Australia	CXO	Australian Dollar	70000	
9	Australia	Manager	Australian Dollar	36000	
10	Australia	Anaylst	Australian Dollar	20000	

Reference: Chapter 3.12 : Lookup and Reference functions, Chapter 1.10: Importing data into Excel, Chapter 3.10 : Summarizing Functions

Ans: • To compare the salaries across different countries / job types, we will first convert the salaries in a single currency, that is, USD (US Dollar).

 • First step is to get the live exchange rates using the import from web feature of Excel, as done in the previous example #13 (refer to 'Using Live

Currency Exchange Rates' heading). The exchange rate data is loaded in the Excel sheet as given below.

	A	B	C
1	US Dollar	1.00 USD	inv. 1.00 USD
2	Euro	0.926658	1.079147
3	British Pound	0.810498	1.23381
4	Indian Rupee	76.189335	0.013125
5	Australian Dollar	1.562877	0.639846
6	Canadian Dollar	1.414476	0.706976
7	Singapore Dollar	1.42122	0.703621
8	Swiss Franc	0.975447	1.025171
9	Malaysian Ringgit	4.323712	0.231283
10	Japanese Yen	106.141336	0.009421
11	Chinese Yuan Renminbi	7.104658	0.140753
12			

- Now we will use this exchange rate data to convert the salaries in USD using the function VLOOKUP in the formula as shown below, like what we did in the previous example #13.

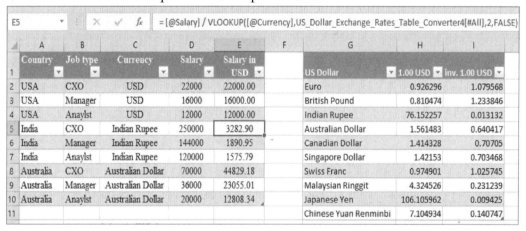

For example, the value in cell E5 is calculated using the formula, "=[@Salary] / VLOOKUP([@Currency],US_Dollar_Exchange_Rates_Table_Converter4[#All], 2, FALSE)"

Since the data is in Excel Table format the column names are referred in the formula. In simple terms the formula used is "= D5 / VLOOKUP(C5,G1:I11,2,FALSE)", that is, "= 250000 / 76.152257" where the VLOOKUP function is searching for the key="Indian Rupee" (cell C5) in the 2nd column of the exchange rate data range G1:I11.

- To find the average salaries country wise / job type, we will use the AVERAGEIF function, that is,

AVERAGEIF(range, criteria, [average_range])

where,

range – one or more cells to average

criteria – expression or text that defines which cells are averaged

average_range - actual set of cells to average

AVERAGEIF is like AVERAGE except that it returns the average (arithmetic mean) of all the cells in a range that meet a given criteria.

	A	B	C	D	E	F
1	Country ▼	Job type ▼	Currency ▼	Salary ▼	Salary in USD ▼	
2	USA	CXO	USD	22000	22000.00	
3	USA	Manager	USD	16000	16000.00	
4	USA	Anaylst	USD	12000	12000.00	
5	India	CXO	Indian Rupee	250000	3282.69	
6	India	Manager	Indian Rupee	144000	1890.83	
7	India	Anaylst	Indian Rupee	120000	1575.69	
8	Australia	CXO	Australian Dollar	70000	44820.54	
9	Australia	Manager	Australian Dollar	36000	23050.56	
10	Australia	Anaylst	Australian Dollar	20000	12805.87	
11						
12			Average Salary in USD for:			
13			Country	India	2249.73	=AVERAGEIF(Table2[Country], D13,Table2[Salary in USD])
14						
15			Job Type	Manager	13647.13	=AVERAGEIF(Table2[Job type],D15,Table2[Salary in USD])

- In cell D13, enter the Country for which you want to see the average salary.

- And in the cell E13, enter the function "=AVERAGEIF(Table2[Country],D13, Table2[Salary in USD])", which is equivalent to "–AVERAGEIF(Λ2:Λ10, D13, E2:E10)". This function averages the salaries based on the country name specified.

- In cell D15, enter the Job Type for which you want to see the average salary.

- And in the cell E15, enter the function "=AVERAGEIF(Table2[Job type], D15, Table2[Salary in USD])"])", which is equivalent to "=AVERAGEIF(B2:B10, D15, E2:E10)". This function averages the salaries based on the job type specified, irrespective of the country.

Note: Since the data is in Excel Table format the column names are referred in the AVERAGEIF function. Table2 refers to the cell range A2:E10, as shown in the preceding screenshot.

Qs 15. Puja has the salary numbers of two different groups. She wants to find if the mean of two group's salaries is significantly different or not.

	A	B	C	D
1				
2		Group A	Group B	
3		6,07,892.00	7,29,800.00	
4		2,67,810.00	3,42,421.00	
5		5,70,067.00	9,61,383.00	
6		6,60,227.00	10,45,148.00	
7		3,62,602.00	6,87,665.00	
8		3,39,245.00	8,70,090.00	
9		5,17,290.00	6,62,820.00	
10				

Reference: Chapter 9: Complex Data Analysis using ToolPak

Ans:
- We will use the T-test function of Excel for this analysis. T-test function is used for calculating the probability of significant difference between two data sets whether any or both are under the same population with the same mean.

- Go to "Data -> Data Analysis", select "t-Test: Paired Two Samples for Means" in the Data Analysis dialog box and click OK.

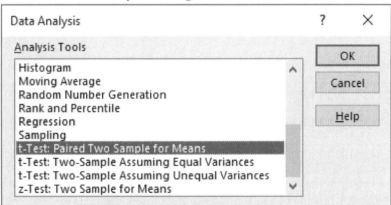

- In the t-Test dialog box, select the Variable 1 Range and Variable 2 Range as the salaries of Group A (i.e., cell range B2:B9) and Group B (i.e., cell range C2:C9).

- Specify the Output Range (i.e., E2) where you want the t-Test results and click OK.

- Detailed report is generated and shown in worksheet as given in screenshot below. It shows the mean of each data set, their variance, how many observations are taken into consideration, correlation, and P value. The p-value is the most important statistic, and that is what we are also interested in.

	A	B	C	D	E	F	G
1							
2		**Group A**	**Group B**		t-Test: Paired Two Sample for Means		
3		6,07,892.00	7,29,800.00				
4		2,67,810.00	3,42,421.00			Group A	Group B
5		5,70,067.00	9,61,383.00		Mean	475019	757046.7143
6		6,60,227.00	10,45,148.00		Variance	22797654631	53980635881
7		3,62,602.00	6,87,665.00		Observations	7	7
8		3,39,245.00	8,70,090.00		Pearson Correlation	0.681970002	
9		5,17,290.00	6,62,820.00		Hypothesized Mean Difference	0	
10					df	6	
11					t Stat	-4.386930352	
12					P(T<=t) one-tail	0.002316667	
13					t Critical one-tail	1.943180281	
14					P(T<=t) two-tail	0.004633333	
15					t Critical two-tail	2.446911851	

- In the example above, the P value is less than the alpha level selected (0.05), which means that Group A and Group B have less than 5% chance of belonging to the same population.

Qs 16. Puja wants to print the t-Test detailed report that got generated in the above example #15. She wants to print the complete report in a single page but currently it is coming in four pages, as shown in Page Break Preview below.

	A	B	C	D	E	F	G
1						Automatic Page Break	
2		Group A	Group B		t-Test: Paired Two Sample for Means		
3		6,07,892.00	7,29,800.00				
4		2,67,810.00	3,42,421.00	Page 1		Group A	Group B
5		5,70,067.00	9,61,383.00		Mean	475019	757046.7143
6		6,60,227.00	10,45,148.00		Variance	22797654631	53980635881
7		3,62,602.00	6,87,665.00		Observations	7	7
8		3,39,245.00	8,70,090.00		Pearson Correlation	0.681970002	
9		5,17,290.00	6,62,820.00		Hypothesized Mean Difference	0	
10					df	6	
11					t Stat	-4.386930352	
12				Page 2	P(T<=t) one-tail	0.002316667	Page 4
13			Cell below Page		t Critical one-tail	1.943180281	
14			Break		P(T<=t) two-tail	0.004633333	Manual Page Break
15					t Critical two-tail	2.446911851	

Reference: Chapter 1.7.2 : Print File

Ans:
- Excel inserts automatic page breaks based on the paper size, margin settings, scale options, and the positions of any manual page breaks. To print a worksheet with the exact number of pages that you want, you can adjust the page breaks in the worksheet before you print it.

- In the above example, the sheet is divided into four pages. The dashed line is the page break Excel automatically added. Solid line is the page break that was added manually.

- Now to print the complete report on a single page, we will need to remove the page breaks.

- For this example, we will work in the "Page Break Preview". To enable this view, go to "View" tab and select "Page Break Preview" under the "Workbook Views" group.

Removing Manual Page Break

- To delete a horizontal page break, select the row below the page break that you want to delete.

- Select any cell in the row below the manual page break, say D9, as shown in the preceding screenshot. Go to "Page Layout -> Breaks -> Remove Page Break" to delete the selected page break. Now we are left with just two pages.

▲	A	B	C	D	E	F	G
1							
2		**Group A**	**Group B**		t-Test: Paired Two Sample for Means		
3		6,07,892.00	7,29,800.00				
4		2,67,810.00	3,42,421.00			Group A	Group B
5		5,70,067.00	9,61,383.00		Mean	475019	757046.7143
6		6,60,227.00	10,45,148.00		Variance	22797654631	53980635881
7		3,62,602.00	6,87,665.00		Observations	7	7
8		3,39,245.00	8,70,090.00		Pearson Correlation	0.681970002	Page 2
9		5,17,290.00	6,62,820.00		Hypothesized Mean Difference	0	
10					df	6	
11					t Stat	-4.386930352	
12					P(T<=t) one-tail	0.002316667	
13					t Critical one-tail	1.943180281	
14					P(T<=t) two-tail	0.004633333	
15					t Critical two-tail	2.446911851	

Removing Automatic Page Break

- You cannot delete the page breaks added automatically by Excel, but you can move it.

- To move the page break, drag the page break to a new location. Place your mouse cursor over the automatic page break, that is, the dotted line. Mouse cursor changes to a double headed arrow, that enables you to drag the dotted line to end of the column G.

▲	A	B	C	D	E	F	G
1						Mouse cursor ◄►	
2		**Group A**	**Group B**		t-Test: Paired Two Sample for Means		
3		6,07,892.00	7,29,800.00				
4		2,67,810.00	3,42,421.00			Group A	Group B
5		5,70,067.00	9,61,383.00		Mean	475019	757046.7143
6		6,60,227.00	10,45,148.00		Variance	22797654631	53980635881
7		3,62,602.00	6,87,665.00		Observations	7	7
8		3,39,245.00	8,70,090.00		Pearson Correlation	0.681970002	Page 2
9		5,17,290.00	6,62,820.00		Hypothesized Mean Difference	0	
10					df	6	
11					t Stat	-4.386930352	
12					P(T<=t) one-tail	0.002316667	
13					t Critical one-tail	1.943180281	
14					P(T<=t) two-tail	0.004633333	
15					t Critical two-tail	2.446911851	

- Note that moving an automatic page break changes it to a manual page break.

- On removing both the page breaks, the complete report is now displayed in a single page.

Enabling cell drag-and-drop feature

- Note that to enable dragging of page breaks to another location in a worksheet, make sure that the cell drag-and-drop feature is enabled. If this feature is not enabled, you may not be able to move any page breaks.

- Go to "File -> Options" and in the Advanced category, under Editing options, select the "Enable fill handle and cell drag-and-drop" check box, and then click OK.

Printing the report

- To print the report, go to "File -> Print" or press CTRL+P on your keyboard to launch the Print dialog. You will notice that the detailed t-Test report is printed on a single page.

▲	A	B	C	D	E	F	G
1							
2		Group A	Group B		t-Test: Paired Two Sample for Means		
3		6,07,892.00	7,29,800.00				
4		2,67,810.00	3,42,421.00			Group A	Group B
5		5,70,067.00	9,61,383.00		Mean	475019	757046.7143
6		6,60,227.00	10,45,148.00		Variance	22797654631	53980635881
7		3,62,602.00	6,87,665.00		Observations	7	7
8		3,39,245.00	8,70,090.00		Pearson Correlation	0.681970002	
9		5,17,290.00	6,62,820.00		Hypothesized Mean Difference	0	
10					df	6	
11					t Stat	-4.386930352	
12					P(T<=t) one-tail	0.002316667	
13					t Critical one-tail	1.943180281	
14					P(T<=t) two-tail	0.004633333	
15					t Critical two-tail	2.446911851	

Printed in Great Britain
by Amazon

59542073R00235